DIVINE

SEX

DIVINE
SEX

A COMPELLING VISION FOR
CHRISTIAN RELATIONSHIPS
IN A HYPERSEXUALIZED AGE

JONATHAN GRANT

Brazos Press
a division of Baker Publishing Group
Grand Rapids, Michigan

© 2015 by Jonathan Grant

Published by Brazos Press
a division of Baker Publishing Group
P.O. Box 6287, Grand Rapids, MI 49516-6287
www.brazospress.com

Printed in the United States of America

Library of Congress Cataloging-in-Publication Data
Grant, Jonathan, 1973–
    Divine sex : a compelling vision for Christian relationships in a hypersexualized age / Jonathan Grant.
        pages cm
    Includes bibliographical references and index.
    ISBN 978-1-58743-369-6 (pbk.)
    1. Sex—Religious aspects—Christianity. I. Title.
    BT708.G676 2015
    233′.5—dc23   2015001679

17   18   19   20   21   7   6   5   4

For Esther

Contents

Foreword

James K. A. Smith

When you write a book on desire, people expect you to talk about sex. When you talk about *agape* as rightly ordered *eros* and describe human beings as "erotic" creatures, the temperature in the room clicks up a couple of degrees, and people are waiting for a libidinous turn in the conversation.

But I'm the *last* person who should be writing about sex. Indeed, in that respect, I am a complete square, an alien from another age. I was married when I was nineteen years old and have had sex with exactly one person—the lovely woman who has been my wife for twenty-five years. While I can recall pages of dirty magazines floating around the locker room, my formative years were not haunted by the ubiquity of pornography we know today. I attended a Bible college where women were allowed into the men's dorm rooms for exactly two hours *per semester*, under close surveillance. So the worlds of *Sex in the City* or Lena Dunham's *Girls* are pretty much unimaginable to me.

Still, I have four children (which I hope is some proof that I *like* sex!) and have a deep awareness that they have grown up in a foreign country. While we have open lines of communication and we talk about both the gifts and guardrails of healthy sexuality from a biblical perspective, I sometimes fear that their mother and I must sound like those parents in Charlie Brown movies: a kind of droning "Wah wah wah wah waaaah" that, however well intentioned, is a language that makes no sense to younger Christians in the twenty-first century. This isn't because the transcendent norms of biblical discipleship are passé but rather because the world in and from which our children hear them has radically changed. This doesn't mean we need to revise or reformulate a biblical understanding of sex, but it does mean we need to recontextualize it so that it can be heard anew for what it is: an enduring gift for human flourishing.

This is why I'm so grateful that Jonathan Grant has written *Divine Sex*. He displaces the reductionistic way traditional Christian morality is usually articulated: as though sufficient knowledge coupled with (Herculean!) willpower are all we need. This kind of "thinking-thing-ism" tends to forget that, in discussions of sex, there are other organs beyond the brain that might be, shall we say, *relevant* to the discussion. Our sexual lives don't just play out in rational, deliberate choices we make, as though sex is the conclusion to some syllogism. Our sexual lives are ways of life we live into because our hearts and minds have been captivated by a picture of the so-called good life. As Grant rightly emphasizes—resonating with my argument in both *Desiring the Kingdom* and *Imagining the Kingdom*—our sexual being-in-the-world is affected by the formation of our imagination. We are creatures of habits, and such habits are formed in us by the rhythms and rituals we are immersed in, even (indeed, even more so) if we don't realize it. Our loves and longings and desires—including our sexual longings—are not just biological instincts; they are learned. But the pedagogies of desire that train us rarely look like lectures or sermons. We learn to love on the register of the imagination.

Grant sympathetically recognizes the ways in which Christians are embedded in cultural patterns that shape us without our realizing it. We have to appreciate, he rightly points out, "the extent to which the modern self, with its focus on being free in the negative sense of being free *from* other people, has seeped into the Christian imagination and distorted our vision of sexuality and relationships." Or as he puts it a little later, "The red thread running throughout this book is the conviction that we are, more than we realize, *made* by our context." This is why the first half of *Divine Sex* is focused on a diagnosis of the cultural milieu that forms and shapes our imagination—including how we imagine sex in ways we might never articulate. And Grant's analysis is stellar: it is pointed and honest without being alarmist and despairing. Drawing on (and lucidly translating) the important work of scholars and social scientists like Charles Taylor, Christian Smith, and Mark Regnerus, as well as engaging some of my own work, Grant helps us understand how and why the world that forms us has changed—and hence what effective Christian *counter*formation would look like. The diagnosis of our cultural condition is not then taken as license for revision of biblical norms; instead, it provides the impetus for a fresh articulation of why those norms could be received as liberating us from the enslavement that parades itself as sexual "freedom" today.

The result is pastoral theology *as* ethnography, written from the front lines of our secular age and growing out of ministry in London and else-where. Grant isn't writing from some protected enclave where traditional plausibility structures are alive and well. No, this book is written from the trenches of ministry in some of our most pluralistic—and hedonistic—global cities. Its voice is at once theological and pastoral: a brilliant work of cultural analysis that seems to always keep embodied names and faces in view. (I also have to admit that I am jealous of Grant's uncanny facility with metaphor, simile, and the word pictures that paint his argument. As my Pentecostal sisters and brothers like to say, "This stuff will *preach*!")

This is a book that needed to be written. I pray that it will make its way into the hands of not only pastors and parents but also the wide array of those leaders who care for the body of Christ in the twenty-first century. It speaks both to those who are single and to those who are married. And it is a must-read for anyone working with young people today; it should be read by youth pastors and university chaplains as well as by student-life divisions at Christian colleges and universities. Absorbing Grant's insight, analysis, and constructive argument should not only deepen how we are talking about sex and discipleship; it should also give us new in-tentionality about the church as a formative community, enabling us to live into a different script that is good news: our sexual lives are hidden with Christ in God.

Acknowledgments

When you embark on a major faith project, there are many people who wish you well but a much smaller group who genuinely travel with you on the journey. This book belongs to them.

Studying and writing is a stage of life that involves a lot of plowing, sowing, and watering without yielding immediate fruit. In this hidden time, Donald Dewar, Josh and Carly Arnold, Steve and Rachel Cole, Clare Gates, Julie Noon, and Debs Paterson provided generous financial support without ever being asked. For their practical love and support I am eternally grateful.

I am also hugely appreciative of great friends in Vancouver who were a constant source of encouragement and fun: JJ and Lisa Kissinger, Dan and Krista Carlson, and our home group, including Sarah Clarke, Lisl Baker, and John Gardner, who provided a willing "laboratory" for the live-testing of many of the ideas contained in this book! I am privileged to have had mentors in Don Lewis and Reid Johnson, who were always available for conversation and prayer.

Anne Cochran and her formidable group of praying women in North Carolina have tracked with me every step of the way, while Kathy Gillin and Pauline Kirke provided invaluable contributions to the manuscript from different ends of the earth.

The concept, research, and academic spine for this book took shape as a ThM thesis at Regent College, Vancouver, BC. Many people provided input into that project, but I especially want to thank Professor Bruce Hindmarsh for his generous encouragement.

Special thanks also to our dear friend Cherith Fee Nordling. She has been a kindred friend and cheerleader for some years, as well as an inspiring example of the rare phenomenon of one who wholeheartedly pursues life in Christ. It was Cherith's personal commendation that led to James Ernest at Baker Publishing graciously receiving and considering an earlier manuscript of this book. Thank you, James!

The simple truth is that this book would not exist without the determination and huge contribution of my wife, Esther. It was together that we first began to work and minister in the area of relationships, and this book is a continuation of that partnership.

Esther has carried the vision for this book as deeply as I have, and each time this project looked to have foundered on yet another reef, her tenacity and inspiration kept the project afloat and moving forward. Esther has a unique ability to make abstract ideas tangible and practicable in real lives, and without her contribution this would be a much less readable and useful book.

Indeed, the reason I believe passionately in the beauty and hope of Christian relationships is in large part because of her friendship, love, and perseverance through these last twenty-one years of marriage.

Finally, I want to thank my parents, Ian and Mary Grant, who have modeled a life of trusting obedience to God.

1

Adjusting Our Vision

*Christian Formation and Relationships
in a Sexualized Age*

A few years ago, while celebrating our fifteenth wedding anniversary, my wife, Esther, and I stayed at the base of the twin mountains of Whistler and Blackcomb, the mammoth ski resort on Canada's West Coast. Our hotel was right at the foot of the ski fields, so that these huge mountains shot straight up outside our window. The view was spectacular, and it was mesmerizing to watch the many gondolas and chairlifts climb the slopes before passing over vertiginous ridges and out of sight. As the spring sun glistened off the icy slopes, it was easy to forget that this is rugged terrain, exciting and terrifying in equal measure. Deaths are common during the ski season here because of the huge *off-piste* area and constant avalanche risk.

Looking up at the awe-inspiring scene that morning, I was struck by the parallels between this environment and the state of relationships today, even within the church. Like those imposing mountains, love and romance have become alluring but risky places. Our culture's romantic idealism encourages us to boldly explore the boundless playground of sex and relationships. Yet we quickly succumb to "exposure" when faced with the corrosive elements of our culture's hypersexuality and its fatalism about lasting commitments. This combination of factors has turned romantic relationships from places of adventure and exhilarating risk into crevasses of death and despair.

Having tossed away the map and abandoned the network of chairlifts and gondolas that could orient us and safely guide us in our sexual lives, our culture finds itself lost and desperate in a veritable whiteout. The prevailing wisdom says, "Find your own way," and yet these mountains are no place for the creative novice. The evidence is in, and it's compelling. Our cultural experiment has left a trail of relational wreckage, and it has left us in a state of denial about where we stand.

As a society, we have encouraged powerful sexual scripts that shape the narrative world in which modern relationships unfold. We have, for instance, put our confidence in sex but lost our faith in marriage. Young people are encouraged to delay "settling down" while becoming sexually active at ever-younger ages. Research suggests that for many young people, dating and sex are becoming synonymous—one simply follows from the other. Fully 84 percent of American 18- to 23-year-olds have had premarital sex, while this figure rises to 95 percent for all Americans (of any age) who have had sex outside of marriage.[1] Beyond the realm of real-life relationships, virtual sex—thanks to the wildly successful innovation of online pornography—is flooding into mainstream culture.

All this unfolds against a backdrop of failed marriages that, over several generations, has undermined the imaginative possibility of marriage as a permanent form of relationship. This cultural environment makes the Christian vision of sexuality and marriage seem naive, unreasonable, or at least unworkable as a real-life philosophy—even for many Christians.

And yet in the midst of this cultural fatalism lies the strong hope of the Christian vision of relationships. In our hotel room that morning, I read about the origins of the Whistler ski resort. In its beginnings in the 1960s, critics argued that these mountains were too hostile for a commercial ski resort; they were simply too inaccessible, wild, and unpredictable. But through a massive network of roads, chairlifts, and gondolas, an otherwise

1. Mark Regnerus and Jeremy Uecker, *Premarital Sex in America: How Young Americans Meet, Mate, and Think about Marrying* (New York: Oxford University Press, 2011), 1.

impenetrable context has become an exhilarating place to explore and enjoy—even becoming a venue fit for the Winter Olympics. We face a similar challenge in relation to sex and relationships today. With lifelong committed marriages no longer considered "natural," we are tempted by the warmth of the spring sun to get involved and explore—and yet the weather seems to quickly change as we find ourselves getting deeper into uncharted territory.

7. Tragically, the church has absorbed many of the same perspectives and so has come to reflect the surrounding culture rather than transform it. Yet this need not be our fate. Within this crisis, God's vision of life is a plan for comprehensive human flourishing in all its fullness. Just like those chairlifts and gondolas, it provides orientation, know-how, and momentum for exploring and enjoying the depth, breadth, and glory of God's creation, particularly in our romantic relationships.

The seeds of this book were planted several years ago when Esther and I were pastors at a church in London. The vast majority who attended the church were young, single adults in their twenties and thirties. As we got to know their many different stories over a period of years, we felt a growing sense that addressing the area of relationships and sexuality was one of the biggest challenges we faced. Because of our responsibility to disciple and shepherd this generation within that church, we couldn't ignore their confusion. Relational issues were commonly the most difficult and vexing aspects of their lives. For many, intimate relationships were a major source of confusion, frustration, disappointment, anger, and often despair as they moved through their thirties and into their forties without any "success" in finding love. This often resulted in a crisis of faith: "How could God lead me into this lonely pit when I've followed him and all his rules about sex?" Others seemed to marginalize their Christian faith and sexualize their relationships while not knowing what to do with the guilt that followed. At the same time, we were shocked by the number of friends, Christian and otherwise, whose marriages were splitting apart after only a few years.

In addition, a relatively toxic atmosphere was developing in the church between the sexes. Each side pointed across the divide, blaming the other side for what was going wrong. The men seemed to have all the choices of partners but couldn't commit to one relationship, while the women only wanted to be approached by the "right" guy and treated anyone they perceived as "wrong" with disdain. The likelihood of rejection made guys reluctant to risk themselves by initiating relationships. Couples who subsequently split up found it difficult to be in church together, and so one or both would usually leave.

It was not a universally grim picture, of course. People were still getting together, and the church was an exciting place to be, both spiritually and socially. But we realized that the church's discipleship needed to address this critical issue, or else we were just putting our heads in the sand. We were seeing a disconnect between people's spiritual worlds and their Friday- and Saturday-night lives. They seemed to be getting their view of God from the church and their view of sex and relationships from popular culture.

We also saw that churches across the board were struggling to address this complex issue. It is, I believe, a critical challenge for the church, as this generation of young adults becomes ground zero in the sea change brought about by the modern world and its approach to intimate relationships. We, as the church, need to catch up. We must work to understand the needs of this generation as it deals with the brokenness and fragmentation of modern sexuality.

This recognition was the beginning of a journey for me, both in thought and in ministry, to explore and address some of these issues. There seemed to be courses and information available but not a lot of writing about how to approach this area in a way that might be transformational. Esther and I began by hosting a course focused on relationships—strictly for "nonmarrieds," which was loudly cheered when we announced it in church! The course struck a resonant chord within our community and attracted people from other churches, which confirmed to us the hunger that exists in this area of life. More recently, I have sought to understand and answer some key questions: What is it about our cultural moment that has led to such a complex dysfunction in sexual relationships? In what significant ways is our secular context shaping our sexuality? And, in response to this, what is the Christian vision of relationships, and how can Christian leaders give that vision power in people's real lives? This book is an attempt to address these questions.

The importance of this area is confirmed to us almost every week. Recently, my wife and I spent an evening helping a couple prepare for their approaching marriage. Although both appeared to have a mature Christian faith, they described some weighty issues that they were struggling to come to terms with. He had a long-standing addiction to online pornography, and they both were concerned about how this would affect their marriage. In addition, the bride-to-be had suddenly become uncertain whether she was attracted to her fiancé at all. The previous week, we had met with three single friends, all eligible women in their late thirties. Each expressed a deep sadness about the fading reality of their long-held dreams to be married and have a family. The following night, our home-group meeting was dominated by conversation and prayer around issues of relational uncertainty and angst. In light of this widespread neurosis, what is the task at hand, and where do we start?

Come with me on a thought experiment for a moment. Let us assume for the sake of argument that the priority of Christian leaders and pastors is to encourage and bring about, by every means possible, the steady growth, maturity, and integrity of those in their care. Now let's assume that these leaders are also able to categorize and prioritize the obstacles and challenges that these same disciples face in their normal lives. Perhaps they could loosely rank each issue on the basis of its *frequency*: for instance, "faced every day," "once per week," "once per month," and so on. Perhaps they could further categorize each issue on the grounds of its *severity*, such as "ability to resist or resolve this issue from 1 to 10." To complete our thought experiment, the leaders might rank how much time and attention they give to each issue within the teaching and discipleship of the church: for instance, "focus by the church from 1 to 10."

Now it's time for me to place my poorly concealed cards on the table. Surely we can affirm the assumptions described above: that the goal of Christian leaders is indeed to pursue growing maturity within their churches, and that they can also understand and rank the issues that Christians are facing in their everyday experiences. My strong suspicion is that issues relating to sexuality and relationships, for young Christians in particular, would appear right at the top of these lists as the most frequent and the most severe. And yet these same issues would most likely rank near the bottom of our lists regarding the amount of focus we give these challenges within the church. Why is that? The answer is complex, but it demands our attention and a response.

The beginning of that answer lies in the fact that we are already deeply formed within our modern cultural context. These issues, we are told, are "private," to be left up to the conscience of each person acting in isolation. The core conviction of this book is that we can only get to the heart of these most important issues and address them effectively by means of a Christian conscience that is freed from the limitations of the modern imagination.

An old Irish joke tells how a tourist in the County of Cork asks a local man how to get to the big city of Dublin. "Ah," responds the local man with a deeply furrowed brow, "I wouldn't be starting from here." There is a temptation in the context of discipleship to make the same mistake, to start with the question, "What is the Christian vision of sexuality and relationships?" and then move directly to the final question, "How do we live that out within our church communities?" Yet this practice avoids the most important aspect of contemporary formation. The question we must first address is contextual: "What is it about our cultural moment that makes the Christian vision of sexuality seem naive and unrealistic at best and downright repressive at worst, even to many young Christians? Why does the church's view of sexuality, with all its 'rules' and 'restrictions,' fail to resonate with so many contemporary believers?"

Only once we have understood the nature of the present challenge can we fully answer the other two questions. Surely we need to know where we stand before we can plan our journey toward the place we want to be. If we think of our pastoral vocation as being akin to that of a spiritual physician, then we can see the importance of making an accurate and insightful diagnosis of the illness so that we can apply the gospel most effectively to the formative cause.

We must guard against two common mistakes in this complex arena. At one extreme, without a critical diagnosis we can too easily accept the way things are, simply absorbing our cultural understanding as our own worldview. The most compelling conviction in this regard is the idea that the quality of love between two people—whoever they are and whatever they do together—should be the only consideration when taking a relationship into the sexual realm. Many Christians have no coherent way of countering this open-ended moral imperative. They either accept it as being self-evident or reject it by proof-texting Scripture.

At the other extreme, without a careful diagnosis of the issues, we can fall into the trap of rejecting all modern cultural norms. A common example is the modern quest for self-fulfillment. If we view this as purely self-centered and problematic, we will be tempted to discard it entirely. Yet the problem is not with self-fulfillment per se but rather with the fact that it has come to be placed above all other priorities. This impulse needs to be rebalanced within the other prerogatives of the Christian life: obedience to Jesus, patience in suffering, and self-giving *agape* love within the community of faith. The temptation to reject modern culture in all its forms is like prescribing a broad-range antibiotic to treat a specific infection. The patient may be healed, but her immune system will be greatly weakened.

[handwritten margin note: sex placed on a pedestal over God]

The Formative Power of Context

One of the most influential legacies of modern politics and philosophy is the conviction that personal identity is premised on the individual's freedom to choose his or her own source of meaning and form of life, largely free from outside influences. This conviction has seeped so deeply into Western consciousness that it has become part of the religious landscape. Many Christians, for instance, believe they can simply build their self-identity entirely on Scripture over against, and parallel to, secular culture. Such confidence is deceptive. American sociologist Robert Wuthnow observes, "The basic premise of social science research is that religion is embedded in a social environment and is thus influenced by this environment," so that "broad social trends do define how people think about themselves."[2] James K. A. Smith further suggests that pervasive "secular liturgies"—our regular cultural practices, such as going to the mall or the movies—represent the "affective dynamics of cultural formation," which are shaping the identities of everyone who lives within Western culture, Christians and non-Christians alike.[3] Such secular liturgies, Smith argues, represent a powerful *mis*formation of the self that undermines the gospel.[4]

Charles Taylor describes this "cultural formation" of the self using the notion of the "modern social imaginary."[5] It represents the sum total of

2. Robert Wuthnow, *After the Baby Boomers: How Twenty- and Thirty-Somethings Are Shaping the Future of American Religion* (Princeton: Princeton University Press, 2007), 20.

3. James K. A. Smith, *Desiring the Kingdom: Worship, Worldview, and Cultural Formation* (Grand Rapids: Baker Academic, 2009), 88.

4. Ibid.

5. Charles Taylor, *Modern Social Imaginaries* (Durham, NC: Duke University Press, 2004), 23–30.

how we collectively imagine our social life in the Western world, including our economy, community, family, intimate relationships, environment, and politics. For most of us, this social imaginary is not primarily expressed or received as a collection of intellectual ideas or beliefs but is carried in "images, stories, and legends" that embed themselves deep within our consciousness and practices.[6] Through this process of cultural formation, the modern world's conception of the human self makes it difficult to imagine alternative ways of seeing and being in the world. This view, as Taylor says, has "come to count as the taken-for-granted shape of things, too obvious to mention."[7] The problem is that this modern self is not well equipped for sexual fidelity and committed relationships.[8]

Christians are not immune to this problem. Wuthnow points out that certain trends in American society have influenced religious groups, including young evangelicals, particularly in the areas of premarital sex, delayed marriage, and divorce.[9] While religious beliefs strongly shape young people's *attitudes* toward sex, relationships, and marriage, Wuthnow suggests that there is a significant gap between what evangelicals *believe* and what they *do* in this area. For instance, while young American evangelicals have become more likely over the last generation to say that premarital sex is "always wrong," fully 69 percent of unmarried evangelicals in this group said they have had sex with at least one partner during the previous twelve months.[10] The hugely influential "abstinence pledge" among young people in the United States has had muted success in changing the sexual behavior of young Christians.[11] We are also told that one in two Christian marriages in America will now end in divorce. By some measures, this is higher than the national average.

6. Ibid., 23.

7. Ibid., 29.

8. Robert N. Bellah et al., *Habits of the Heart: Individualism and Commitment in American Life* (Berkeley: University of California Press, 1996).

9. Wuthnow, *After the Baby Boomers*, 20.

10. Ibid., 139–40.

11. Mark Regnerus sums up this phenomenon: "While religion certainly *influences* the sexual decision-making of many adolescents, it infrequently *motivates* the actions of religious youth. In other words, religious teens do not often make sexual decisions for religious reasons. The ones who articulate religious reasons and act in step with their stated beliefs are the exception, not the rule. Most religious adolescents remain influenced by their faith tradition and practices, but not motivated by them." See Mark D. Regnerus, *Forbidden Fruit: Sex and Religion in the Lives of American Teenagers* (New York: Oxford University Press, 2007), 184.

During the relationships course we led at our church, nearly five hundred attendees responded to an anonymous survey that asked a number of questions concerning issues of sexuality. In matters of pornography and sex before marriage, among others, it was difficult to tell whether the survey had been conducted within a church context or in a purely secular one. This is a crisis needing attention. Whichever way you slice and interpret the social data, experience confirms that the church has a genuine problem. Something in our approach to discipleship is not getting to the heart of things.

Although a number of influential Christian leaders have addressed issues relating to sexuality, the church has often struggled to perceive and effectively come to terms with the significant *mis*formation of the self that occurs within the (post)modern world. The common approach of teaching people to live according to Scripture, without giving due attention to the formative influence of our cultural context, unwittingly and ironically succumbs to the modern illusion that we can choose our own reality, largely free from external influences. This myopic approach to cultural formation runs the risk of incorporating secular assumptions about human identity into our models of discipleship. Although this may be unintentional, it undermines the formation of mature Christians who are able to sustain sexual practices that are faithful to the Christian vision of life. Basically, our inability to perceive the influence of cultural *mis*formation is undermining the power of the Christian gospel to guide and form people so they can walk its pathway to sexual maturity.

Christian leaders tend to use the Bible as their exclusive source for framing Christian speaking and living. Yet only through a kind of "thick description" of our present circumstances, being attentive to both the world and the church, can we deeply understand the hope of the gospel in redefining and reforming the self within our complex times.[12] Understanding the nature of the modern self has enormous significance for spiritual leaders because it cuts to the heart of Christian identity and mission within our culture. Is Christian identity being formed by the church, or is it being formed by the culture at large? Only by getting to the root of this issue can we effectively pursue the task of allowing God to reshape people in the gospel.

12. James K. A. Smith, series editor's foreword to Graham Ward, *The Politics of Discipleship: Becoming Postmaterial Citizens* (Grand Rapids: Baker Academic, 2009), 12.

Adjusting Our Vision

When my grandparents were in their eighties, their television developed a fault that made the screen permanently bright green. It was good for viewing garden shows or nature programs, but it was pretty disconcerting the rest of the time. Being a thrifty Scotsman, my grandfather never got it fixed! Although it's tempting to caricature culture's influence on us in this way, its effects tend to be more subtle. Culture gradually adjusts our vision, rather than completely changing it. When you cover one eye, for instance, you still can see everything clearly, but your depth perception is compromised. Basically, you no longer see in 3-D. Our cultural context works in a similar way. It is a lens through which we view life, shading and adjusting how we see things. And yet, because we tend to look *through* it rather than *at* it, we are often unaware that this cultural lens is affecting our vision at all.

Modern culture has this sort of influence on our way of seeing life. If Christian vision involves seeing with two eyes—one divine and the other human—modern culture covers one eye so that we begin to see only from the human perspective. In essence, it compromises our spiritual depth perception and tempts us to become the center of gravity of our own lives. One of the critical roles of Christian leaders, including parents, is to be guardians of the lens. We need to attend to the lens because Scripture calls us to see with new eyes, from the perspective of eternity. Consequently, this book is an attempt to describe the significant ways in which our cultural lens is shaping our identity and relationships and how we can refocus the church's vision through the lens of the gospel.

Making Disciples as Our Core Priority

Like the early church, we need to nurture a passion for making disciples who reflect the image of our Master and stand distinct from the world around them. Genuine and tangible personal change is not only possible; it is an imperative of the gospel. Indeed, the priority of Paul's ministry was to present his congregations at Christ's return as mature communities of disciples—without "blemish."[13] This is not the defeatist language of "sin-

13. Eph. 5:27; Col. 1:22.

ners saved"; it is an energetic expectation that these communities would truly become temples of the Holy Spirit and living epistles of the message to those around them.[14] Paul was more of a tent-making discipler than a tent-meeting evangelist. He spent much of his time teaching and mentoring his converts in the way of life appropriate to the new community of Christ.

Attending to people's sexual and relational lives is a critical part of this journey of discipleship because we are *connectional beings*. As Mark Regnerus and Jeremy Uecker say, "Relationships are a large playing field upon which other life contests and struggles get worked out."[15] Focusing on discipleship in the area of relationships, then, is not just about checking a box in a program of spiritual formation or helping Christians to live happier lives. It is important precisely because the whole purpose and target of the gospel is reconciled relationships. Good relationships within the community of faith are about living into our future destiny now. Romantic relationships are an important area of focus because in these relationships we are called to commit ourselves most fully and sacrificially—and yet it is here where we run into such trouble. We cannot afford to let sexual and relational formation remain a secondary concern within the church, one that we deal with in the occasional sermon or specialist course. Sustaining faithful relationships and encouraging the ability to live disciplined sexual lives may be one of the most influential missional tasks of the contemporary church as we witness to the kingdom of God in the midst of a sexually confused and relationally fatalistic culture. This should make equipping men and women to live whole and healed lives in the area of sexuality and relationships a key priority and passion for Christian leaders.

The basic conviction of this book is that Christian faith and secular culture exist in complex interrelationship. This creates both challenges and opportunities for discipleship. The first part of the book considers the following questions: What is the modern self, and how does it approach sexual relationships? How has our cultural moment shaped what we think and do in this area? Having identified the signs of the times and their influence, the second part will propose an alternative Christian vision of personal identity as the basis for a practical model of formation, one that integrates issues relating to sexuality and relationships.

14. 2 Cor. 3:1–3.
15. Regnerus and Uecker, *Premarital Sex*, 138.

PART 1

MAPPING
THE MODERN
SEXUAL
IMAGINARY

2

Seeking the Truth Within

*Love, Sex, and Relationships within
the Culture of Authenticity*

During my years working in corporate finance in London, a friend and colleague used to have vivid and often comic dreams, which he would recount over lunch at the office. One of the most poignant involved him cycling through central London on his daily commute. As he stopped at a red light, the crosswalk became a parade of every woman in the city. The premise, he explained to us, was that he could choose any one of four million women for a relationship. The bind, of course, was that having so many options made any choice impossible.

Sadly, this dream summed up my friend's real-life vision of relationships. Although he had been in a long-term relationship and was already a father, his imagination was captured by that parade of infinite choice. The idea that there might be someone "better" out there, perhaps just around the next corner, put an impossible strain on his relationship. It eventually crumbled.

Unfortunately, this is the reality for vast numbers of relationships within our modern culture. Captured by the tantalizing idea that personal integrity calls for freedom and ongoing choice, people see commitment as a barrier to achieving that freedom. Tragically, many within the church have also been captivated by the romantic myth and its promise of a perfect "soul mate" somewhere out there.

again, biased

This popular mentality arises from the recent movement of the "culture of authenticity" into mainstream society. Modern authenticity encourages us to create our own beliefs and morality, the only rule being that they must resonate with who we feel we *really* are. The worst thing we can do is to conform to some moral code that is imposed on us from outside—by society, our parents, the church, or whoever else.[1] It is deemed to be self-evident that any such imposition would undermine our unique identity.

Ultimately, this form of expressive individualism, with each person doing his or her own thing, leads to a form of soft moral relativism: we should not criticize each other's "values" because each person's right is to live as they wish. The only sin we cannot tolerate is intolerance.[2] This expressivist revolution became a mass phenomenon through the cultural and sexual revolutions of the 1960s and has come to focus, in particular, on issues of sexuality. Since then, there has been a progressive movement to further encourage sexual freedom, aided by the courts' increasing protection of our "privacy." As the Canadian prime minister said in reforming the country's criminal code in the 1970s, "The State has no business in the bedrooms of the nation."[3] For many Christians this has translated into the idea that the church has no business in the bedrooms of believers. The authentic self believes that personal meaning must be found within ourselves or must at least resonate with our one-of-a-kind personality. We must, as we often hear, "be true to ourselves."

The modern authentic self is also romantic. It focuses on feeling, sensuality, and intuition as the deepest and most important parts of human identity, the places where we experience real meaning. As a result, in our quest for authenticity we prioritize intimate relationships as *the* place where

knap Press of Harvard University

cieties during the 1970s, the legal egalization of abortion, divorce

is the author suggesting that modern view is bad?

we can most fully express and actualize ourselves. We must not settle for anything less than complete emotional happiness and sexual satisfaction. All this is commonly expressed in the language of personal "health" and "wholeness." Almost everything we read in the popular press about sexuality rehearses this conviction that a relationship can and should be powered by romantic feelings and sexual experiences alone. If the mood changes or our sex lives become less than thrilling, then our emotional integrity requires us to give the relationship a decent burial. Indeed, why settle for less when the crosswalk of infinite choice beckons? Worse still, if we stay together in the face of this romantic eclipse, then our children, if we have them, will be polluted by our hypocrisy. It is really in *their* best interests that we should move on to new things.

In his significant study of the moral and spiritual lives of "emerging adults," identified as 18- to 23-year-olds, sociologist Christian Smith observed the vague moral relativism of modern authenticity at work among non- or semi-religious young Americans. They tended to emphasize personal emotion as the main way to discern the truth without any real conviction that there is an identifiable and objective reality relevant to everyone. One interviewee's response is typical of this vague approach to moral reasoning:

> Morality is how I feel too, because in my heart, I could feel it. You could feel what's right or wrong in your heart as well as your mind. Most of the time, I always felt, I feel it in my heart, and it makes it easier for me to morally decide what's right and wrong. Because if I feel about doing something, I'm going to feel it in my heart. And if it feels good, then I'm going to do it.[4]

Smith suggests that this popular version of morality was most often described by those he interviewed as "karma"—their general idea that the good and bad things they do will be paid back during this life, often expressed as "what goes around comes around."

So how did this combination of authenticity and romanticism, known as *expressive individualism*, become so important within our culture, and how does it influence our relationships? How, in other words, did our emotional intuition become our primary arbiter of truth?

4. Christian Smith with Patricia Snell, *Souls in Transition: The Religious and Spiritual Lives of Emerging Adults* (New York: Oxford University Press, 2009), 51.

The Culture of Authenticity

The strong tradition of individualism in the Western world, and especially in North America, has led to placing personal freedom at the core of personal identity. The "American Renaissance" among poets like Walt Whitman focused on self-exploration and personal expression, especially of the soul and sensuality, as the way to find genuine meaning and make sense of life. Within this culture of expressive individualism, each person seeks his or her own unique core of feeling and intuition. Although this is an individual journey, it is possible to join together with others through intuitive feeling, and so relationships can become part of this quest for personal authenticity. Despite the importance of relationships, the focus and priority is always the journey of each individual self.

Although this way of thinking had its genesis among cultural elites—poets, artists, and intellectuals—over the course of the twentieth century it became mainstream, and it is now one of the dominant ways by which we see ourselves. This culture of expressive individualism has become the moral wallpaper of the modern world.

Touching the Void: Personal Transcendence as the New Religion

The American philosopher William James was a cultural prophet speaking at the cusp of this major change, and his voice sounds surprisingly contemporary and resonant. In 1900, writing about what he called "true religion," James summed up the coming culture of authenticity.[5] At the time of his writing, there still was a popular conviction that certain moral ideas provided the building blocks for our lives and communities. Sex, for instance, was seen as essential for sustaining marital intimacy and producing children, and so it needed to be kept within marriage. Marriage, for its part, created a stable environment in which children could best be raised, both for their sakes and for that of society. This gave marriage a position of privilege, so that it needed to be encouraged and protected as a lasting partnership. Not everyone played by these rules and not all marriages were

5. See Charles Taylor, *Varieties of Religion Today: William James Revisited* (Cambridge, MA: Harvard University Press, 2002).

happy, of course, but there was a general belief that these fundamental, unquestioned realities were handed down by the church for the good of society. This stance informed people's sexual lives, with the result that they entered into marriages and had children not just for their own fulfillment but also for the sake of the wider community.

Speaking into those times, James wanted to preserve true religion by drawing a stark contrast between "primary religious experience," which he described as the powerful spiritual intuitions and experiences of individuals, and "secondary religion," the weak secondhand faith received from the church and its traditions. For James, true religion was the cornerstone of personal identity and could only be found in "primary religious experience," which he described in highly individualistic and subjective terms as "the feelings, acts and experiences of individual men in their solitude, so far as they apprehend themselves to stand in relation to whatever they may consider to be the divine."[6]

James argued that our strong personal feelings and spiritual intuitions are most important in shaping who we are and how we live.[7] This important move sets us free from traditional sources of authority such as the church, our family, or wider society, which had previously told us what to think and how to live our lives. The key, according to James, is to be guided by our own moral intuitions and aesthetic values: what seems best to us, without too much regard for other people's views.

Although James still linked spirituality to an experience of transcendence, he saw this as purely personal and emotional, and so he opened up the way for people to find transcendence *within* themselves rather than in something above and beyond them, such as God. This new perspective created an infinite spectrum of personal creeds, both within Christianity and in combination with other religions. Indeed, James turned out to be a strangely accurate cultural prophet, summing up the spiritual zeitgeist of our times. It has become completely natural to put together a personal mash-up of different beliefs—to combine Catholicism with Buddhism, to be a "HinJew" or an evangelical who doesn't *do* church. Within our "mosaic" culture, religion, faith, and spirituality have truly become what we make them. In our culture

6. William James, *The Varieties of Religious Experience: A Study in Human Nature* (Oxford: Oxford University Press, 2012).

7. Taylor, *Varieties of Religion*, 7.

and churches today, James's vision has become thoroughly mainstream. As Charles Taylor observes: "For many people today, to set aside their own path in order to conform to some external authority just doesn't seem comprehensible as a form of spiritual life. The injunction is, in the words of a speaker at a New Age festival: 'Only accept what rings true to your own inner Self.'"[8]

This vision creates significant challenges for churches, particularly in relation to people's sexual lives. If spirituality is no longer intrinsically connected to the church and Scripture, then we are tempted to customize our entire way of life.[9] Whereas the traditional Christian conviction is that Scripture is our primary text, so that we seek to interpret and align our lives with its truth, our culture of authenticity has reversed this dynamic. Within the modern mind-set, our lives and personal experiences have become the primary text; we seek to interpret and align Scripture in accordance with *this* truth. Indeed, the influence of authenticity is clearly demonstrated by the way in which biblical teaching on every aspect of sexuality has been disciplined, chastised, and reinterpreted in recent times. In this critical area it seems that Scripture cannot be allowed to contradict our deepest impulses.

Living within the age of authenticity, then, we can make whatever we want of our spiritual experience and moral convictions. We may not even need to be part of a church; technology encourages us to personalize our religious experience, podcast our favorite speakers, plug in a suitable solo worship experience, and attend church simply for the social interaction and romantic prospects. If things don't turn out well, we can always find a new place to worship in the competitive spiritual marketplace.

Authenticity and Sex

Just as we customize our religious experience, we are tempted to personalize our sexual choices without too much regard for Scripture or the views of our spiritual leaders. So how did this happen? Clearly, sexual relationships have become a critical part of modern identity and an important way in which we express ourselves.[10] Sexuality and intimate relationships

8. Taylor, *Secular Age*, 489.

9. Ibid., 102.

10. Ibid. See also Charles Taylor, "Sex and Christianity: How Has the Moral Landscape Changed?," *Commonweal* 134 (2007): 12–18.

are front and center in our quest for personal authenticity. An important early influence in this development was the Protestant Reformers' affirmation of ordinary life, particularly work and family, as the most important places where we are called to serve God. The Reformers wanted to connect the individual believer directly to God, and so they rejected much of the mediating role of the church, including its sacred times and spaces, as well as its "higher" vocations such as monastic celibacy.

Reflecting God's affirmation of all creation as *good* per Genesis 1, the Reformers' theology formed the critical foundation for the modern focus on ordinary life as the place where we find meaning.[11] This "sanctification of the ordinary" allowed ordinary believers to serve God by participating in the redemption of every part of his creation and to serve others by working for the common good—that is, raising children and providing a stable platform for society. The mutual comfort that marriage provided included sex, which gave sexual pleasure a positive role, although its main purpose remained having children. "Unnatural" sexual acts were defined as those that did not serve this purpose.

Later on, the Victorians emphasized the importance of sex on the basis of different grounds. Sex was still described in Christian terms, but sexual ethics came to be justified in terms of science, so that medical experts' pronouncements were given as much authority regarding God's will in this area as those of Christian leaders. Whereas the world had previously been thought of as part of a cosmos connected to and sustained by God, it came to be seen as a divinely ordered machine. God's will for humanity came to be understood as the maximization of human happiness, discerned through pleasure and pain according to the design of nature. Scientists as well as ministers could now discern God's will from this design rather than from the character of God as most clearly revealed in Scripture.[12] This opened the way for sexual ethics to be naturalized, or medicalized, without any sense of conflict with Christian faith.

But the underlying assumptions had radically changed from earlier approaches. Whereas the Reformers believed that we could only live good sexual lives via God's radical grace and a journey of spiritual transformation,

11. Taylor, *Secular Age*, 218.
12. Taylor, "Sex and Christianity."

the medicalized view saw sexual health as being available to everyone as part of everyday experience. The identification of virtue/sanctity with "health" provided the key justification for modern sexuality to develop along independent lines. It remains an influential idea today, as demonstrated by most sex-education programs.

At the beginning of the twentieth century, social science began to break its alliance with religion. Thinkers such as Freud saw sexual gratification either as a good in itself or at least as an unstoppable force. Freud birthed a lasting legacy by ascribing medicinal power to sexual expression, making it a potential cure for a host of dysfunctions and pathologies. These developments led to increasing sexual freedom and exploration in the 1920s. Whereas marriage, family, and work had been seen as spiritual "vocations" in which people engaged for the sake of God's kingdom and the good of society, sex and relationships soon became central fulfillments in their own right. For many, they became things to be pursued for their own sake, ends in themselves rather than means to greater ends. This shift placed sexual relationships right at the heart of modern identity. They became the sun around which everything else revolved.

Sex was no longer something we chose to engage in or abstain from but was now a natural force that was either embraced or denied, leading to either health/wholeness or a repressed/diseased self. This sexualization of personal identity involved the bringing together of desire, morality, and a sense of integrity. The coming out of several influential homosexuals during this time highlighted the change in perspective.[13] The shift was not just about putting aside a false mask but also involved recognizing that the disguise was a wrong that had been committed against the individual and must be thrown off for the individual's own sake and for the good of society. Integrity came to be about discovering one's personal identity, particularly in terms of sexuality, and expressing that freely and confidently.[14]

All these developments came to full expression in the cultural and sexual revolutions of the 1960s. A whole set of social and philosophical dynamics combined to create a societal powder keg. This included new social factors

13. Taylor, *Secular Age*, 475.
14. Ibid.

36

such as women in the workforce and contraception, combined with a changing moral landscape and a growing desire among young people to throw off the stifling conformity of their parents' generation. Although it is often characterized as an outbreak of hedonism, the sexual revolution was also shaped by core convictions that placed it squarely within the culture of authenticity. Four moral changes took place among young people especially: the resurgence of the idea of sex as a good in itself (witness Freud); the new ideal in which men and women would come together in sex as equal partners free of gender roles; a widespread view of sex as liberation from authority; and a new insistence that sexuality was a core part of individual identity.[15] Several generations later, we still live with the powerful legacy of this revolution. Our society generally believes that "being true to ourselves," especially in our sexual lives, is critical to living full and happy lives. Much of this is taken for granted and goes unquestioned.

Within the church, however, we profess to live according to a different script. Yet if this social environment and its distinctive vision of sexual integrity forms the moral wallpaper of our lives, how does that impact our relationships?

Implications for Sexuality and Relationships

Living in the age of authenticity has placed heavy burdens on intimate relationships and has left couples striving to build security and meaning on its hopelessly weak foundations. Because of our culture's move away from transcendence, or a belief in God as the source of reality, we have come to place the full weight of our personal identity on ordinary life—our material, here-and-now existence. Rather than becoming free and expansive, our relationships have become narrow and constrained, having no purpose *atheistic POV* beyond themselves. This exclusive focus has seismically destabilized them in two ways: (1) the burden they bear becomes overwhelming because of the expectation that all of our psychological, emotional, material, and sexual needs will be met by one remarkable soul mate; and (2) the very bond we crave is undermined by the inwardly focused nature of the "authentic" self. We do not so much give ourselves to a relationship as expect the relationship to give to us.

15. Ibid., 502.

37

Our most intimate relationships are looked to by each partner as a primary source of happiness and self-actualization, measured in the narrow terms of personal gratification. *Am I getting what I need from this relationship? Does it make me happy? Do the benefits to me outweigh the costs?* The assumption is that a relationship may last until death if it continues to fulfill each person, but to make a lifelong commitment at the beginning makes no sense.[16] The cruel irony is that contemporary men and women view intimate relationships as essential to their personal identity, but they struggle to commit themselves fully to these same relationships. The reality is that our identities cannot be built on this inadequate notion of fundamentally tentative relationships.[17] We can only find genuine personal meaning by making strong commitments beyond ourselves.[18] Because relationships are no longer seen from a transcendent perspective, they are divorced from any greater purpose than one's own personal happiness and intimacy.

Traditionally, marriage was based on Aristotle's three characteristics of friendship—affection, mutual benefit, and shared commitment to the common good. Modern culture emphasizes the first two aspects but makes the third—shared commitment to the common good—irrelevant or even threatening.[19] Yet for the traditional church, as for Aristotle, this commitment to something bigger than the relationship itself enabled marriages to last through the vagaries of life and love and so provided the foundation for strong families, church communities, and a good society.[20]

Why does he hate modern culture so much?

Unfortunately, many modern Christians have been deeply formed within the surrounding culture, so that they have also come to see their relationships and marriages in purely individualistic terms. Their <u>marriages</u> are perceived as solely <u>for their own benefit rather than existing also for the sake of the church and its witness in the world</u>. It is no wonder, then, that Christian relationships are often not clearly distinguishable from those in the culture at large.

16. Charles Taylor, *The Malaise of Modernity* (Concord, ON: Anansi, 2001), 43.
17. This disturbing trend is compellingly demonstrated by the increasing rates of cohabitation among contemporary 20- and 30-_____ evidence that this model un_____ett and W. D. Mosher, "Coh_____States," *Vital and Health St___*
18. Taylor, _____
19. Ibid., 1_
20. Ibid.

For instance, although the rates of divorce among American evangelicals have been consistently lower than the national average on most measures, evangelicals still track with the general cultural trend. The proportion of divorced or separated evangelicals almost doubled from the 1970s to the 2000s, from 25 percent to 46 percent—which is below the national average but hardly a victory for the distinctive witness of the church.[21]

The Problem of Desire: The Distraction of Attraction

Along with these issues, we need to understand the inner workings of our culture's quest for romantic authenticity. When we unchain sexual and emotional desires from greater commitments, we find something within ourselves that is more unstable and complex than we imagined. Especially in relation to sexual attraction, we can find ourselves pulled in many directions at once.

Anthropologist Helen Fisher observes that romantic love has been an essential part of every civilization we know of. She describes the dynamics of falling in love in compelling terms:

> Romantic love is an addiction: a perfectly wonderful addiction when it's going well, and a perfectly horrible addiction when it's going poorly. . . . Romantic love is an obsession. It possesses you. You lose your sense of self. You can't stop thinking about another human being. . . . The main characteristics of romantic love are craving: an intense craving to be with a particular person, not just sexually, but emotionally.[22]

Fisher describes three different "brain systems," or stages of attachment, within intimate relationships. These are (1) the obsession of early romantic love, (2) sexual intimacy, and (3) deep emotional attachment. To better understand how these stages affect us, Fisher interviewed people at

21. Bradley Wright, *Christians Are Hate-Filled Hypocrites . . . and Other Lies You've Been Told: A Sociologist Shatters Myths from the Secular and Christian Media* (Minneapolis: Bethany House, 2010), 135.
22. Helen Fisher, "Why We Love, Why We Cheat," *TED Talks*, February 2006, http://www.ted.com/talks/helen_fisher_tells_us_why_we_love_cheat.html. See also Helen Fisher, "Broken Hearts: The Nature and Risks of Romantic Rejection," in *Romance and Sex in Adolescence and Emerging Adulthood: Risks and Opportunities*, ed. Ann C. Crouter and Alan Booth (Mahwah, NJ: Lawrence Erlbaum Associates, 2006), 3–28.

various stages of a relationship while taking functional MRI brain scans. The first phase, essentially infatuation, has a surprisingly powerful influence on the brain. She found that "falling for someone" impacts the same brain centers as cocaine, and with similar intensity. This area is the "motor" of the mind, associated with basic drives such as wanting, motivation, hunger, craving, and focus. It works beneath the regions that deal with cognitive thinking and emotion. Romantic love, it turns out, is a powerful drug that connects with our basic drives.

But infatuation has a short natural life cycle. Like the boosters on the space shuttle, it burns bright for a time and then falls away. This explains why we feel so "alive" in this early romantic stage and why people make such significant sacrifices—of careers, reputations, and existing relationships—in obedience to these feelings. The infatuation drug is so strong, Fisher explains, that anything associated with the object of our affection will seem to glow—his car in a crowded parking lot or her sweater hanging over a chair. It explains why the grass seems greener when we "fall in love."

The second stage Fisher describes is the bonding experience of sexual intimacy. Besides the spiritual-emotional attachment that develops during these encounters, a strong physiological attachment also occurs. This, she says, is why there is no such thing as "casual sex." Sexual climax releases a rush of certain neurotransmitters and hormones. The neurotransmitter dopamine intensifies the sensation of romantic love, while the hormones oxytocin and vasopressin deepen our emotional attachment to the other person. Oxytocin is also released when a mother breastfeeds a baby, which bonds mother to child. As Fisher explains, this is partly why we can experience such a strong sense of cosmic union with somebody after making love with them.[23]

The final phase of relational attachment is the deep sense of peace, warmth, and security we can feel with a long-term partner. This is the consolidation phase of a relationship, wherein the bond is deepened through emotionally warm experiences such as sharing a walk along the beach or watching a movie together.

Neuroscience obviously can only take us so far, but it does shine a light on the power of these three "brain systems" in consolidating a relationship,

23. Fisher, "Why We Love, Why We Cheat."

as well as on an essential problem with our culture of authenticity. Fisher points out that these three stages can be held together and become self-reinforcing if we so choose, but they can also move in different directions if we allow them to. We can find ourselves in the painful position of feeling a deep attachment to our spouse while longing for someone else. Believing that we must be true to ourselves, especially our strongest feelings, increases our vulnerability to the infatuation cycle, which can pull us in ever-new directions.

Fisher is surely right in saying that romantic love is one of the most addictive substances we can experience. Indeed, faced with the choice between an existing relationship and a fresh romantic attachment, the latter will always feel the most *real* while it burns brightly. But these natural stages of love also show us how the Christian vision of committed relationships works itself out in our lives. Infatuation is a divine gift that helps us to find and commit to a potential partner, and it can act like a pathfinder in the dense forest of potential partners. But it is not infallible, and if we fail to "guard our affections"—in the words of Proverbs—then infatuation can become distorted and attached to the wrong person. We need to exercise caution and discernment in weighing our affections for someone before these feelings become fully engaged.

Once we have navigated the complexities of this first stage in a relationship, we can also see the power of intentional love for building deep and resilient marriages. The other two stages of attachment—sexual and emotional bonding—act like glue that seeps ever deeper into the fabric of a relationship, working out the commitment to progressively become "one flesh." At the same time, we need to recognize the importance of guarding these dynamics from becoming detached from this exclusive context. A new attachment, even one that may seem like an innocent infatuation, will eat away at that exclusive bond. Love, it turns out, is both a feeling and a choice.

A few years ago I met with a friend for lunch, during which he explained that he had made a terrible mistake. A year previously he had started taking the occasional coffee break with his secretary, and over time these catch-ups had become more frequent. Although he hadn't noticed at the time, a mutual attraction had started to develop. Sadly, this culminated in a night in a hotel together after a party at their law firm. His wife, who was pregnant at the time, eventually discovered the truth. This, of course, had a devastating impact on their marriage. As my friend explained all this, his demeanor was one of deep sadness and regret. He would have done anything to go back and avoid the chain of little decisions that led to such a moment of madness.

We often focus on the big decisions in our relationships, and yet it is the "little foxes that spoil the vines."[24] It was the small decisions that had softened my friend's resilience. I believe one of the most important roles pastors have is teaching practical discernment in this area. Within our culture of authenticity, a key pastoral concern is how to offer practical ways to safeguard Christian marriages and relationships. How do we envision practices and habits that help to foster fidelity rather than enslavement to the recurring cycle of infatuation?

Authentic Relationships in Practice

Caught between Intimacy and Autonomy

The two most influential characteristics of the modern self—radical individualism and expressive authenticity—create a perfect storm for relationships. One social observer argues that we should embrace new ideas regarding romance and family and relinquish traditional marriage as society's highest ideal.[25] She reflects on her personal experience of pursuing a career straight out of college rather than settling down with one of the many eligible men she met there as a student. Now in her thirties and unable to find a suitable man in a greatly diminished pool, she reflects on why she ended so many relationships in her twenties with perfectly "marry-able" men.

As a typical example, at twenty-eight she ended a three-year relationship for no good reason. Her friends were bewildered, and so was she. She says, "To account for my behavior, all I had were two intangible yet undeniable convictions: something was missing; I wasn't ready to settle down." Ten years later she concludes, "The decision to end a stable relationship for abstract rather than concrete reasons ('something was missing'), I see

24. Song of Sol. 2:15 (KJV).
25. Kate Bolick, "All the Single Ladies," *The Atlantic*, November 2011, http://www.theatlantic.com/magazine/archive/2011/11/all-the-single-ladies/308654/.

now, is in keeping with a post-Boomer ideology that values emotional fulfillment above all else. The elevation of independence over coupling ('I wasn't ready to settle down') is a second-wave feminist idea I'd acquired from my mother."[26] In other words, she found herself caught between the contradictory forces of intimacy and autonomy.

She observes that America has a high divorce rate compared with other Western countries because it combines a strong culture of marriage with an equally powerful commitment to individualism. This inevitably generates opposing tectonic forces, one propelling the popular desire to be married, the other tearing at those very relationships. Sadly, she, along with most secular commentators, suggests that this contradiction should be resolved by weakening our commitment to marriage. This vividly underlines our culture's fatalism about the possibility of committed and sacrificial bonds between people. Yet we still place a high priority on finding "true love." These contradictory forces create heightened expectations as well as deeper grief when a relationship inevitably unravels.

Caught between Fantasy and Fatalism

Indeed, for all the talk about career, most people ultimately measure fulfillment in life through their closest relationships. Although work may take up most of our time, most of us still long to share life with a kindred companion. Here again the contradictory forces of modern authenticity pull us in different directions. While we yearn for an intimate soul mate, we tend to hold that person at arm's length, unsure whether he or she will continue to fulfill our needs for all time.

This quest for a perfect soul mate combines fantasy and fatalism and butts up against some hard realities. A 2012 study by a group of US-based psychologists concludes that "people with a strong belief in romantic destiny are especially likely to exit a romantic relationship when problems arise, even when they are involved in rewarding relationships." It seems that believing in soul mates tends to lead to what the researchers call "romantic dysfunction."[27] This illusory quest for meaning in romantic

26. Ibid.
27. Eli J. Finkel et al., "Online Dating: A Critical Analysis from the Perspective of Psychological Science," *Psychological Science in the Public Interest* 13, no. 1 (January 2012): 50. See

fulfillment is difficult to address because it sits at the heart of so many modern relationships. Indeed, the vast majority of emerging adults—94 percent in one survey—want their marriage partner, first and foremost, to be a "soul mate."[28]

This dynamic is exemplified in the phenomenon of the celebrity marriage. We see the stark reality of many modern relationships caricatured in the grandeur of the bold and the beautiful. Public fanfare or a small private ceremony in Maui tends to give way to separation after twelve long months of trying to make it work. If the fairy-tale wedding ceremony stands for the fantasy, the phrase "irreconcilable differences" as a rationale for ending the relationship stands for modern fatalism. There are, of course, legitimate reasons for relationships to break up—but are there really such things as irreconcilable differences? Notice how we have turned a dynamic verb into a static adjective. Rather than refusing *to reconcile* our differences, we have turned these disagreements into fixed realities independent in themselves—irreconcilable differences—objects that exert a force on us as irresistible as gravity.

Far from being a unique category of relationships, celebrity marriages reveal the inner dynamics of our culture of authenticity and hold a mirror up to our own relationships. The divorce of supermodel Heidi Klum and the musician Seal provides a poignant example. Their separation was a shock to many because they had been married for seven years, had three biological children together, and had a well-known tradition of renewing their wedding vows every year. They were seen as a famous couple who had managed to navigate the pressures of celebrity marriage.

In part, what bolstered the image of their romantic staying power was their annual renewal of love. Yet what seemed to be their relationship's greatest strength turned out to be its weakest point. By prioritizing emotional fervor and continuity as the critical hinge for sustaining their marriage, they undermined the very bond they were affirming. Rather than creating a covenant of commitment through thick and thin, they inadvertently turned their marriage into a rolling twelve-month contract with an annual right of renewal or, by implication, a right of cancellation.

---

also Kate Englehart, "True Loves: The Search Will Soon Be Mobile, Transparent and Constant," *Maclean's*, January 30, 2013, http://www.macleans.ca/society/life/true-loves/.

28. Regnerus and Uecker, *Premarital Sex*, 192.

It is not, of course, that we should remove romance and sexual desire from our relationships. Quite the opposite. As Fisher's theory of the "three brain systems" demonstrates, becoming "one flesh" is a holistic journey in which we give ourselves to each other in joyous and intentional communion. Romantic attraction, sexual intimacy, and emotional bonding are divine gifts that we need to pursue, encourage, and protect within marriage. And yet the one-dimensional nature of the romantic myth, which sees emotional force as a sufficient engine to carry all other aspects of the relationship, undermines the very thing it seeks to build.

The "Definitely Maybe" Approach to Commitment

The tension between autonomy and intimacy is most clearly evidenced in the trend toward cohabitation. Today, between 50 and 70 percent of American couples are cohabiting before or instead of marrying.[29] Living together is now seen as the only mature way to begin an intimate relationship while preserving one's personal integrity. This is the "definitely maybe" approach, whereby covenant is replaced with "wait and see" and "try before you buy." If intimate relationships were mortgages, we might call these sub-prime commitments. They are high-risk projects with little or no collateral security. Unfortunately, just like sub-prime mortgages, these relationships are designed to fail.

What is most startling about the trend of living together outside of marriage is that it is becoming increasingly popular, even though research shows overwhelmingly that cohabiting ultimately undermines relationships. Indeed, the evidence completely contradicts the popular belief that "testing" a relationship first is the best way to secure its future. As a path to marriage, cohabitation is extremely unreliable, with only one in five cohabiting relationships ending in marriage, and these figures are getting worse over time.[30] Even in those cases where living together does subsequently lead to

29. Galena K. Rhoades, Scott M. Stanley, and Howard J. Markman, "Couples' Reasons for Cohabitation: Associations with Individual Well-Being and Relationship Quality," *Journal of Family Issues* 30 (2009): 233–58; Sheela Kennedy and Larry Bumpass, "Cohabitation and Children's Living Arrangements: New Estimates from the United States," *Demographic Research* 19 (2008): 1663–92.

30. Robert Schoen, Nancy S. Landale, and Kimberly Daniels, "Family Transitions in Young Adulthood," *Demography* 44 (2007): 807–24.

marriage, cohabiting significantly increases the likelihood of an eventual divorce.[31] Not surprisingly, serial cohabiters show radically higher rates of divorce in their subsequent marriages; women who cohabit multiple times before marrying divorce more than twice as frequently as those who live only with their future husband.[32]

The notion that sexual chemistry is critical to a long-term relationship has led to the "search theory," which drives people to explore more sexual relationships in order to increase their chances of finding the "right" person (the soul mate). But research reveals the exact opposite. It shows that serial monogamy—that is, a string of consecutive sexual relationships—actually hinders eventual marital satisfaction, while sexual experience before marriage is a good indicator for an increased likelihood of infidelity within marriage. It turns out that "settling down" later is a nice idea but a challenging reality. As sociologists Mark Regnerus and Jeremy Uecker write, "Repetitive relationships—including repetitive experiences with cohabitation—don't lead to better marital odds, they just lead to more sex."[33]

Numerous research studies, including meta-analysis of those studies, show that men and women report the highest levels of satisfaction within marriage if they are married in their twenties—ages 20–27 for women and 23–27 for men. This stage of life for women coincides with their peak fertility, and so there seems to be a close fit—by design, you could say—between the best time to be married *and* to have a family.[34] Yet in the face of this overwhelming evidence, Regnerus and Uecker observe that the vast majority of emerging adults in America are convinced that marrying in their twenties heightens the chance of divorce while cohabiting is the safest route to ensuring the resilience and longevity of a relationship.[35]

Embracing the Shifting Self

Another significant barrier to young adults in their twenties pursuing permanent relationships is the conviction that they will change over time

31. Regnerus and Uecker, *Premarital Sex*, 202.
32. Ibid.
33. Ibid., 191–92.
34. Ibid., 181.
35. Ibid., 204.

as they discover their authentic personal identity. This narrative of instability and dynamic change is considered both inevitable and impossible to navigate within a relationship. Regnerus and Uecker found this common perspective in their interviews with young adults. "What is clear, is that emerging adults expect to *change* what they think and feel and want as they move through college and their early adult years *and* that such change will move them from being who they are now—the product of their parents and peers—to who they'll become: their true selves."[36]

Whereas Christianity views personal transformation as a necessary and reliable platform for relationships, the modern script of "authenticity" sees personal change as an inherent threat to relationships and vice versa. Young people often describe a dualism in how they see their lives across time. Their twenties are seen as the time for discovery and change, with their thirties the decade for stability and settling down: now is for "self," and later is for "others."[37] It is a mystery, though, how this transition is meant to take place. It is akin to the Olympic hopeful who decides to leave training until the event itself.

Modern Authenticity within Christian Relationships

The culture of authenticity has indeed become the moral wallpaper of our lives, deeply shaping our personal identity, sexuality, and relationships. It affects our willingness to enter relationships as well as our ability to sustain them. Sadly, these trends have influenced our church communities as thoroughly as the secular culture. The "authentic" self, it turns out, is sitting in the sanctuary. We can see this among both single and married Christians.

Soul Mate Salvation

One of the most influential myths nourished by the culture of authenticity is that we will be "saved" or made complete when we meet the right-shaped

36. Ibid., 184.
37. Ibid., 185.

soul, that perfectly complementary person who can fulfill all of our needs and desires. Like Morpheus in *The Matrix* we find ourselves asking, *Is he or she "the one"?* Within the church we have tended to supercharge this fantasy by spiritualizing it, so that "the one" becomes the single human being that God has fashioned into perfect compatibility with all of our needs and longings. God is just waiting for the perfect moment to release this person into our lives, along with an associated relational epiphany just to make sure we don't miss the moment.

The problem is that we are likely to experience a keen sense of frustration and despair as this paragon fails to materialize. Some personality trait or quirk always mars our idealized image. Despite this reality, modern authenticity encourages us to search for Dante's Beatrice: the perfect soul who can lead us into the beatific vision of the heavenly realm. This search, like my friend's dream about the parade of infinite choice, locks us into a quest for a sanctuary that does not exist. Rather than focusing on the potential relationships standing in front of us, we keep our eyes focused on the elusive possibilities on the road ahead.

Our real experience reveals that the perfect image of "the one" is a chimera. In marriage, we discover that the person we exchanged vows with has been a mere host body for our projection of "the one," who plainly left the building shortly after the wedding ceremony! It is not, of course, that God is not involved in our relational lives. Our loving Creator, who has numbered every hair on our heads, is intimately concerned with every part of our lives. We can trust his provision in our relationships as much as in any other area of life. The risk, however, is that, fueled by our culture's obsession with "soul mates," we can easily turn the Christian vision of love into a fantasy.

Toward the end of the first relationships course we led at our church, one of the speakers talked about the need to smash the idol of "the perfect partner." At the end of her session, she asked everyone to close their eyes and invited those who knew they were clinging to this idol to stand up and receive prayer. We were amazed that in a crowd of around five hundred mostly 20- to 35-year-old singles, at least half stood up. We realized then the extent to which the elusive search for "the one" held a powerful grip over our collective imagination. It seems we have unwittingly sanctified the culture of authenticity, including its focus on soul mates.

Emotional Authenticity as Our Moral Guide

A few years ago Christian friends of ours, after several years of marriage, came to see Esther and me to explain that their relationship had reached an impasse and that they could see no alternative but to end it. After a downward spiral of conflict and loss of trust, they struggled to have a civil conversation with each other and had begun to form romantic attachments with other people.

They were surprised when we said that they had simply reached a normal stage in every marriage, the stage where going on together seems impossible and unthinkable, where you wonder what you saw in each other in the first place. This was a stage that we had reached early on in our own marriage and had repeated several times since. If happiness or emotional resonance had been our main interpretive dials for navigating our relationship, we would have split up many times. Over the following weeks, we worked through some practical ways in which our friends could turn around the destructive dynamics that had taken hold in their relationship and, in their place, foster trust, intimacy, and commitment to each other. Many years later, their marriage is on a solid footing, and they are thriving with a family.

The tragedy is that so many Christian marriages never recover from the same downward spiral. We in the church have not spoken and ministered effectively into our culture's prioritization of authenticity above all else in matters of sexuality and relationships. When a marriage ceases to make us happy or the traveling becomes heavy going, we have no other master story to navigate us through the storm. So we take this as a sign that it simply "wasn't meant to be"—that we are not among the lucky ones when it comes to marriage.

Christian tradition emphasizes courage and perseverance in the face of suffering, but even within the church, seeking happiness and avoiding emotional pain have become our highest virtues. Yet this impossible foundation for Christian sexuality and relationships must be challenged. Allowing emotional authenticity to guide us in our long-term relationships is like trusting ourselves to the schizophrenic Gollum—sometimes loyal and sometimes treacherous but ultimately bent on our destruction. Christian marriage has a different genetic makeup, built upon covenant and imaging

Jesus's love for the church. We are called not only to seek deep friendship, intimacy, and companionship but also to give of ourselves in faithful love.

Concluding Thoughts: Creativity, Sin, and Suffering

The risk that goes along with strongly critiquing a cultural phenomenon like authenticity is that we are tempted to throw out the proverbial baby with the bathwater. Instead, by equipping ourselves to understand the contours of modern authenticity, the Christian community can discern right responses. We should not, for instance, abandon human feeling and intuition as hopelessly unreliable guides in our spiritual and sexual lives. Indeed, redeemed desire lies at the very heart of the Christian self. It is only through God's ongoing healing and reorientation of our deepest longings that we can live wholeheartedly within the gospel. What is most alluring and corrupting about the modern quest for personal authenticity is that it taps into the legitimate Christian search for truth and transcendence—that is, to know and experience things as they *really* are. But the modern self seeks authenticity via the shortcut of attempting to make peace with ourselves rather than making peace with God and allowing him to change us.

This distortion of Christian authenticity is a dangerous illusion. The Christian story claims that genuine personal wholeness is made possible only through the crisis of the gospel, which required nothing short of God himself taking on flesh to overcome human sin and self-deception. Living faithfully within a Christian sexual ethic requires a radical personal transformation, whereby we walk the same journey into death and new life that Jesus walked. In *The Problem of Pain*, C. S. Lewis explains that the way to the promised land must pass Sinai, where Israel received God's moral guidelines for the good life.[38] The wilderness is a necessarily challenging place where our old ways of thinking and living and our former sources of identity wither, die, and are gradually replaced by an understanding of God's path for us.

Idolatry is commonly described as the objectifying of the human will and worshiping it in place of God. Self-creators essentially become idolaters

38. C. S. Lewis, *The Problem of Pain* (San Francisco: HarperSanFrancisco, 2001).

who worship themselves, including their desires, purposes, and wills. They give themselves the status of God and exalt their own wills as of supreme worth.[39] This understanding can help to explain our cultural obsession with creativity, because it is the ultimate expression of our unique independent selves and it gives us status as primary creators—gods. In contrast, genuine Christian creativity is something quite different. Seeking to discern and reflect God's truth, goodness, and beauty, we are striving not to be creative per se but to imitate God so that our lives and talents reflect and serve him. Even our sexuality and intimate relationships are a response to God. As C. S. Lewis describes, aside from God himself,

> the duty and happiness of every other being is placed in being derivative, in reflecting like a mirror. Nothing could be more foreign to the tone of Scripture than the language of those who describe a saint as a "moral genius" or a "spiritual genius" thus insinuating that his virtue or spirituality is "creative" or "original." If I have read the New Testament aright, it leaves no room for "creativeness" even in a modified or metaphorical sense. Our whole destiny seems to lie in the opposite direction, in being as little as possible ourselves, in acquiring a fragrance that is not our own but borrowed, in becoming clean mirrors filled with the image of a face that is not ours. . . . The highest good of a creature must be creaturely—that is, derivative or reflective—good.[40]

The idea of reflective or derivative creativity is an affront to the modern vision of life, which has rejected the ideas of sin and suffering. In regard to sin, our culture of authenticity has sought to deny its existence and to rise above it. This subtly distorts the gospel by offering us the counterfeit of personal resonance and self-discovery without deep transformation.

This should lead us into deep compassion rather than judgment over our culture, because behind the confident mask of the "authentic" self often lies self-hatred or a lack of self-acceptance. These issues can run so deep that we would rather go into hiding than face up to fundamental questions of identity. The false self lives to avoid suffering. Indeed, we are increasingly becoming an anesthetized society that will do anything to avoid pain. We

39. Paul C. Vitz, *Psychology as Religion: The Cult of Self-Worship* (Grand Rapids: Eerdmans, 1994), 93.

40. C. S. Lewis, "Christianity and Literature," in *Christian Reflections*, ed. Walter Hooper (Grand Rapids: Eerdmans, 1967), 6.

have many ways of self-medicating the physical, emotional, and spiritual pain in our lives—compulsive behavior, consumption of food, sexual encounters, highly dependent relationships, pornography—although, inevitably, we find that these false comforts send us further into hiding, increasing our sense of shame and isolation. Ironically, beneath the assured culture of authenticity we find a generation of people unsure of their right to exist. This insecurity undermines intimate relationships through a host of compulsive behavioral patterns. As Gerald May puts it: "Psychologically, addiction *uses up* desire. It is like a psychic malignancy, sucking our life energy into specific obsessions and compulsions, leaving less and less energy available for other people and other pursuits. Spiritually, addiction is a deep-seated form of idolatry. The objects of our addictions become our false gods. These are what we worship, what we attend to, where we give our time and energy, *instead of love.*"[41]

Our culture also refuses to take suffering or personal sacrifice seriously. These are rarely seen as having any positive meaning, and we think that we must seek to avoid suffering at all costs. This helps to explain why relationships have become so brittle. We would rather end a challenging relationship or marriage than enter into the long, costly journey necessary to sustain a long-term partnership.

The reality is all around us, however. Modern "authenticity" cannot, in the end, remove or give genuine significance to the inevitable difficulty and suffering that life brings. The epidemic use of prescription and over-the-counter painkillers—especially antidepressants—is startling testimony to this phenomenon.[42] Our culture has chosen as one of its highest priorities the anesthetic prerogative to numb emotional pain. Yet just as our physical nerves help us to navigate the world safely, our emotional and spiritual "nerves" help us to discern truth and to live within it. In contrast, the modern quest to be authentic obscures the problem by "solving" it—simply accepting ourselves as we are—without addressing its causes. Because it does not acknowledge and get to the heart of the human condition, modern

41. Gerald G. May, *Addiction and Grace: Love and Spirituality in the Healing of Addictions* (New York: HarperOne, 1988), 13.

42. Antidepressants have become the most prescribed drug in the United States, even exceeding blood pressure medication, with their usage tripling during the 1990s. National Center for Health Statistics, *Health, United States, 2006: With Chartbook on Trends in the Health of Americans* (Hyattsville, MD: National Center for Health Statistics, 2006).

authenticity begins in optimism but ends in pessimism as it inevitably moves from fantasy to fatalism.

⌐The walk of Christian discipleship, by contrast, involves understanding who God is and walking with him in trusting obedience. Only through this journey of confession, repentance, and restoration do we allow ourselves to be remade in his likeness, allowing the false self of self-consciousness to be reordered and reoriented toward the true self of God-consciousness.[43] Richard Rohr provides insight into why the autonomous self cannot sustain relationships:

> Only the great self, the True Self, the God Self, can carry our anxieties. The little self cannot do it. People who don't pray basically cannot live the Gospel, because the self is not strong enough to contain and reveal our delusions and our fear. I am most quoted for this line: "If you do not transform your pain, you will always transmit it." Always someone else has to suffer because I don't know how to suffer; that is what it comes down to. Jesus, you could say, came to show us how to suffer, how to carry "the legitimate pain of being human," as C. G. Jung called it.[44]

The hope of the gospel is that it invites us out of hiding, not to expose us and parade our pain in front of everyone, but to heal it and root us within real community. The gospel ushers us into the *true* culture of authenticity. Christianity takes suffering seriously and treats it as an important, inevitable, and even necessary part of our spiritual and moral development. Our faith, as exemplified in the cross, begins in suffering and sacrifice but ends in joy.

43. Rom. 8:5; Eph. 4:22–24.
44. Richard Rohr, "The Rent You Pay for Being Here," *Richard Rohr's Daily Meditations*, August 1, 2013, http://conta.cc/1aY7HeA.

3

Three Paths
to Freedom on the
Road to Nowhere

The Dead End of Modern Liberty

The phenomenon of "private" sexuality has deeply infiltrated the Western church. I recently read about a Christian leader who was mentoring a younger student in catechism. The leader had a girlfriend, and one day the student accidentally stumbled upon them having sex together. Deeply confused, the student later asked his mentor what was going on, whereupon he was told that it was "none of his business." This story typifies the prevailing sense among contemporary Christians that we do not have any legitimate moral claims on each other's lives, especially our sexual lives. This is *private* business.

The all-conquering narrative of modern freedom has driven a wedge of confusion into the sexual lives of Christians as they find themselves increasingly caught between two scripts: a cultural one and a Christian one. Regnerus and Uecker describe the moral ambiguity surrounding sex and relationships that is typical of many young Christians.

> They're *selectively permissive*: the moral rule remains right and good and in effect, yet it does not apply to them at present, for reasons too nuanced and difficult for them to adequately describe. It's not that they're hypocritical. Rather, they feel the powerful pull of competing moral claims upon them: the script about what boyfriends and girlfriends in love want or are supposed to do for and to each other, and the script about what unmarried Christian behavior should look like. They want to satisfy both but find themselves rationalizing.[1]

It is little wonder that confusion reigns. The right to be "free" has become our consummate cultural cliché, a banner under which we live our entire lives. Yet we give little attention to what it actually means, beyond the shallow, open-ended sense of being able to do whatever we want. The idea of freedom, though, has assumed some particular meanings in our time that are quite distinct from previous understandings and that pose profound challenges for Christian discipleship and sexual formation.

Three Ways to Be Free

Utilitarianism and Expressivism — I hate for modern Culture? But like... why.

Right at the heart of modern culture is the ideal of personal freedom: that we can live well and truly be ourselves only if we are free from outside influences. Where did this pervasive idea come from, and how has it become sacrosanct? In contrast with the Christian conviction that personal freedom is possible only by receiving God's grace and living in step with his commandments, the Enlightenment split freedom into two very different visions of life that eventually morphed into two mainstream forms of individualism, *utilitarian* and *expressive*.

The *utilitarian* mode sees the world as a great field of competition, within which other people may be used to further our own pleasure and self-interest. Rather than living in open communion with each other,

1. Regnerus and Uecker, *Premarital Sex*, 35.

we learn rules by which to euphemistically "win friends and influence people." We become masters of the universe, self-made people who express our freedom through control and manipulation. Things and people become pawns that we move on the strategic chessboard of our lives. When I worked in finance, my boss's favorite book was *Zen and the Art of Warfare*, which shaped a philosophy that he applied to his clients, colleagues, and competitors alike. Within this worldview, everyone is a rival to be feared.

This utilitarian perspective is founded on basic human fears and desires. The philosopher Thomas Hobbes introduced the idea that essentially we all fear being controlled by others, and we in turn desire to exert power over them.[2] Within this "war of all against all," redemption is provided by the state and other social institutions, which act as referees and policemen, essentially protecting us from each other.[3]

This bleak conception of human life, later reinforced by the general acceptance of social Darwinism, has put modern relationships on shaky foundations, so that even within the church we fear making lasting and sacrificial commitments. The popular media powerfully reinforces the primacy of hostility and competition. Many of the most acclaimed miniseries on our TV screens paint a dark social vision that is compelling and pervasive. Violence, drugs, crime, terrorism, paranoia, political machinations, broken relationships, and the dog-eat-dog dynamics of the corporate world feed our imaginations with a bleak vision of relationships—a dystopian society rather than a utopian one. The binge-watching "box set" model of TV-series consumption encourages us to enter into and inhabit these worlds for hours at a time, further shaping our moral and social imaginations. This social imaginary has come to resemble the *realpolitik* of Vladimir Lenin's assertion that in relationships "trust is good, but control is better."

Modern *expressivism*, not surprisingly, reacted against this imbalanced view of personal identity by seeking a more genuine freedom, tuning into the voice within, especially emotions and sexuality. This formed the basis for the culture of authenticity that we explored in the previous chapter.

2. Thomas Hobbes, *Leviathan*, ed. C. B. Macpherson (London: Penguin Classics, 1985), xiii.
3. Stanley Hauerwas, *A Better Hope: Resources for a Church Confronting Capitalism, Democracy, and Postmodernity* (Grand Rapids: Brazos, 2000), 13–14.

These contrasting visions of freedom, utilitarian and expressive, caused a head/heart split within modern identity that has created profound rifts in our social and sexual relationships. This duality is vividly symbolized by the stereotypical daily commute from the soft leafy suburbs, which represent the warmth of home, love, and family, into the hard efficient spaces of the city, which stand for the rational utilitarian way of surviving in the business world.

Postmodernism as a Vision of Total Freedom

In addition to these two modern pathways to freedom, a third route emerged toward the end of the twentieth century. Growing out of the other two, but also in reaction to them, *postmodernism* represents a yet more extreme form of freedom. Whereas expressivism seeks to be faithful to an inner core of personal identity, postmodernism focuses solely on the flow of human experience. Within postmodernism, the connection between what we *do* and who we *are* becomes less clear. The emphasis is on expressing freedom rather than on what that freedom expresses.

The most influential thinkers within postmodernism, shaping its basic ideas, are Michel Foucault, Jacques Derrida, and Jean-François Lyotard. Foucault, for instance, embraced the negative side of Nietzsche's philosophy, a rejection of any higher reality that might make sense of life. On this basis, Nietzsche had argued that all interpretations are arbitrary, so that power and the force of the human will inevitably fill the void. Within this vacuum, Foucault argued, the individual does not have a genuine core or self but is a product of the ideas and disciplines imposed upon him or her by those who hold power.[4] In other words, each of us is like soft putty to be molded by politicians, spin doctors, advertisers, spiritual authorities, and therapists. For Foucault, since all these forms of control and authority are artificial, our goal should be to throw them off as oppressive restrictions on our right to be free.

Jacques Derrida pictured the individual as surrounded by language that he or she cannot control or escape. Derrida challenged traditional

---

4. As Charles Taylor describes, Foucault presented the individual as "constructed through relations of power and modes of discipline." See Taylor, *Sources of the Self: The Making of the Modern Identity* (Cambridge, MA: Harvard University Press, 1992), 488.

hierarchies between clarity and confusion, truth and falsehood, so that all interpretations of reality are misinterpretations or, at best, merely contextual and provisional. We never can say with any certainty that we have found "the truth."

So both Foucault and Derrida rejected any comprehensive vision of reality, which led by default to a celebration of the completely unrestricted freedom of the self. Jean-François Lyotard especially came to see this form of total freedom as the essence of postmodernism. Yet as Tom Wolfe wryly observes, whenever these philosophers needed bypass surgery or a root canal, they were not in the habit of challenging the oppressive institutions of medical knowledge or dental accreditation but would put their trust in the authority of these "experts."[5]

Laden with inconsistencies, the "free play" of postmodernism has caused confusion and havoc in the arena of modern sexuality. It emphasizes the importance of embodiment and sexual experience but at the same time takes away any coherent basis for choosing *which* experience. Whereas expressivism generally seeks authenticity and intimacy, so that sexual encounters are at least directed toward these goals, postmodernism seeks sexual experience merely for its own sake, serving no greater purpose. In his snapshot of American life at the dawn of the third millennium, Wolfe suggests that postmodernism, despite its obvious flaws, has become the dominant way of thinking, not because it makes sense of life, but because it affirms the highest modern priority: unconstrained liberty.

On the basis of his wide-ranging study of 18- to 23-year-olds, sociologist Christian Smith makes some important observations about this generation as it is caught up in the vortex of postmodern freedom. Smith ends his sociological narrative with a prophetic portrait of these emerging adults as "sovereign individuals lacking conviction or direction."[6] They value freedom but are confused about what to do with it. They value information but have no coherent lens through which to organize it, and so they find themselves overwhelmed by it. They value diversity but have no standard for evaluating differences, which become fuzzy and gray. They want to keep their options open, but openness easily becomes a void filled by default

5. Tom Wolfe, *Hooking Up* (New York: Farrar, Straus & Giroux, 2000), 13.
6. Smith, *Souls in Transition*, 292–94.

imperatives: the easy rush of pornography, consumerism, uncommitted relationships, the next big experience, and so on.

Critiquing Modern Freedom

Although these three contemporary visions of freedom are quite different and battle with each other, what gives them so much combined force is that they are built on a shared foundation. At their core, they agree that each of us should be free to define and pursue life as we see fit. This idea of unrestricted personal choice is positively encouraged through the ever-expanding options offered by the novelty-machine that is consumerism.

Although this context has become our unquestioned horizon, theologian Stanley Hauerwas argues that it has hopelessly distorted our vision of who we are and how we relate to one another. This liberal/capitalist matrix permeates every part of our lives, he says, imposing its own comprehensive vision of the "good life" and making it difficult to appreciate any alternative to this way of living. Indeed, this vision is so pervasive that even most Christian thinking about ethics, including sexual ethics, operates unquestioningly within it. The church's first task, then, is to recognize and name the rival gods.[7]

Hauerwas develops his critique of modern freedom by pointing to the common moral discussion of "values." In particular, liberal social contexts form people within the perspective of "normal nihilism," meaning a shared acknowledgment that our moral values can only ever be contingent.[8] Regardless of how strongly we hold these values, in the end, they stand only on the strength of our personal convictions and not on any external truth. It is fine to have strong beliefs, of course, as long as we do not claim any special authority for our way of life or try to impose it on anyone else.

This perspective is rooted in the modern project itself, which cuts people off from any overarching story, such as God's creation, redemption, and progressive restoration of his creation as described in Scripture. The denial

7. Stanley Hauerwas, *A Community of Character: Toward a Constructive Christian Social Ethic* (Notre Dame, IN: University of Notre Dame Press, 1981), 12.

8. Stanley Hauerwas, "Preaching as though We Had Enemies," *First Things* 53 (May 1, 1995): 45–49.

of any sort of metanarrative encourages the illusion that we can create our own story and personal identity out of thin air, simply through our personal choices.[9]

One member of the US Supreme Court described this vision of modern freedom succinctly: "At the heart of liberty is the right to define one's own concept of existence, of meaning, of the universe, and of the mystery of human life."[10] We would be hard pressed to find many within mainstream culture who disagree with this vision. Yet this story is deceptive. Although it masquerades as the neutrality of free choice, it actually promotes its own vision of life and so seeks to manipulate the choices we make.

The Modern Vision of Sexuality: Two Myths but One Illusion to Live By

In the realm of sexuality and relationships, the modern vision of freedom is expressed under two myths, the "romanticist" and the "realist," both of which have become pervasive in our culture. Romanticism describes the freedom of the *expressive* individual. It says we should freely express with our bodies what we feel in our hearts; how we feel about someone should determine how far we go with him or her sexually. This is encouraged by the recent creation of "sexuality" as a type of distinct and core part of our identity that we must actively express to become a whole self. Sexual expression becomes an issue of personal integrity, of being true to the inner testimony of our desires, especially the sexual ones.

Realism, in contrast to romanticism, represents the freedom of the *utilitarian* individual. Realism tries to "demystify" sex by reducing it to a sort of "happiness technology" that offers fulfillment in the most immediate sense.[11] Sex becomes an important pursuit within the utilitarian priority of seeking pleasure and avoiding pain. Realism further demystifies sex by acknowledging that premarital sex is happening whether we like it or not, and so claims that the best we can do is to limit the potential damage, in the narrow terms of preventing pregnancy or disease.

9. Ibid., 48.

10. See the plurality opinion of Justices O'Connor, Kennedy, and Souter, Planned Parenthood of Southeastern Pennsylvania v. Casey, 505 U.S. 833 (1992).

11. Stanley Hauerwas and Allen Verhey, "From Conduct to Character: A Guide to Sexual Adventure," *Reformed Journal* 36, no. 11 (November 1, 1986): 12–16.

*note: we need to instead of having a set thing for a relationship create your own. Do whatever works for you.

Three Paths to Freedom on the Road to Nowhere

Although romanticism and realism appear to be opposites, Hauerwas says that these expressive and utilitarian paths to "freedom" both spring from the same underlying philosophy. Despite claiming to be morally neutral, realists accept the modern moral imperative that each person should do what seems best to him or her. Meanwhile, romanticism says that "love"—in the limited sense of passionate or affectionate feeling—is the necessary condition for both sex and marriage. Realism and romanticism also both insist that we should respect sex as a "private" matter. They both assert the basic moral premise that sex should be merely consensual.[12]

Although accepted as permanent features on the sexual landscape, romanticism and realism fail to go to the heart of the issue; they do not establish any solid ground on which to build their own visions of "authentic" relationships. In other words, they refuse to make the connection between personal character and authentic sexuality. Indeed, lurking beneath modern notions of what we should *do* in our sexual lives is the more fundamental question of who we should *be*. The key weakness of romanticism is that it seeks intimacy but refuses to encourage the habits that form people who are able to enter into and sustain genuinely intimate relationships. This is because real intimacy requires giving ourselves faithfully and permanently to another person in vulnerable trust. It is only in this context of safety that genuine intimacy, as opposed to just a powerful romantic or sexual attraction, can develop.

This puts young women, in particular, in a "double bind." Emerging adults today are expected to want to be in traditional committed relationships, but they are also encouraged to want sex "without strings attached." Marrying in their early twenties is no longer attractive to many young women with potential careers ahead of them, and so they are taught to avoid getting too emotionally attached. They don't want to be "tied down" to one person for the long run, but they want to enjoy companionship and sex in the meantime.[13]

12. In a wide-ranging survey of American college women, for instance, nearly 90 percent agreed with the statement "I should not judge anyone's sexual conduct except my own." See Norval Glenn and Elizabeth Marquardt, *Hooking Up, Hanging Out, and Hoping for Mr. Right: College Women on Dating and Mating Today* (New York: Institute for American Values, 2001).

13. Regnerus and Uecker, *Premarital Sex*, 149.

This creates a difficult scenario for both men and women, generating cognitive and relational dissonance. It is also questionable whether this sort of relational formation can suddenly be set aside at some point in the distant future. Our society's approach to sexual formation within emerging adulthood has wildly underestimated what is required to enter into and sustain these sorts of durable partnerships.

In a nationwide survey of American men, 62 percent of unmarried 25- to 29-year-olds and 51 percent of unmarried 30- to 34-year-olds said they were "not interested in getting married anytime soon." Eighty-one percent of the younger group and 74 percent of the older one agreed that "at this stage of your life, you want to have fun and freedom."[14] It is stunning to think that in previous generations most of these men would already be married fathers of multiple children.

To sum up, romanticism and realism agree that our sexual lives should be founded upon personal freedom, but they each fail to perceive that we are not as free as we think.

An Argument from the Outer Limits: Consensual Degradation

The problem with consent as the basic moral premise for sexuality is highlighted at the extreme end of the spectrum in the area of hard-core pornography. An essay highlighting the challenges of this philosophy caused a storm in the blogosphere.[15] The writer described going to a basement studio in San Francisco to watch, in the company of a small participating crowd, the filming of an explicit film. The choreographed narrative involved scenes with particularly extreme levels of degradation, abuse, and even mild levels of torture, such as electrocution.

The author describes a regular-looking crowd primarily made up of couples having a night out. She also notes that the lead actress had signed a detailed consent form and left the studio feeling upbeat and report-edly keen to repeat the experience. Obviously, this incident raises some important questions. On the basis of the modern principle that consent is king, it is difficult to challenge this filming on moral grounds because everyone involved was a willing participant and left feeling "happy." Yet

14. Ibid., 171.
15. Emily Witt, "What Do You Desire?," *n+1* 16 (Spring 2013).

the incident demonstrates the deep inadequacies of our cultural vision of freedom and sexuality.

Rod Dreher commented, in the ensuing debate, that there is nothing new about people seeking degrading sexual experiences. The problem is that this is becoming increasingly acceptable and even mainstream because our society now lacks a coherent moral framework within which these desires can be identified as deviant. In the modern moral void, "You can have whatever you desire," writes Dreher. "If you choose hell, then we will call it good, because it is freely chosen, and brings you pleasure."[16]

Yet this is not a "morally neutral" principle. It actively degrades and undermines the dignity of human sexuality while spreading this vision through the internet. In fact, the sex industry's evangelistic zeal is such that most explicit online content—fully 90 percent—is consumed free of charge. So, far from being a private consensual transaction, pornography is publicly and formatively shaping modern sexuality. That basement in San Francisco seems a long way from the church's vision of sexuality. Yet as Christians we too have been wooed by the idea of sexuality as a private matter, purely a concern between consenting adults behind closed doors. Increasingly, then, the church has no place in the bedrooms of believers.

The Private Self in Our Midst

Church leaders have often failed to understand how distinctive the Christian vision of sexuality really is and to articulate this vision as a convincing alternative to secular norms. As a result, Christian sexual ethics also appear to be operating out of the same romantic/realist fallacy as the secular perspective.[17]

In the epilogue to his book *Sex God*, former pastor Rob Bell describes a marriage he blessed in an unconventional wedding ceremony that lasted only seven minutes.[18] At one point in the service the couple released a

16. Rod Dreher, "Slouching towards Googletopia," *The American Conservative*, May 13, 2013, http://www.theamericanconservative.com/dreher/slouching-towards-googletopia/.

17. Stanley Hauerwas, "Sex in Public: How Adventurous Christians Are Doing It," *The Hauerwas Reader*, ed. John Berkman and Michael Cartwright (Durham, NC: Duke University Press, 2001), 481–504.

18. Rob Bell, *Sex God: Exploring the Endless Connections between Sexuality and Spirituality* (Grand Rapids: Zondervan, 2007), 174–75.

cluster of helium balloons as symbols of their previous failed marriages, terminated pregnancies, affairs, and unsuccessful relationships. They made this gesture as a picture of starting afresh together. Bell observes that they walked into an adjoining field, "just the two of them, holding hands, standing in knee-high grass, exchanging words that only they could hear," before letting go of the balloons. Unfortunately, the marriage ended acrimoniously a few years later. This haunting story simply shows, Bell tells us, that "life is messy" but that God's grace and healing are endless.

This story truly *is* a tragedy; it points to the desperate quality of so many relationships today, even within the church. But there is a far greater tragedy underlying the tale. Christian marriages should be built on a fundamentally different vision of personal identity and relationships than their secular counterparts. Rather than representing a contract between two ultimately independent people, Christian marriage is a covenant entered into sacrificially, within and for the benefit of the church. It is only within a committed community of faith that our intimate relationships can be properly supported and find their ultimate purpose.

Given the couple's messy history of relational failure, one wonders whether the marriage's sad end was anything but inevitable without greater support from the church community, both before and after their wedding. Yet there is no mention of the role of their church community. The book consistently emphasizes the private dynamics within marriage as being the critical determinant of success. For Bell, the priority of Christian marriage is the pursuit of sexual and emotional intimacy, exclusivity, and trust. At one point in the book he says, "A marriage is between those two people, not us. It's not ours, it's theirs."[19]

Although its overall intention is to tie Christian sexuality into the greater story of God's redemption and reconciliation of all creation, the book ironically depicts marriage and sexuality as private matters to be protected from outside influence or inquiry. But framing Christian relationships in the terms of modern romanticism, isolated from the corporate life of the church, actually is a reflection of cultural conformity—not of the transformation that Bell is aiming for.

19. Ibid., 138.

If the radically free modern self is also sitting in the sanctuary, then the question is, how did this vision of freedom become so pervasive among the very people who are called to live according to a different vision?

The Evolution of Radical Individualism

In the 1830s, French social philosopher Alexis de Tocqueville made some insightful observations about what he called the "habits of the heart" of the American people, which gave them and their country its specific character.[20] He focused on the American emphases on family life, religious traditions, and participation in local politics as practices that would create the sort of person who could sustain committed relationships and a connection to the wider community. But he also worried that American "individualism" (he was one of the first to use the term) was a force that could eventually isolate people from each other and undermine the very freedom they prized so highly.

With this warning in mind, a group of sociologists from the University of California at Berkeley undertook a comprehensive survey of American identity and relationships, interviewing people from all walks of life. Reflecting on their findings, they observed that the earlier forms of individualism observed by Tocqueville had, indeed, morphed into a radical individualism that saw the individual as the *a priori* reality of life—a self-sufficient atomic particle amid a cloud of other atoms.[21] Psychologist Paul Vitz calls this outlook "selfism," which he says is supported by modern psychology's vision of personal identity.[22] Rather than seeing the self as necessarily connected to other people, so that we can become our full selves only within relationships, "selfism" views each person as an autonomous being and often locates the source of our problems in formative relationships with our parents and siblings. Within this model, true freedom involves becoming self-sufficient and freeing ourselves from the control and dysfunction of other people.

Picking up on Tocqueville's prediction, the Berkeley sociologists observe that today's radical individualism has become cancerous, undermining the

20. Alexis de Tocqueville, *Democracy in America*, trans. George Lawrence, ed. J. P. Mayer (New York: Doubleday, 1969).

21. Bellah et al., *Habits of the Heart*, vii.

22. Vitz, *Psychology as Religion*, 57–58.

very significance we seek by cutting us off from meaningful relationships and broader social commitments. It is, they say, an influential cultural illusion that implies we can—and must—come to our deepest beliefs in the isolation of our private selves.[23] This has led to the endemic notion that love and marriage primarily have to do with personal gratification, a notion that has stripped relationships of their traditional social function of providing people with stable, committed contexts that tie them into the larger society.[24]

Creating Private Space

The modern conviction that our private lives are entirely our own, to be lived as we see fit, has a specific and quite recent history. The Enlightenment created a separation between "public" and "private" spaces, so that public spaces such as universities, legislatures, and courts could become places of reasoned debate, free from the prejudices of religion and the vagaries of emotion. The private realm—especially the home and the local church—was the place where love and faith, the things of the heart, could be freely expressed according to personal taste.

What was critical for Enlightenment thinkers was the idea that these spaces needed to be kept separate so as not to encroach upon each other. The utilitarian philosopher John Stuart Mill implanted the then controversial but now unquestioned idea that our private lives are nobody else's business, unless we directly hurt someone else. This became known as the "harm principle," meaning that no one has a right to interfere with me for my benefit, but only to prevent direct harm to others.[25]

Although there has always been a tension between the individual and social aspects of personal identity, the Enlightenment decisively created the concept of "private life" that has become so sacrosanct in our culture. But this separation is clearly illusory, because our so-called private lives are already deeply formed by social and cultural practices that shape us in every way. But this is a two-way dynamic. What goes on in our bedrooms—or on our computer screens, for that matter—will also ultimately influence our collective vision and approach to sexuality and relationships.

23. Bellah et al., *Habits of the Heart*, 65.
24. Ibid., 83.
25. Taylor, *Secular Age*, 484.

During my time in ministry in London, one of my pastoral responsibilities was to recruit, mentor, and oversee small-group leaders in the church. On more than one occasion, some of the seemingly mature Christian leaders approached us to let us know that they were living together, although they were not yet married. What was most surprising in each case was that they came forward not in order to resign their positions as leaders or to seek counsel but just "to put us in the picture."

Similarly, over the years, a number of Christian couples confided in us that they had made private marriage vows before God or been married legally in secret sometime before their "public" wedding. This idea that our sexual lives are purely private spaces has become a cardinal conviction among many modern Christians, as well as within the broader culture. Indeed, there often now appears to be no sense of connection between our personal relationships and the greater purposes of the wider church community.

why do we have to include the community.

Only God

Drowning Narcissus: The Narrowing of Self-Identity and Relationships

An ironic consequence of the emergence of this radically free self is that instead of making us more rounded individuals by exposing us to a more diverse range of people and influences, it has actually narrowed our social horizons and led to what Francis Fukuyama calls our "moral miniaturization."[26] As we have abandoned extended families and larger social organizations such as the church as our primary communities, we have simultaneously replaced them with smaller affinity groups, such as the gym, work colleagues, wine clubs, niche or single-generation churches, and even marriages. These can all become "lifestyle enclaves."[27]

These small voluntary associations enable us to pick and choose our own values, allowing us to reconcile the contradictory desires for autonomy and community. In other words, we choose to be with people we like, people we are comfortable with . . . people like us. This is intensified by the transition to "virtual" relationships—via social media, chat rooms, and online

26. See Francis Fukuyama, *The Great Disruption: Human Nature and the Reconstitution of Social Order* (New York: Touchstone, 2000), 49, 243, 281–82.
27. Bellah et al., *Habits of the Heart*, 71–75.

pornography—that encourage us to further fragment ourselves as we select different virtual sources to meet our desires and personal needs. We can even create multiple avatars of ourselves to inhabit infinite virtual contexts.

In Greek mythology, the youth Narcissus became so captivated by his own reflection in the water that he eventually fell into the image and drowned. This ancient insight helps describe what is happening within modern relationships. The narrowing of our social horizons reflects a similar tendency toward self-absorption as we seek out those in our own image. We are told that this path leads toward personal freedom, but it is creating a society made up of individuals who are drowning in their own personas.

The enduring appeal and fascination of Jane Austen's *Pride and Prejudice* is the mystery of love, which could cross even the watertight boundaries of the nineteenth-century English class system. The subversive power of romantic love is that it calls us to move beyond ourselves, to put ourselves at risk for the sake of something broader than our personal horizons. Despite the modern imperative to be radically free, we still yearn for intimacy that draws us beyond the confines of ourselves. This is in step with the trajectory of the gospel, which calls us into sacrificial relationships within a community of people who are not like us. Paul's churches were complex because they were diverse, including Jews and gentiles, slaves and their owners, rich and poor. This unity in diversity, which was operating within and resisting a highly stratified society, was the miracle of the gospel and was only possible through the Spirit.

"Going Solo"

In his challenging book *Going Solo*, sociologist Eric Klinenberg says that although we have tracked the growing numbers of single, cohabiting, and unmarried people in America, one of the most important trends over the last fifty years has gone largely unnoticed: the growing number of people who are choosing to live alone.[28] The change has been dramatic.

In 1950, there were about four million Americans living alone, a little less than 10 percent of all households. Today there are more than thirty-two million "singletons," as Klinenberg calls them, accounting for about

28. Eric Klinenberg, *Going Solo: The Extraordinary Rise and Surprising Appeal of Living Alone* (New York: Penguin Books, 2012).

28 percent of all American households.[29] The fastest growing age group of people living alone is those under thirty-five, and this trend is even more pronounced in big cities, where singletons are closer to one-half of all households. It seems that we are increasingly willing to pay a premium for the privilege of living alone, which is becoming the quintessential modern expression of personal freedom.

Klinenberg discovered that these singletons, although living alone, did not for the most part feel isolated or lonely. In fact, he says, they tended to be more socially engaged than married peers. Only a small minority found themselves locked in a downward spiral of isolation and depression.

Although Klinenberg puts a positive spin on these social developments, we can also see this trend from a different angle. The Christian invitation into self-giving relationships stretches us beyond the narrow concerns of our personal preferences and reflects Jesus's pouring himself out for the sake of others. The gospel beckons us beyond the detached safety of personal sovereignty and relationships on our own terms, into the demands and rewards of genuine community.

My concern is not that "going solo" removes us from relationships but that it changes the *nature* of our relationships. As Klinenberg says, the main impulse for choosing to live alone is that it offers us freedom to do what we want, when we want to, without concern about someone else's eyes looking over us and passing judgment.[30] Lying at the heart of this important "solo" trend is the modern desire to be in control of our lives, especially our relationships. Although Klinenberg sees this trend as a positive social development, it is hard to see how it fosters the sort of character and rhythms that enable us to form and sustain lasting relationships. Rather than enhancing our relationships, surely the narrowing of our social and moral horizons impoverishes them in the long run.

In a similar vein, Christian Smith makes some interesting observations about emerging adults and their view of personal freedom. Smith observes that this 18–23 age group includes the least religious adults in the United States today, with only about 20 percent attending a religious service weekly.[31] It is not that they are much less spiritually or religiously engaged than

29. Ibid., 5–6.
30. Ibid., 17, 89.
31. Smith, *Souls in Transition*, 94–95.

previous generations; traditionally, this stage of life is one in which religious commitments are loosened, when young people explore the freedom that comes after leaving home and before the responsibilities of marriage and family. What is of more concern is that this open-ended, freewheeling stage of life is becoming longer.[32] There are even signs that, for some, this stage can morph into a prolonged adolescence that lasts well into their forties and beyond. What used to be a brief transitional phase is becoming a permanent lifestyle choice.

This trend has important implications for pastors. People are delaying or avoiding any greater commitment to their faith or to the demands of committed relationships such as marriage and family. Within the dazzling array of choices available, our consumerist mentality tempts us to keep our options open for as long as possible.

This "Peter Pan" syndrome is most enticing in big cities, where the possibilities appear endless. We can find a kindred group to suit any stage of life and make us feel at home. What is tragic about this social phenomenon, something that my wife and I observed at close quarters among our predominantly young congregation in London, is that most people did not consciously choose to remain in this stage of life. Many people found themselves trapped in a cycle that they seemed unable to understand or break out of. For instance, their romantic relationships would break down for similar reasons at similar stages. One of our key challenges as pastors of this generation is to help people progress through this stage of life into more mature stages of development.

Freedom at the Altar: The Crisis in Christian Relationships

Within the church, the tragedy of the "freedom trap" has dramatically affected our approach to both marriage and singleness. Along with the secular world, the church has fallen into the snare of sanctifying personal autonomy as a virtue. We are, for instance, becoming accustomed to watching the breakup of Christian marriages with genuine but resigned sadness. Yet within the church we seek to resist and rise above modern fatalism. Jesus's work of atonement involved reconciling, or putting back together, what had been fractured—our relationships with God, ourselves, each

32. Ibid., 6, 56.

other, and creation. We seek to embody this thoroughgoing reconciliation within the community of faith as the "firstfruits" of the kingdom of God. If Thomas Hobbes's bleak vision represents the social fragmentation of Babel, the Christian vision seeks the social reconciliation of Pentecost.

It is perhaps in our marriages that we can most clearly witness to the gospel of peace and reconciliation. Paul expresses the stunning conviction that Christian marriage should stand as a living metaphor for the self-giving love between Christ and his church.[33] This is the profound mystery of Christian sexuality. We are called to walk a radical middle path, resisting both the saccharine fantasy of modern romanticism and the grim fatalism of Hobbes's realism.

Although marriage offers many wonderful benefits, we also need to teach the essential crisis that lies at the heart of marriage. The task of weaving together two different stories, personalities, and family backgrounds is costly work that we cannot take lightly. Children, although a blessing and gift, provide even stiffer challenges. If marriage is like an earthquake that shakes our world, then the demands of young children are more like a city-leveling tsunami. We need to stand firmly on both feet, then, in our approach to and teaching about marriage. Marriage is a *gift*, but it's also a *crisis*.

Ties That Loose: Getting Caught in the "Freedom Trap"

The modern vision of freedom encourages us to keep our options "in play" and to be skeptical about entering into ties that bind us. Today independence is dressed up as the ultimate form of maturity, so that living alone is becoming *de rigueur* for sophisticated urbanites who can afford it. Although we still crave intimacy and connection, self-sufficiency is lauded as the cardinal modern virtue.

This has made it difficult for men, in particular, to take the ultimate risk of entering a committed relationship. There may be many different reasons for this, depending on the person and his specific circumstances. Young men who have not had constructive male exemplars—usually a father—and who have not been positively initiated into adulthood often face real challenges. They can become confused about how to make the bold step into a permanent relationship. This pathway to maturity is a journey in which

33. Eph. 5:31–33.

we need guidance from those who can most deeply affirm our identity. The modern myth is that we can become whole and mature on our own.

Yet every known civilization throughout history has placed enormous significance on the rites and rituals that affirm boys and usher them into adult maturity and responsibility, as well as those that initiate girls into womanhood. Sadly, our culture's vision of personal freedom and its adoration of youth are prolonging adolescence, creating significant challenges in nurturing mature relationships within the church.

Concluding Thoughts: Liberty at What Cost?

The second part of this book will discuss how we might address the complex matrix that has been created by the "freedom trap." At this stage, I want to highlight the extent to which the modern self, with its focus on being free in the negative sense of being free *from* other people, has seeped into the Christian imagination and distorted our vision of sexuality and relationships. The "freedom trap" is one of the major challenges facing the church and its formation of mature disciples today.

4

We Are What We Acquire

Consumerism as a Corrupting Dynamic

On our way home from a family wedding in California, we flew out of the city of Reno, Nevada. Viewed from the sky, the sparse desert surroundings threw the human-made landscape into sharp relief. What was unmistakable looking down was the dominance of retail strip malls within the city and suburban limits. There seemed to be only limited space between these monstrosities of conformity. On our drive north from Seattle later that Sunday afternoon, we passed a giant outlet mall. It seemed as if the whole Pacific Northwest had crowded into this cavernous but now claustrophobic shrine.

Does it make you wonder, given the pervasive presence of these places, what influence they have on us? If retail therapy is our new religion and the regional mall is our place of worship, how does it influence who we are, including our sexual lives?

Capitalism is probably the most formative structural reality within our society. It sets the course for most of our lives, shaping what we consider to be worth having and giving us a context in which to pursue those things. Certainly for most in the Western world, capitalism has become the taken-for-granted shape of things, as permanent and unquestioned as the sealed roads and power lines outside our houses.

One of the most influential church fathers, Augustine of Hippo, viewed the human person as enmeshed in a complex web of desires. For Augustine, as "desiring creatures" we cannot escape our magnetic attraction to whatever we ultimately love. The key is not *whether* we love but *what* we love. We are fundamentally characterized by an attraction toward our Creator, as expressed in Augustine's prayer, "You have made us for yourself and our hearts are restless until they find their rest in you."[1] Nothing else can satisfy this longing, although these desires can become misdirected when they attach to objects and ultimate goals other than God.

In fact, the Christian conviction goes even further than this. Sin has already bent our desires out of shape—witness the age-old temptation of idolatry—and these can be set straight only by God's radical grace.[2] Our lives are essentially shaped by what we are drawn toward as a vision of ultimate human flourishing—the "good life."[3] I will develop this view of human identity in the second part of this book. In the meantime, this brief sketch will help show how capitalism distorts our fundamental desires.

Given the power of our cultural context to shape us, we need to look critically at those aspects of life in which modern culture has invested heavily, such as economics and sexuality. Daniel Bell argues that the "megapolis" of global capitalism has replaced the nation-state as the most pervasive influence in our lives.[4] Capitalism, he says, now controls all aspects of our lives and must therefore be challenged by the church as a form of idolatry. Bell suggests that capitalism's "technologies of desire" impose on us a regime of disciplines and practices that seek to shape us within a certain vision of human flourishing: *acquisition* and *consumption*.

Using Augustine's terms, we can say that capitalism seeks to orient our fundamental desires to accept other gods that can never satisfy our essential longing.[5] In the language of the Old Testament, consumerism offers us

1. Augustine, *Confessions*, trans. Henry Chadwick, Oxford World's Classics (Oxford: Oxford University Press, 2008), 3.
2. Steven Shakespeare, *Radical Orthodoxy: A Critical Introduction* (London: SPCK, 2007), 119.
3. Taylor, *Secular Age*, 16.
4. Daniel Bell, *Liberation Theology after the End of History: The Refusal to Cease Suffering* (London: Routledge, 2001), 17.
5. Ibid., 245.

bread that can never satisfy our hunger and broken cisterns that can never hold thirst-quenching water.[6] No matter how much we gorge on this food, it leaves us malnourished. Sadly, the Western church accepted the Trojan horse of capitalism into its midst because it accepted capitalism's claim to religious neutrality. But that is a false claim. The underlying assumptions of capitalism's autonomous, competitive, and free-choosing self carry a normative vision of the self and the world, a world that is closer to Babel than Pentecost.

The market economy is marked not by social reconciliation but by competition, and it shapes us in two important ways. At the big-picture level, it seeks to capture our imagination about what we should be aiming for in life, that is, our telos or essential purpose. As well as giving us a goal to live for, a happiness target, capitalism also provides clear pathways and disciplines to help us reach our destination.

The Disciplining of Modern Desires

The fallacy at the heart of the modern world is the conviction that we are free to do whatever we want. The truth is that we are deeply influenced by secular scripts that subtly shape our vision of life and our deepest desires. We are not, it turns out, as free as we think. Even in those places where we seem to be freest, such as in gargantuan shopping malls with their boundless choices, we are being formed by what James K. A. Smith calls "secular liturgies."[7] These are visions of what life is all about: what will bring us satisfaction, what will save us, what will give our lives meaning and significance, what will add up to the "good life." Smith warns that we can avoid overtly religious liturgies by not attending church, but we cannot avoid cultural ones. They are all around us, and they seek to capture our imaginations, to tap into our deepest desires, and to direct our worship toward rival gods.

The business of advertising perhaps best understands the energizing core of personal identity. This comes into clear focus in the cutting-edge field of "neuromarketing." Developed in the late 1990s by Harvard psychologists, neuromarketers use brain scans (fMRIs) to understand how people respond

6. Isa. 55:2; Jer. 2:13.
7. Smith, *Desiring the Kingdom*, 86–88.

to various marketing images, focusing on those that evoke the strongest emotional response. What makes this field most disturbing is its focus on manipulating *subconscious* brain activity, which accounts for most human thinking—over 90 percent—including our emotions. Developed under the sci-fi-sounding patent Zaltman Metaphor Elicitation Technique (ZMET), the best-known neuromarketing method engages the human subconscious with specially selected sets of images that cause a positive emotional response, activating hidden images and metaphors that are likely to stimulate a purchase. In other words, advertisers seek to harness our subconscious emotions in order to sell us things. Consumerism promises us experiences that will set our desires free, but in reality it intentionally manipulates our passions toward its own ends.

Secular Liturgies as Formative Practices in the Mall

Smith offers a practical example of how consumerism shapes our desires by describing the devotional practices we encounter at the shopping mall.[8] These disciplines encourage us to yearn and quest for our destination, as travelers on the road to the good life. Smith suggests that shopping malls have become places of retreat, transcendence, and worship, as medieval cathedrals were in their time. The architecture of the enclosed mall shuts us off from the frantic world outside and vaults our vision up to the sky through its glass ceiling, hinting at the promise of a higher reality.[9] In the mall, "pilgrims" walk between chapels that compete for their devotion, each offering its own distinctive vision of the satisfied life. Referring to each shop's mannequins, Smith says, "Unlike the flattened depictions of saints one might find in stained-glass windows, here is an array of three-dimensional icons adorned in garb that—as with all iconography—inspires us to be imitators of these exemplars. These statues and icons embody for us concrete images of 'the good life.'"[10]

In this way, the "new global religion" of consumerism taps into our embodied nature by appealing, via our senses, to our imaginations. The rich physical visions of these beautiful, happy people invite us to imagine ourselves in their image and so to enter into the disciplines required to

8. Ibid., 20.
9. Ibid., 21.
10. Ibid.

achieve this transformation: *acquisition* and *consumption*. Unlike the dull moralizing of the church, the shopping mall's religion trades in beauty. It appeals to our deepest desires and aspirations. Although Smith admits that his lush description borders on tongue-in-cheek, he insists that this cultural exegesis acts as a form of "apocalyptic," seeing through and revealing the true nature of something that presents itself as benign and normal.[11]

Rather than being a "neutral" space, Smith says, the mall is religious and formational. It shapes our ultimate desires by presenting a vision of human flourishing embedded, and thereby concealed, within its social imaginary.[12] This vision carries an implicit notion of personal brokenness equivalent to "sin," so that its icons present an image of the perfect life that highlights the gulf between them and us. The mall taps into legitimate human drives, such as the quest for happiness, progress, and beauty, but it exploits these desires by creating a sense of insufficiency in our lives that needs to be filled. Within the identity crisis that it creates, consumerism offers us hope of redemption through its own gods: again, acquisition and consumption.

However, the practice of consumption presents us with a confused vision of reality. At one extreme, it invests almost transcendent meaning and life-changing power in physical things, while it also teaches us to devalue and discard these same things almost immediately, as they fall out of fashion or move to the clearance rack.

As with all idolatries, consumerism is a corruption of something good. As divine image-bearers, we are drawn to beauty. When rightly oriented, beautiful things reveal something about God's own form and character and so point us toward the kingdom beyond. Scripture tells us that the first person "filled with the Spirit of God" was Bezalel, the artisan who adorned Solomon's temple where Yahweh dwelt among his people.[13] Together with artistic creativity, God gave Bezalel wisdom, understanding, and knowledge. We should not, then, reject beauty but rather seek to reappropriate it as a window onto divine reality. Consumerism, in contrast, offers us beautiful things as sacred substitutes.

Modern consumerism both exploits and distorts our sexual natures, making consumerism and sexualization powerful partners. Within this

11. Ibid., 23.
12. Ibid., 94.
13. Exod. 31:1–5.

nexus, promises of sexual fulfillment sell almost everything by evoking our longing for transcendence and then, in a move of substitution, channeling that desire into a consumer product. This formative process affirms us as sexual beings but turns us into sexualized consumers.[14]

The biblical model of personal identity is entirely different. It describes us as holistic beings who cannot compartmentalize ourselves into different selves for different contexts. So consumerism distorts not just our view of sex but our very sexual nature; our longing for God and relationship with others is collapsed into sex and dead objects.[15] In this way, consumerism becomes the social imaginary that shapes our vision of human flourishing in every aspect of life, including our sexual lives.

Making the Perfect Woman: Consumerism as a Religious Narrative

The religious nature and significant influence of consumerism in our lives is made all the more powerful by the way in which it mimics the religious narrative. In Gregory of Nyssa's spiritual classic *The Life of Moses*, Gregory uses Moses's journey as an allegory for the Christian life. At a certain point in the story, Moses, representing the Christian disciple, ascends the mountain toward God. Every time Moses glimpses God, God disappears farther up the mountain into "divine darkness," which represents the infinite mystery of God. Through this allegory, Gregory is expressing the never-ending nature of our journey into knowing God. Our deepening experience of him increases our desire and appetite for more, drawing us farther up the eternal mountain. In other words, the more we taste the goodness of God's presence, the more of it we yearn for. Consumerism, through the unattainability of its saints and icons, also offers us an ever-ascending and yet never-ending journey toward satisfaction.

Jesse Epstein's short documentary *34 x 25 x 36* provides a philosophical window into a company that makes female mannequins. As the firm's owner declares at the outset, "There are no perfect bodies out there . . . we make the perfect body." The goal, he says, is to "stir up the adrenaline

14. James K. A. Smith, *Introducing Radical Orthodoxy: Mapping a Post-Secular Theology* (Grand Rapids: Baker Academic, 2004).

15. Smith, *Desiring the Kingdom*, 76.

in the buyer to say, hmmm, I could look like that." Describing a sculptor creating a template from a real human model, the chief designer says, "He's taking the essence of her [the human model] and capturing what her features are about into an image that is actually more than what she is. We have the ability to alter things." Comparing his work to medieval religious art, which captured the form of saints, he goes on:

> We replicate what the perfect girl is for the times because actually it's a continuation of the same thing [i.e., religious art]. I can see where it would be believing in something or, in a way, worshiping something because it's something that you aim for. Do we worship perfect women? Do we worship people that dress in very expensive clothes? It's playing with people's minds about what their ideal is. In religion the ideal is salvation. What is salvation in our current society? Is it being looked upon, being photographed everywhere you go? To some people it is very important. People have to believe in something.[16]

This modern "religious art" presents idealized saints to be emulated, and yet they are always out of reach. Whereas the purpose of medieval art lay in spiritual emulation, salvation within the lower horizons of the modern world is now found through embodied perfection.

This notion points to the myth of attainability within consumerism. Although this myth seeks to mimic and displace the religious narrative, there is a critical difference between them. Whereas Gregory's vision is fueled by the progressive satisfaction of our spiritual yearning, which spurs us on to experience more of God, consumerism—like all forms of idolatry—is driven by intensifying promises that end up giving us nothing. Happiness and fulfillment always lie just out of reach.

In contrast to the progressive fulfillment of the Christian journey, consumerism is a form of institutionalized dissatisfaction that whets our appetite but leaves us hungry, revealing the myth of freedom within consumerism. Having presented themselves as priests offering salvation, consumption and acquisition become gods in their own right. As we follow these false gods up the mountain, they offer us progressive self-realization and control through personal choice. In reality, we are caught in a downward spiral of provisional commitments.

16. *34 x 25 x 36* (Los Angeles: New Day Films, 2009).

Consumerism and Sexuality

Consumers of Everything, Producers of Nothing

Stanley Hauerwas argues that capitalism's approach to human identity and social relations undermines the formation of sexual fidelity by shaping our choices along purely consumerist lines. Capitalism, he says, creates "sexual identities through the construction of our bodies by economic forces that make us willing consumers capable of producing nothing."[17] As our sexuality has become increasingly detached from its essential purposes—relationships, marriage, and children—it has become simply a mode of consumption. As a result, human sexuality has become part of the entertainment industry—a choice to be catered to rather than a vocation that serves any greater goal. Our sexual choices are seen as just different modes of consumption within an infinite spectrum of choice, without any one choice having an intrinsic priority over the others.[18]

As part of the entertainment industry, sexuality has fallen prey to consumerism's scheduled obsolescence, which thrives on short-term commitments and so inherently favors transient human relationships. Consumerism trains us to acquire, consume, and move on, with novelty as our guiding impulse. The sad reality, though, is that what we do with things, we will inevitably do with people. The modern world has taught us to compartmentalize our lives, so that we can be different people at work, at home, in church, or in the shopping mall. But we cannot avoid the reality that each of us is a socio-psycho-somatic whole.

Loving the World, One at a Time

Popular media and social commentators have made much of the idea that we're living in a "hook up" generation, meaning that sex "without strings attached" is becoming the cultural norm. In reality, though, this trend has been greatly exaggerated. Most people still believe that sex should go hand in hand with an ongoing relationship and that it is important to be

17. Hauerwas, *Better Hope*, 50.
18. Ibid. See also Nicholas Boyle, *Who Are We Now? Christian Humanism and the Global Market from Hegel to Heaney* (Notre Dame, IN: University of Notre Dame Press, 1988), 59.

faithful while in a relationship. In fact, the dominant sexual script today, the narrative that rules above all others, is *serial monogamy*.[19]

This represents a subtle but tectonic shift in the dynamics of modern relationships. Although most people still believe in monogamous relationships, these have become brief and tenuous, so that people move in and out of them more readily. The prevailing wisdom tells us, "No matter the number of relationships, so long as they're one at a time!"[20]

This clearly lines up with the disciplines encouraged by our culture's consumerist matrix. Within this environment we are trained to desire things but also to remain aloof from the very products and services that promise us fulfillment. We must continually seek the option that offers the most features at the lowest cost. We salivate over the latest smartphone, but only until it is usurped by a slimmer and more loaded model. And so with relationships. The consumerist self is taught to seek the most features for the lowest price, as well as to hold open all future options.

Most of the young people surveyed by Regnerus and Uecker believe that they can swim with the fast-flowing current of this sexual script in their twenties and thirties and then, at the appropriate moment, simply choose to swim in the opposite direction—that is, to enter into a permanent relationship and raise a family. This is surely dangerous hubris. It would seem obvious that serial monogamy, as an expression of the consumerist self, forms the sort of person who is unable to enter into anything permanent, let alone the demands and sacrifices of marriage and family.

Breaking Down Artificial Walls

The bottom line is that as Western Christians we tend to compartmentalize our lives, especially our sex lives. We might ask, "What on earth could the market economy or shopping malls have to do with our sexual decisions?" Or, if we *do* see the connection, we take the existence of capitalism as a positive and unquestionable part of a Christian belief structure. Calling this assumption into question, Mark Regnerus demonstrates how tightly and dubiously connected our consumerist outlook is with our vision of

19. Regnerus and Uecker, *Premarital Sex*, 70.
20. Ibid.

sexuality. He observes the clear "antifamily sentiment" within the social science research community, which sees marriage and family as an optional extra once a person's education is complete and his or her career and financial trajectory are secure.[21] Rather than being essential, families are merely additions to the unrestricted individual.

What is most striking, though, is that even the so-called defenders of the family—religious conservatives—often play by the same rules. Regnerus critiques the Christian Right's thin vision of marriage and family as it fights to protect certain legal definitions and rights for the traditional family while the Christian community fails to address the causes that undermine the health and resilience of families within the church. We focus on the *law* of the family rather than on the *life* of the family, which is what makes it worth protecting in the first place. Connecting this specifically to consumerism, Regnerus notes that "family-focused conservatives want to have their cake (no sex before marriage) and eat it too (delayed marriage and family formation—the triumph of free market consumer-oriented individualism)."[22]

If we in the church are serious about marriage and family, we need to acknowledge that we have encouraged this generation to exist in an untenable space by asking them to remain chaste within a prolonged and, for many, unrealistic time frame. This situation tends to breed hypocrisy and shame rather than vision and mature faith. We need to creatively and practically prepare young people for marriage and family, to resist the formation of the consumerist self within our congregations, to support younger marriages, and to nourish families. But more of that later.

Sexuality and Technology

"The Dirty Mind and Lonely Heart of John Mayer"[23]

If consumerism is shaping our sexual lives today, then its influence is nowhere more powerful than within the disembodied realm of cyberspace.

21. Regnerus, *Forbidden Fruit*, 213.
22. Ibid., 214.
23. Erik Hedegaard, "The Dirty Mind and Lonely Heart of John Mayer," *Rolling Stone*, June 6, 2012, http://www.rollingstone.com/music/news/the-dirty-mind-and-lonely-heart -of-john-mayer-20120606.

Popular musician John Mayer gave a brief, honest, and culturally prophetic interview to *Playboy* magazine in 2011. An important aside about Mayer is that he is not perceived as a seedy fringe figure. He is a young, handsome, and influential musician who has dated many of the sirens of the pop and celebrity world. Yet in this interview he describes a world where fantasy effortlessly trumps real experience on any given day. Mayer's interview illuminates the growing influence of the virtual sexual mall. As he describes himself,

> I'm a self-soother. The Internet, DVR, Netflix, Twitter—all these things are moments in time throughout your day when you're able to soothe yourself. We have an autonomy of comfort and pleasure. By the way, pornography? . . . You wake up in the morning, open a thumbnail page, and it leads to a Pandora's box of visuals. There have probably been days when I saw 300 [naked women] before I got out of bed. Internet pornography has absolutely changed my generation's expectations. How does that not affect the psychology of having a relationship with somebody? It's got to. This is my problem now: Rather than meet somebody new, I would rather go home and replay the amazing experiences I've already had. What that explains is that I'm more comfortable in my imagination than I am in actual human discovery. The best days of my life are when I've dreamed about a sexual encounter with someone I've already been with.[24]

Mayer makes his point with frightening clarity: we cannot keep sexual fantasy as a separate compartment in our lives, neatly sealed off from our other relationships. That is an illusion. Online pornography makes it difficult for a user to stay present in his or her flesh-and-blood relationships. Sexual fantasy generates a destructive loop by shaping our expectations for real-life relationships while also displacing those relationships.

It's no wonder that Jesus made such a point of reconnecting our sexual imaginations with our practical lives when he warned that lusting after a woman is tantamount to sleeping with her.[25] This extreme teaching was a typical rabbinic form of moral instruction, meant to shock the listener. In other words, our imagination shapes the contours of our lives.

24. Full transcript of interview available at http://www.thepaparazzis.com/john-mayer-playboy-interview-full-text-apology-video/.
25. Matt. 5:28.

Embracing Erotic Robotics: The Future of Technological Intimacy

Unfortunately, John Mayer does not have the final word on the future of detached intimacy. David Levy is a former world chess champion, computer scientist, and CEO of a leading computer software company that specializes in "smart" toys for children. These toys, such as robotic pets, mimic the experience of looking after, talking to, and playing with live pets. They train us at an early age to see these artificial interactions as "real." Levy's firm has won the world's most prestigious award in conversational software for convincing people that they were speaking with another person and not a machine.

Levy wrote a book with the arresting title *Love and Sex with Robots: The Evolution of Human-Robot Relationships*. He predicts that within forty years, sexual intimacy with robots will become as common as with humans.[26] Instead of being alarmed by this, Levy says that it will offer us many benefits, such as an infinitely more creative sex life! It will actually enhance our real-life relationships, he says, by allowing us to practice friendship and intimacy with machines. But Levy goes even further by suggesting that marriage to robots may be better than human relationships, offering the upsides of normal marriage without the downsides of infidelity, illness, conflict, and complex differences (robots don't grow up in dysfunctional families). For Levy, the only question we should ask is, "Does the robot make me happy?"

MIT professor Sherry Turkle describes being disturbed by Levy's book because of its blindness to the critical differences between human intimacy and robotic interaction, which is not "intimacy" at all. Intimacy, she says, is possible only with a mutual "other." Intimacy requires a certain type of consciousness, a genuine core of feeling, which allows us to interact and identify with each other. Aping "humanness" does not create genuine human interaction.[27] Turkle negatively reviewed Levy's book, only to be accused by an angry *Scientific American* reporter of "species chauvinism"; that is, she was denying robots their right to "realness" and their own distinctive qualities.[28]

26. David Levy, *Love and Sex with Robots: The Evolution of Human-Robot Relationships* (New York: HarperCollins, 2008), 303–10.
27. Sherry Turkle, *Alone Together: Why We Expect More from Technology and Less from Each Other* (New York: Basic Books, 2012), 5–6.
28. Ibid., 7–8.

For the agitated reporter, the marriage robot was not just "better than nothing," a mere substitute for the real thing, but potentially "better than something," a genuine alternative to messy human relationships. Although this all sounds like something from a dystopian science-fiction movie, these are some of the most respected voices in their fields and, in Levy's case, someone who is playing an influential role in modern childhood formation.

Turkle's observations are particularly poignant in assessing our culture's changing expectations for personal relationships. What is most important, she says, is not whether Levy's predictions come true but what they say about our present willingness to accept the soothing balm of false intimacies in place of genuine companionship. Turkle describes an encounter with a young woman at a conference where she was giving a presentation on anthropomorphism (when robots do humanlike things that cause us to think of them as an "other"):

> During a session break, the graduate student, Anne, a lovely, raven-haired woman in her mid-twenties, wanted specifics. She confided that she would trade in her boyfriend "for a sophisticated Japanese robot" if the robot would produce what she called "caring behavior." She told me that she relied on a "feeling of civility in the house." She did not want to be alone. She said, "If the robot could provide that environment, I would be happy to help produce the illusion that there is somebody really with me." She was looking for a "no-risk relationship" that would stave off loneliness. A responsive robot, even one just exhibiting scripted behavior, seemed better to her than a demanding boyfriend. I asked her, gently, if she was joking. She told me she was not.[29]

Genuine feeling was not essential to this young woman as long as the performance of feeling seemed genuine. As this sad encounter suggests, technology is most seductive when it offers to salve our human vulnerabilities. And we are at our most vulnerable in our intimate relationships.

Connection without Communion: Relational Detachment in a Digital World

As much as we need each other and yearn for genuine friendship, the digital world offers an infinite variety of contexts that allow us to hide from

29. Ibid., 8.

each other by controlling the types of interactions we have.[30] One of the risks posed by social media, for instance, is that it offers wide but shallow relationships. It creates a veil, which allows us to mediate our exposure to other people. This inevitably tempts us to become pseudo-avatars, or slightly adjusted versions of ourselves. As we spend increasingly more time "connecting" with each other online, it raises the question of whether social media is *stimulating* genuine relationships or just *simulating* them. Are we sharing our lives with others, or are we just broadcasting them? Are we learning the rhythms of intimacy, or are we too busy pleasing the adoring crowd? These are important questions because we are increasingly "doing relationships" virtually.[31]

In 2014 the social media giant Facebook had 1.31 billion users, and Nielsen Research found that American teenagers are sending 3,146 messages per month, which translates to over 100 every day. Even those under twelve years of age are sending 1,146 messages per month. These staggering findings suggest that young people today are hyperconnected; at the same time, they spend less time in face-to-face relationships.[32] Turkle describes the weakening of friendship that is occurring among young people today as a result of the "flattening" out of our forms of communication.

> We are connected as we've never been connected before, and we seem to have damaged ourselves in the process. A 2010 analysis of data from over fourteen thousand college students over the past thirty years [in the US] shows that since the year 2000, young people have reported a dramatic decline in interest in other people. Today's college students are, for example, far less likely to say that it is valuable to try to put oneself in the place of others or to try to understand their feelings. The authors of this study associate students' lack of empathy with the availability of online games and social networking. An online connection can be deeply felt, but you only need to deal with the part of the person you see in your game world or social network. Young people don't seem to feel they need to deal with more, and over time they lose the

30. Ibid., 225.
31. Ibid., 202.
32. Roger Entner, "Under-Aged Texting Usage and Actual Cost," *Nielsen Newswire*, January 27, 2010, http://www.nielsen.com/us/en/newswire/2010/under-aged-texting-usage -and-actual-cost.html. Nielsen analyzes more than forty thousand mobile bills every month in the United States to determine what consumers are spending their money on.

inclination. One might say that absorbed in those they have "friended," children lose interest in friendship.[33]

As the researchers suggest, this generation is so absorbed with self-concern and saturated in media that they have very little time for empathizing with others. This is one of the most significant formational and relational challenges facing both pastors and parents today. How can we promote genuine communities of friendship within a frenetic world of online connections? How do we encourage face-to-face social contexts that slow the communication down, allowing empathy, trust, patience, kindness, and joy to develop, both as personal capacities and as social dynamics within our churches? Indeed, it is these virtues and environments that provide the foundation for genuine Christian discipleship and relationships.

And so we come full circle in our conversation about consumerism and the formation of personal identity. Consumerism's glorification of things and commodification of people comes into full view with both the sociable robot and the mechanization of friendship through social media. We are left with a worrying symmetry whereby, as Turkle says, we are increasingly "determined to give human qualities to objects and content to treat each other as objects."[34]

This phenomenon reflects our cultural zeitgeist and reveals the way moderns think about sexual and relational intimacy within the utilitarian mind-set. In this pragmatic-efficient way of thinking, sexual desire and our quest for intimacy are simply human needs that can be met in different ways. Just as we can receive essential vitamins from vegetables or a convenient pill, our relational needs can be met by any number of purpose-made products.

The key within this consumerist mind-set is not *what* we are connecting with—another person, digital imagery, or a physical humanoid—but the satisfaction of our perceived needs. We are increasingly complicit with the illusion of intimacy as long as it appears to satisfy those needs. Like John Mayer, we are becoming more willing to trade the messy but rich reality of human relationships for the false allure of simulation, which promises "intimacy" without risk.

33. Turkle, *Alone Together*, 292–93.
34. Ibid., xiv.

Getting Together in the Ether: Online Dating as Cupid in a Brave New World

One of the most significant trends influencing relationships and sexual behavior today is online dating. Digital matchmaking looks set to become the most important theme shaping modern relationships, via the growing influence of dating websites, including Christian providers. Whereas in the early 1990s less than 1 percent of relationships started online, that figure has risen to over 20 percent in recent years. Between thirty and forty million people in North America now use one of over fifteen hundred internet dating websites, and the number of users in the United States is growing by 70 percent every year. It has become an industry worth over $1.5 billion, tempting other big online players like Facebook to move into the market.[35]

Online dating offers an alluring promise. By selectively matching us up within a virtually unlimited pool of prospects, internet dating promises that we are all but assured of finding true love. This is not just a secular trend. Christian websites have been quick to embrace this new phenomenon, with the extra allure of divine destiny to sugar the pill. Whether we like it or not, online dating is here to stay. Trends over the last decade suggest that digital matchmaking will soon be *the* dominant way that relationships come into being. One author says that online dating represents a shift as significant as the sexual revolution of the 1960s in changing our approach to love and romance.[36]

It cannot be denied that online dating has some important benefits. My wife and I know several married couples who met online across far-flung continents and cultures to form lasting partnerships. For other friends who had been traumatized by past relationships, dating websites were safe environments to test the waters again without fully exposing themselves to the risks of rejection. Online dating also offers broader horizons to those who are socially or geographically isolated. As a result, many Christians and church leaders seem unable to conceive of any reason why we might pause for thought at the prospect of online dating. If it works, what could possibly be wrong with it?

35. Ibid., 46.
36. Dan Slater, *Love in the Time of Algorithms: What Technology Does to Meeting and Mating* (New York: Current, 2013), 120.

But how is this bustling marketplace subtly shaping our underlying thinking about intimate relationships? In particular, given the consumerist dynamic at its heart, how does online dating affect the Christian vision of relationships as committed, mutually sacrificial, and resilient partnerships? What if online dating makes it *too* easy to meet someone new? What if it raises the bar for a "good" relationship *too* high, while constantly dangling attractive alternatives in front of us? What if the prospect of an ever-more-compatible mate just a click away tempts us to chase the elusive end of the rainbow?

interesting thought

When Love Becomes a Commodity

Online dating is a business. It is designed around a purpose, and we need to understand how it seeks to shape its users according to that purpose. If consumerism thrives on short-term commitments, we see these incentives embedded within online matchmaking. Dating sites, particularly those with monthly subscription fees, do best when relationships last long enough to build our trust in the algorithm, but not when we swap dating for the wedding altar. There is an essential conflict of interest between what we ultimately want and what the system requires of us. Within the consumerist model, a permanently paired-off dater is a lost revenue stream. This acknowledgment is embedded in the practices of online dating websites. Well after their accounts become inactive, users on popular websites receive messages that new people are browsing their profiles and want to talk. In the words of a senior Match.com executive, "Most of our users are return customers."[37] Online dating sites offer the promise of romance and companionship, but their success relies on love remaining just out of reach or occurring in a series of short bursts. In this way, they affirm and encourage the modern sexual script of serial monogamy.

These dynamics are reflected also in the interactions between users. Online matchmaking is, at its heart, transactional. On many websites people pay a subscription fee and, in exchange, are presented with people who fit their request. At its most fundamental level, online dating offers

37. Dan Slater, "A Million First Dates: How Online Romance Is Threatening Monogamy," *The Atlantic*, January 2, 2013, http://www.theatlantic.com/magazine/archive/2013/01/a-million-first-dates/309195/.

a convenient and alluring consumer experience. From the safety of our computers or smartphones, we can observe and choose from a wide range of "compatible" options. We even get to make tentative contact and ask questions about each "product" to find out more before we try it on. This echoes Sherry Turkle's earlier warning about the temptation of trusting our intimacies to technology. Given that consumerism has so heavily conditioned our approach to life, it is difficult for us to differentiate between people and things, or people *as* things to be consumed.

In 2011, a consultant to online-dating companies published the results from a survey of thirty-nine of the industry's executives called "How Has Internet Dating Changed Society?"[38] These insiders agreed that online dating had "made people more disposable" and may be partly responsible for a rise in divorce rates. Instead of seeing this as a problem, though, they argued that internet dating is helping people to realize that they can end mediocre relationships. As a result of these higher expectations, "low quality, unhappy and unsatisfying marriages are being destroyed as people drift to internet dating sites."[39] But the question is whether online dating is really saving us from unhappy connections or rather fundamentally reshaping our notion of what love actually is. As online dating becomes more like internet shopping, we should be wary of its claims to offer emotional and relational satisfaction.

In Machines We Trust: Putting Our Faith in the Algorithm

Like most technology-driven services, internet dating has gone through several phases over the past fifteen years. The first phase basically offered users an online shopping mall where they could browse a wide range of profiles from a safe distance. The principles were similar to normal dating, just with massively increased choice and less up-front awkwardness. But the second phase changed the landscape radically. As the horizons of choice increased to unmanageable levels, computer algorithms offered "science based" compatibility screening. That freed users from the tyranny of choice, the sense of becoming paralyzed when faced with thousands of profiles, like in an overcrowded room. All they had to do was describe themselves, their characteristics, and their preferences, and a machine would do the rest.

38. Ibid.
39. Ibid.

A third phase has recently changed the picture again. Dating apps through social media and on smartphones, tablets, and other mobile devices mean that users can now seamlessly incorporate online dating into their everyday lives. They can date on the run. This mobile option offers users a more spontaneous experience; it blurs the boundaries between online and off-line dating.

The most powerful promise of these sophisticated online matchmakers is that we can find a "soul mate" who shares our core preferences, interests, and dispositions. The basic assumption is that similarity between people is the key ingredient for good relationships. But most scientific research, as well as the experience of married couples down through the ages, challenges this idea. A 2012 metastudy of online dating research undertaken by five US-based social psychologists reviewed the results of four hundred research studies.[40] They found little evidence that internet matchmaking services were improving romantic outcomes, and they found in some cases that these algorithms were undermining the results. As they say, "By suggesting that compatibility can be established from a relatively small bank of trait-based information about a person—whether by a matchmaker's algorithm or by the user's own glance at a profile—online dating sites may be supporting an ideology of compatibility that decades of scientific research suggests is false."[41]

Even if compatibility were a firm foundation for relationships, one of the main problems with dating online is the accuracy of the information users offer. Online dating allows us to conceal ourselves by massaging the details of our lives. Research found that 80 percent of people on dating websites misrepresent fundamental information in their profiles, such as their height, weight, or age. It turns out that some of the things people say about themselves are aspirational rather than honest. This is certainly true of a number of our Christian friends, who have admitted to "helping themselves out a bit" because of the huge competition to be noticed by others on dating websites. This places the whole premise of computer-generated compatibility on even shakier ground.

At a more fundamental level, computer algorithms fail to reflect the richer mystery of human identity and romantic attraction. As the thinking

40. Finkel et al., "Online Dating," 51.
41. Ibid.

goes, if a woman has seen a photo and gotten a guy's key stats, career prospects, and political leanings, then she's ready to go. But people and their interactions are far more complex than that. It turns out that people are much more like wine. When we taste something we like, we can describe it—but it's usually not a very useful description. Still, we know whether we like it or not. As with wine, so also with people. It is the complexity and completeness of the face-to-face experience that sums up a whole range of intuitions and preferences. The intuitive aspects of romantic relationships are hard to pin down, but they are our most valuable way of assessing friendships and potential relationships at the outset.

Underneath the practical question of whether online dating actually works, there lie some deeper philosophical issues. Are we really happy to entrust our intimacies to a computer algorithm and its masters? Does online dating encourage a separation between sex and love? Does the allure of an infinite pool of choice render our real relationships contingent and soluble?

The Myth of Infinite Choice

It is tempting to believe that an online matchmaker with a database of millions of potential partners from every corner of the globe can offer something like the perfect soul mate. When we see limited options within our church or among our friends, or if we find ourselves in a complex relationship, this idea of unlimited choice is tantalizing. However, this also leads to the sort of freeze we experience in a supermarket aisle when faced with one hundred varieties of cheese. How can we be sure we will choose the right one? There are just too many options and too many variables.

There is a general acceptance among both social observers and industry insiders that this aspect of online dating is profoundly reshaping our approach to sex, love, and relationships. This idea makes intuitive sense, but it has also been demonstrated by a host of sociological studies over the past twenty years. These studies show that our willingness to commit to a particular relationship depends on our perception of good alternatives. Given that online websites offer us a nearly infinite range of potential partners, this phenomenon seems set to undermine our ability to enter and sustain long-term relationships.

Dan Slater describes the archetypical experience of a thirtysomething named Jacob.[42] Before dating online, he found it difficult to find a girlfriend and was reluctant to let relationships end because of the fear of being left alone. He describes how his experience changed radically when he joined an online dating service. Suddenly he was regularly dating women whom he perceived to be "above" his level. He eventually developed a stable relationship with a "young and beautiful" woman named Rachel. But after a couple of years, the relationship seemed to be coming to an end. Rather than trying to work things out (as he would have done previously), Jacob let the relationship lapse because, having met Rachel so easily online, he felt that he could just as easily find someone else. He even reactivated his online dating subscription on the day they broke up, noting that the options had gotten significantly better during the two years that he had been off the website. He says,

> I'm about 95 percent certain that if I'd met Rachel offline, and if I'd never done online dating, I would've married her. At that point in my life, I would've overlooked everything else and done whatever it took to make things work. Did online dating change my perception of permanence? No doubt. When I sensed the breakup coming, I was okay with it. . . . I was eager to see what else was out there.[43]

Observing that online dating inevitably weakens the mortar within existing relationships, a senior industry executive sees this as a positive development. "Historically relationships have been billed as 'hard' because, historically, commitment has been the goal. You could say online dating is simply changing people's ideas about whether commitment itself is a life value."[44] This view is supported by another executive in Britain who wonders "whether matching you up with great people is getting so efficient, and the process so enjoyable, that marriage will become obsolete."[45]

In his 2004 book *The Paradox of Choice*, psychologist Barry Schwartz indicts a society that sanctifies freedom of choice so profoundly that the benefits of infinite options seem self-evident. He argues that "a large array of options may diminish the attractiveness of what people actually choose,

42. Slater, *Love in the Time of Algorithms*, 109–14.
43. Ibid., 114.
44. Ibid., 121.
45. Ibid.

the reason being that thinking about the attractions of some of the un-chosen options detracts from the pleasure derived from the chosen one."[46] Psychologists who study relationships say that three ingredients generally determine the strength of commitment: overall satisfaction with the relationship, the investment put into it (time and effort, shared experiences, emotions, and so on), and the quality of perceived alternatives. It is hard not to conclude that online dating overwhelmingly undermines the first and third of these key factors. People will become less willing to work through the inevitable rough patches and issues within a marriage or relationship when there is an ocean of alternatives to be explored.

Despite the high ideals of its claims, the ultimate vision of online dating may be shaped by the idea that romance should be a series of existential encounters rather than part of the process of finding a lifelong partner. In light of this, we should be suspicious of the bold claims that online dating will satisfy our longing for love.

But What about the Christian Experience?

Surely, though, Christians march to the beat of a different drum . . . right? It is true that Christian dating websites and their users tend to have a higher vision of marriage and committed relationships than their secular peers. Yet this strength may morph into a disadvantage in the arena of Christian online dating. The less immediate sexual priorities and the smaller pool of potential local partners means that the search tends to extend farther geographically. The majority of our Christian friends who have dated online tended to be in conversation with people in different states, countries, or continents. This significantly changes the nature of the courting and relational discernment process, which tends to be one-dimensional and conducted in private.

One of my friends was due to be the best man at a Christian wedding. Yet as the event approached, the groom decided not to go through with the marriage. Some months later, my friend received an email from the previously reluctant groom announcing that he was now married to someone else whom he had met online. None of his family or circle of close friends

46. Barry Schwartz, *The Paradox of Choice: Why More Is Less* (New York: Harper-Perennial, 2004), 20.

had met the bride or been invited to the wedding. This scenario is highly problematic because it lures us to explore the world of love as an avatar among other avatars rather than as a person embedded within a community. Such isolation bypasses our traditional discernment filters, such as the perspectives of friends, family, and older people whom we trust. We also learn an enormous amount about a potential partner by engaging with their core communities. Although off-line relationships tend to be messy, risky, and sometimes embarrassing, there is a social honesty and accountability about them that is essential during the courting process.

Concluding Thoughts: Consuming Love

Within the overarching vision of modern capitalism, we are truly becoming consumers of everything, including intimacy. We have created a global hypermarket of potential love partners, all just a click away. As this giant romantic matrix (a sort of Franken-cupid) becomes the most common way that relationships are formed, Christian leaders should consider what influence this is having on those they care for spiritually—and on the quality of their relationships. A corrupting dynamic does not inevitably mean that we will be corrupted by it. Yet we have perhaps overplayed the extent to which we are free to make choices over and above our formative contexts and the visions of life they promote.

The promise of infinite choice can easily coalesce, even for Christians, with secular distortions of love. The romantic ideal that a soul mate is waiting out there somewhere becomes, within Christian circles, the mythical notion of "the one"—that perfectly compatible person whom God has been preparing for us. Large-scale dating websites offer us, in one efficient search, the answer to our quest to find this perfect partner within the whole of God's creation. But the question is whether this quest for "the one" weakens our ability to pursue the potential relationships that are right in front of us or to work through a relationship to which we're already committed. The main concern relating to online dating is that it encourages the dislocation of romantic relationships from our natural communities. It tempts us to travel through the world as private and independent consumers of people as much as things. Yet as holistic beings, whatever we do with things, we will inevitably do with people.

5

The Hypersexual Self

Sex and Relationships as Happiness Technologies

A significant contradiction lies at the heart of modern identity. On one hand, sexuality has come to be seen as a core marker of our personal identity within the expressive culture of authenticity. Yet the extreme form of personal freedom envisioned by postmodernism has trivialized sex as a sort of happiness drug, detaching it from those social and relational contexts that traditionally gave sex its meaning and its role within our personal identity.

The combined effect of authenticity and postmodernism has created a tendency toward hypersexuality, empowering social phenomena that threaten to entrap much of a generation. To understand how this affects the formation of personal identity and relationships, we first need to briefly compare the Christian and postmodern visions of sexuality.

Defining Christian Sexuality

Christianity views human identity as holistic, in that our sexuality is an essential part of who we are. Despite attempts throughout history to place

96

sexuality at the edge of human personhood, the doctrines of creation, incarnation, and resurrection—as well as the divine blessing of marriage—all affirm our embodied existence, including sexuality as essential and ongoing, although we will express it differently in the age to come.[1] Our sexuality also goes beyond our physical form to our essential "maleness" and "femaleness." Modern social sciences have confirmed aspects of male and female sexuality that go beyond our different bodies and reproductive capacities. Sexuality is described broadly as "everything in mind, body and behavior that arise[s] from being male and female."[2] We can draw a distinction between a person's physical sexuality and what it means to be a gendered being more broadly— that is, our *social* or *affective* sexuality.[3] Although our culture has sought to "level the playing field" between maleness and femaleness, there are critical differences between how men and women *generally* relate to each other.

Only when we are attentive to these differences of sexual complementarity, free from hierarchical paranoia, can we build a strong foundation for intimate relationships. The holistic nature of human sexuality means that sex engages us in something deeper and more complex than a mere physical encounter. The biblical metaphor of becoming "one flesh" in marital intimacy is consistent with Scripture's holistic view of human identity. We are integrated socio-psycho-somatic beings, and since sex engages our whole selves, sex outside of marriage is an act of personal disintegration.

To reduce sexuality to sex is to miss this deeper essence. The greater part of sexuality is affective or social, including our fundamental need for relational intimacy across a broad range of nurturing friendships.[4] Confusion in this area leads to crossover between sex and the social expression of our broader sexuality. There is, though, an important difference between "desire for sex," which is a physical urge, and "sexual desire," or *eros*, which covers a broad range of human longing, including our yearning to know our Creator.

It is important for Christians to differentiate between these two senses psychologically, emotionally, and in our practical lives.[5] One important

1. Stanley J. Grenz, *Sexual Ethics: An Evangelical Perspective* (Louisville: Westminster John Knox, 1990), 21–27.
2. Ibid., 17.
3. Ibid.
4. Ibid., 17, 196; see also Marva J. Dawn, *Sexual Character: Beyond Technique to Intimacy* (Grand Rapids: Eerdmans, 1993), 21–22.
5. Grenz, *Sexual Ethics*, 21.

aspect in which "sexual desire" is different from "desire for sex" is in what we actually express through sex. The Christian conviction is that in sex we express a desire to join with another person in a deep and complex inter-weaving as "embodied souls and ensouled bodies," to borrow Karl Barth's expression. The complementary nature of male and female sexuality, as a composite image of God, provides both the drive and direction to express our full humanity, meaning that we are drawn beyond ourselves to each other because of our God-ordained differences.[6]

Postmodern Sexual Expression

In contrast to this Christian perspective, postmodern secular notions of personhood locate our essential identity in our nature as free-choosing be-ings. This allows us to separate actions, including sex, from our essential self. We can "self-actualize" through sexual expression, but our freedom to do whatever we want—rather than the type of act we choose or with whom we choose to do it—is the core of who we are. When postmodern-ism's extreme view of personal freedom joins forces with sexual expression, three specific radical freedoms arise: the instrumentalist view of sex, the reshaping of female desire, and, perhaps most significant, the tsunami of cyberporn.

Radical Freedom 1: Unshackling Sex

Outside the church, there is little substantive basis on which to discuss sexual values today. Yet the void created by this new moral ecology is also profoundly influencing Christian ways of thinking and living. The only moral constraint our culture seems to accept in this area is that sexual expression between "adults" should be free and consensual, without any force or manipulation. If people want to have sex and the feeling is mutual, who could object? This approach, which misinterprets both sex itself and the sort of desire expressed in it, is founded on four important myths.[7]

6. Ibid., 20.
7. Roger Scruton, "The Abuse of Sex," in *The Social Costs of Pornography: A Collection of Papers*, ed. James R. Stoner and Donna M. Hughes (Princeton: Witherspoon Institute, 2010).

First, this perspective rests on the foundational belief that sexual desire is simply the longing for a certain type of sensory, physical pleasure. Sex is said to be a natural appetite like eating, and so sexual craving merely seeks to satisfy this physical hunger; it is not anchored in any deeper and more holistic desire toward another person. According to this myth, we could just as easily satisfy this hunger in another way or with another person. By oversimplifying sex, this belief makes it coherent both intellectually and morally within the modern worldview: sex serves a clear physical purpose by satisfying a natural urge, and the lack of any moral imperative frees us from the complicated responsibilities and expectations of relationships. If the other person freely agrees to it, then we have no further obligations.

An important aspect of this myth is the conviction that there is no fall-out or cost from sex with "no strings attached." We can walk away from these encounters unscathed and undiminished. The feminist author Naomi Wolf describes a characteristic discussion about sex and relationships with students at a major university. One young woman explained, "We are so tightly scheduled, why get to know someone first? It is a waste of time. If you hook-up, you can get your needs met and get on your way." The guys agreed. As one said, "Things are always a little tense and uncomfortable when you just start seeing someone. I prefer to have sex right away just to get it over with. You know it's going to happen anyway, and it gets rid of the tension." When Wolf queried whether this removes some of the mystery of sex, he looked at her blankly. "Mystery? I don't know what you're talking about. Sex has no mystery."[8] Tragically, this jaundiced view of intimate relationships is becoming accepted within mainstream youth culture.

The second myth builds on the first. If sex is just about physical pleasure—a happiness technology—then the key to fulfillment is to maximize and intensify this sensation by perfecting technique. The key, then, is not *what* we express in sex but *how* we experience it. We become performers and consumers rather than genuine participants.

The third myth expresses the influential belief that if we "repress" our sexual urges, it will harm us psychologically. Freud gave birth to this view with his hydraulic imagery of sexual desire as a powerfully flowing internal spring tha   it in the end,

8. Naom   g.com/nymetro
/news/trend

if we don't give it positive expression, it will find another way out. Indeed, the longer we shut off and repress our sexual urges, the more serious the dysfunctional eruption is likely to be. Freud's compelling imagery has had a lasting influence on Western culture. Put simply, sexual restraint is like bottling unbearable stress, whereas free sexual expression leads to health and maturity.

Finally, there is a focus within modern culture on freeing ourselves from "negative" or "unhealthy" attitudes and feelings such as guilt, shame, or regret. These feelings are deemed to come from the judgmental views of others, which we internalize and negatively associate with our sex lives. The popular response is to "demystify" sex and to enjoy it as one of life's natural and morally neutral pleasures (witness myth 1). Much modern sex education has focused on teaching young people to reject the irrational guilt they feel in relation to sex and to do what comes naturally. Our only responsibility is to check off a few moral prerequisites, keeping sex consensual and "safe" from pregnancy and disease.

None of this would matter if sex were, in reality, trivial. But nothing could be further from the truth. Sexual intimacy engages our whole selves in a complex way that we cannot fully account for. Undermining the gravity of sex trivializes what sex symbolizes and weakens the bond it consummates—the loving, exclusive, and permanent union between a man and woman in marriage. This plays into the contingent nature of many relationships, which are sustained only if they continue to satisfy each party in the narrow terms of emotional, physical, and psychological happiness.

Radical Freedom 2: The "Liberation" of Female Desire

Another influential trend within contemporary sexuality is the changing expectations of female desire.[9] Some radical strains of feminism in the 1960s saw sexual freedom as a form of female emancipation from the stifling patriarchal culture of the 1950s. Within the brave new world of the sexual revolution, men and women met together in sex as equals, freed from their traditional gender roles.[10] Indeed, Tom Wolfe notes that various shades of

9. Taylor, *Secular Age*, 495.
10. Ibid., 502–3.

feminism encouraged women to be just as bold and active as men when it came to sexual exploration.[11] Nothing typified this more than the popular sitcom *Sex in the City*, which ran for sixteen years. It was a cultural revelation to watch four female friends sow their wild oats across Manhattan in a way that self-consciously resembled traditional male sexuality.

All this has radically changed the dynamics, expectations, and resilience of romantic relationships. Traditionally, female modesty was viewed as an important check on the more unruly nature of male sexual desire. An age-old bargain allowed men and women to trade sexual intimacy for different goals—men primarily to satiate sexual desire, and women to secure relational intimacy and commitment. Sociologist Helen Fisher observes that in the Western world today, as compared to earlier times and other cultures, women begin having sex earlier, have more partners, express less remorse for the partners they leave, marry later, have fewer children, and leave bad marriages in order to find good ones.[12]

Tom Wolfe describes the upending of sexual expectations for young women in particular. "Today," he says, "from age thirteen, American girls [are] under pressure to maintain a façade of sexual experience and sophistication. Among girls, 'virgin' [has become] a term of contempt."[13] A major independent study commissioned by the UK government describes the threat posed by this early sexualization of young people, especially girls. The author concludes:

> While sexualised images have featured in advertising and communications since mass media first emerged, what we are seeing now is an unprecedented rise in both the volume and the extent to which these images are impinging on everyday life. Increasingly, too, children are being portrayed in "adultified" ways while adult women are "infantilised." This leads to a blurring of the lines between sexual maturity and immaturity and, effectively, legitimises the notion that children can be related to as sexual objects.[14]

11. Wolfe, *Hooking Up*, 8.
12. Fisher, "Why We Love, Why We Cheat."
13. Wolfe, *Hooking Up*, 7.
14. Dr. Linda Papadopoulos, *Sexualisation of Young People: Review*, February 2010, https://shareweb.kent.gov.uk/Documents/health-and-wellbeing/teenpregnancy/Sexualisation_young_people.pdf. See also American Psychological Association Task Force on the Sexualization of Girls, *Report of the APA Task Force on the Sexualization of Girls* (2010), http://www.apa.org/pi/women/programs/girls/report-full.pdf.

This is an important trend because research confirms that women generally determine when a relationship becomes sexual. As Regnerus and Uecker conclude, "The bottom line is this: *women are the sexual gatekeepers within their relationships.*"[15] Yet the authors also note that women don't *feel* in control of their sexual decisions today because the "sexual market" they are moving within is changing and redrawing expectations. Ironically, with the so-called liberation of female desire, these expectations have become much more tailored to men's sexual interests than to women's.[16] Indeed, playing by the rules of male desire weakens the legitimate hopes of genuine female sexuality—for love, security, commitment, and, in most cases, family. To the significant detriment of young women, the "price" for sex has become very low among young adults in America within the paradigm of the "sex-relationship bargain," with most relationships involving sex within the first five months (70 percent for men, 62 percent for women) and a significant proportion within the first two weeks (36 percent for men, 21.6 percent for women).[17]

What does this bold new world actually offer young women? Modern sex education has focused on the physical risks of sex, almost completely ignoring its influence on emotional and spiritual well-being. And research reveals that despite the bold promises of *Sex and the City*, young women experience most of the emotional fallout of our culture's "relaxed" sexual ethic. Whereas young men's emotional well-being seems almost unaffected by their sexual conquests, young women experience a close connection between sexual experience and poorer emotional health.

Regnerus and Uecker have found that "a sustained pattern of *serial monogamy*—implying a series of failed relationships—hurts women far more than it hurts men."[18] As they observe, "'No strings attached' language is ubiquitous in contemporary sexual scripts, but it's largely a fiction. For most women, the strings are what makes sex good."[19] This is borne out in the authors' extensive interviews. The common testimony of sexually experienced college women, the researchers say, is a narrative of regret. Indeed, a 2005 study found that young women who had had multiple sex

15. Regnerus and Uecker, *Premarital Sex*, 57.
16. Ibid., 58–59.
17. Ibid., 60.
18. Ibid., 143–45.
19. Ibid., 153.

partners were eleven times more likely than virgins to report elevated depressive symptoms.[20] As Regnerus and Uecker put it, "Drinking 'medicates' depression for many Americans yet is itself a depressant. The same may be true for disconnected sex."[21] The popular script that encourages "sex without security" just doesn't cash out in reality, despite our culture's enthusiastic embrace of this approach.

Radical Freedom 3: Pornography as Sex Education

We cannot talk meaningfully about modern sexuality without considering the advent of online pornography, which has allowed the sex industry to reach far beyond its natural hunting ground in red light districts or on the top shelves of local stores. For many people, Christian or otherwise, pornography is deeply influencing their vision of sexuality and relationships.[22] Family therapist Jill Manning says online pornography is altering the cultural zeitgeist and the lives of men, women, and children in ways we may not fully appreciate until our society has paid significant personal and social costs.[23] As one study puts it, "The influence of the internet on sexuality is likely to be so significant that it will ultimately be recognized as the cause of the next 'sexual revolution.'"[24] In particular, Manning says that the pervasive power of pornography has made it the primary sexual educator of today's adolescents.[25] Many of the young women she has worked with dislike the fact that young men use pornography, but they are conflicted about how to reject the men's behavior while also trying to compete for their romantic attention. Young women no longer have allure and mystery on their side, as young men are inundated with unrealistic images

20. Denise D. Hallfors et al., "Which Comes First in Adolescence—Sex and Drugs or Depression?," *American Journal of Preventative Medicine* 29 (2005): 163–70.

21. Regnerus and Uecker, *Premarital Sex*, 161.

22. For a comprehensive overview of recent research into the personal and social impact of online pornography, see Mary Eberstadt and Mary Anne Layden, *The Social Costs of Pornography: A Statement of Findings and Recommendations* (Princeton: Witherspoon Institute, 2010).

23. Jill C. Manning, "The Impact of Pornography on Women: Social Science Findings and Clinical Observations," in Stoner and Hughes, *Social Costs of Pornography*.

24. Al Cooper et al., "Sexuality and the Internet: The Next Sexual Revolution," in *The Psychological Science of Sexuality: A Research Based Approach*, ed. Frank Muscarella and Lenore T. Szuchman (New York: Wiley, 1999), 516–45.

25. Manning, "Impact of Pornography on Women."

of sexually engaged females. This has dramatically altered the flirtatious dance between the sexes.[26]

Yet it is of grave concern to researchers and professionals that there is so little popular discussion about online pornography's harm to people and their relationships. Indeed, the Western world has embarked on a bold social experiment to leave pornography essentially uncensored, on the basis of the quintessentially modern idea that each person's right to privacy and freedom of consumption sweeps away all other considerations. There is also a common belief, encouraged by the popular media, that pornography is primarily a positive force; allegedly it can relieve stress, reduce pressure on marriages caused by different sexual expectations, and even inject a sense of adventure into a couple's sex life. The popular message is that pornography is everywhere, it is good for you, and it is good for your relationship. It is hip, sexy, and fun.

The Rising Tide of Pornography

Pornography as Pop Culture: Fast Sex for a Fast-Food Nation

The scale of online pornography today is staggering. Nielsen ratings reported that in January 2010 more than a quarter of internet users in the United States, almost 60 million people, visited a pornographic website. Incredibly, this number does not take into account the staggering amount of pornography that is distributed through peer-to-peer downloading networks, shared hard drives, internet chat rooms, and message boards.[27] *Time* journalist Pamela Paul details the broad and increasing reach of pornography:

> Americans rent upwards of 800 million pornographic videos and DVDs (about one in five of all rented movies is porn), and the 11,000 porn films shot each year far outpaces Hollywood's yearly slate of 400. Four billion dollars a year is spent on video pornography in the United States, more than on football, baseball, and basketball. One in four internet users look at a

26. Ibid.
27. Natasha Vargas-Cooper, "Hard Core: The New World of Porn Is Revealing Eternal Truths about Men and Women," *The Atlantic*, January 4, 2011, http://www.theatlantic .com/magazine/archive/2011/01/hard-core/308327/.

pornography website in any given month. Men look at pornography online more than they look at any other subject. And 66% of 18–34-year-old men visit a pornographic site every month.[28]

Despite our culture's easy acceptance of pornography, a growing tide of researchers, counselors, neuroscientists, pastors, and other professionals are ringing alarm bells on the basis of the devastating effects of pornography they see in their clinics, churches, and research studies. Some describe it as the "new tobacco." Just as most people considered smoking benign before the mid-1960s, there is a similar disconnect between scientific research and popular perspectives regarding the influence of pornography.

The meteoric rise and acceptance of pornography also highlights a stunning cultural contradiction. In an age where we expect our daughters to be treated with unprecedented dignity, respect, and equality by their male peers, we have handed the sexual formation of our young people to the sex industry with its dark vision of sex and relationships. Christian leaders need to be at the vanguard of replacing these misperceptions about pornography with reality, starting within our own congregations. Yet we are tempted to ignore the issue because it lurks beneath the surface. The strong stigma of shame attached to pornography means that we will only see it if we are deeply involved in the confessional lives of others. The sad truth is that whether we see it or not, pornography has become a major issue for many people within the church.

As part of a course focused on relationships at our church in London, we conducted an anonymous survey of around five hundred young people in their twenties and thirties within the congregation. The results confirmed our suspicions about the depth to which our culture's approach to sexuality has also become our problem within the church. Consistent with what we discovered, broader surveys show that many Christians, including pastors, struggle with pornography as a problematic habit or compulsive addiction. Indeed, we were most surprised by the number of young women who reported having problems in this area, which also is consistent with trends within the broader culture. These problems may well be exacerbated by the combination of prolonged singleness within the church and Scripture's

28. Pamela Paul, "How Porn Became the Norm," in Stoner and Hughes, *Social Costs of Pornography.*

emphasis on sexual restraint. For many young Christians, sexual fantasy is seen as the only outlet for these strong impulses. Indeed, the apostle Paul acknowledged this bind with his pragmatic counsel that it is better to marry than to burn with lust.[29] Pornography may well be an issue we would prefer to avoid, but its broad reach within the church means that we must address it in order to disciple people effectively.

The Meteoric Rise and Potency of Cybersex

To understand how online pornography has become a major problem in such a short time, we need to appreciate its characteristics and dynamics, which are fundamentally different from earlier forms of pornography from just fifteen or twenty years ago. It is now significantly more available, more neurologically powerful, and more extreme than it used to be. The relatively recent expansion of high-speed internet, wi-fi, and 4G cell networks, combined with almost no online censorship and "no cost" models for explicit content, has made multimedia pornography an integral part of mainstream culture. The three As of the internet drive consumption—availability, accessibility, and anonymity.[30]

Besides these developments, the *type* of pornography being consumed has changed in two important senses: its neurological power and its tendency toward hard-core content. As regards the increased potency of pornography, neuroscience has established that the richer the media—such as high-definition, hyperrealistic moving pictures—the more powerful the effect, particularly on the male brain. This helps to explain why contemporary pornography seems more addictive than earlier forms. Online pornography also naturally drives viewers toward increasingly hard-core forms. Automatic pop-ups and linked advertisements create a fast-moving dynamic environment, which tantalizes the user in the heat of the moment to journey into unintended and increasingly extreme areas.

This progressive dynamic means that *all* online pornography tends toward the hard-core, often taking people to places they had no intention of going when they set out. Clinicians make a distinction here between

29. 1 Cor. 7:9.

30. Al Cooper, *Cybersex: The Dark Side of the Force* (Philadelphia: Brunner-Routledge, 2000), 2.

the decisions we make in "cold" and "hot" states. Because cyberpornography offers dynamic and open-ended choices during "hot" or heightened states, it quickly drives users to places they would reject without question in a cold state. Most people who have developed a compulsive habit in this area confirm this progressive movement from "soft-core" erotica into increasingly extreme imagery and scenarios. In this way, scenes that would initially offend or horrify them soon become acceptable and even desirable.[31]

Pornography and the Plastic Brain

Online pornography is particularly effective in encouraging this journey toward hard-core content because it hijacks a well-understood process in human conditioning.[32] Psychiatrist and neuroscientist Norman Doidge explains this progressive journey in terms of how the brain changes through regular use of pornography. The "addictiveness" of pornography, he says, is not a metaphor; people can become addicted to behaviors as well as substances.[33] All addiction involves long-term, sometimes permanent "neuroplastic" change in the brain. The power of addictive substances/behaviors lies in their hijacking of our dopamine system, so that they give us pleasure without our having to work for it.[34]

Dopamine, known as the "pleasure chemical," is an important neurotransmitter and plays a significant role in permanent changes to the brain. It is involved in reinforcing natural behaviors like eating, drinking, and sex, while it is also the main neurotransmitter stimulated by most addictive drugs. Dopamine is released during sexual excitement, increasing the sex drive in both men and women and activating the brain's pleasure centers. Dopamine's key role in both sex and addiction underscores the magnetic force of pornography.

In terms of changing our brains, Doidge explains that the same surge of dopamine that thrills us also reinforces the attachment to the behavior that enabled us to accomplish our goal. Put simply, when sexual arousal becomes

31. Vargas-Cooper, "Hard Core."
32. Norman Doidge, "Acquiring Tastes and Loves," in *The Brain That Changes Itself: Stories of Personal Triumph from the Frontiers of Brain Science* (New York: Penguin, 2007), 107.
33. Ibid., 106–12.
34. Ibid. For a detailed description of how the male brain interacts with pornography, see William M. Struthers, *Wired for Intimacy: How Pornography Hijacks the Male Brain* (Downers Grove, IL: InterVarsity, 2009), 83–111.

connected to viewing pornography, these two activities become strongly associated in our brains. The more we engage in the habit, the more these connections are fused together in our neural circuits. These channels in our brains become automatic pathways through which sexual interactions, whether digital or real, are routed. Repeated exposure to explicit imagery creates a one-way neurological superhighway, whereby a person's mental life becomes oversexualized and narrow.

Doidge describes this as a "use it or lose it" brain, which means that we long to keep these maps activated once we have developed them. He summarizes this journey into addiction in compelling terms:

> The men at their computers looking at porn were uncannily like the rats in the cages of the National Institute of Health, pressing the bar to get a shot of dopamine or its equivalent. Though they didn't know it, they had been seduced into pornographic training sessions that met all the conditions required for plastic change of brain maps. Since neurons that fire together wire together, these men got massive amounts of practice wiring these images into the pleasure centers of the brain, with the rapt attention necessary for plastic change. They imagined these images when away from their computers, or while having sex with their girlfriends, reinforcing them. Each time they felt sexual excitement and had an orgasm when they masturbated, a "spritz of dopamine," the reward neurotransmitter, consolidated the connections made in the brain during the sessions. Not only did the reward facilitate the behavior; it provoked none of the embarrassment they felt purchasing *Playboy* at a store. Here was a behavior with no "punishment," only reward. The content of what they found exciting changed as the Web sites introduced themes and scripts that altered their brains without their awareness. Because plasticity is competitive, the brain maps for new, exciting images at the expense of what had previously attracted them—the reason, I believe, they began to find their girlfriends less of a turn-on.[35]

Pamela Paul describes in practical detail how these addictive habits played out in the real lives of several hundred men she interviewed:

> Men told me that they found themselves wasting countless hours looking at pornography on their televisions and DVD players, and especially online.

35. Doidge, "Acquiring Tastes and Loves," 109.

They looked at things they would have once considered appalling. . . . They found the way they looked at women in real life warping to fit the pornography fantasies they consumed onscreen. . . . They worried about the way they saw their daughters and girls their daughters' age. It wasn't only their sex lives that suffered—pornography's effects rippled out, touching all aspects of their existence. Their work days became interrupted, their hobbies were tossed aside, their family lives were disrupted. Some men even lost their jobs, their wives, and their children. The sacrifice is enormous.[36]

As William Struthers explains, the one-way "neurological superhighway" created by viewing pornography has many on-ramps but almost no off-ramps. It is built for speed and hemmed in by high containment walls that make escape almost impossible. No wonder, then, that online pornography has drawn so many into its addictive snare.[37]

A Shadowy Harem of Imaginary Brides

All this leads us to the important question: How does pornography affect our vision of and approach to relationships?

One of the most destructive effects of online pornography is on marriages. Married men outnumber single men in internet use. Research suggests, surprisingly, that the majority of people struggling with sexual addictions and compulsive online habits are married men.[38] This trend is not just harming marriages; it's destroying them. Family lawyers are seeing a growing influence of pornography in divorces. At a meeting of the American Academy of Matrimonial Lawyers—comprising the nation's top sixteen hundred divorce and matrimonial law attorneys—nearly two-thirds said they had seen a sudden increase in divorces related to the internet, with 56 percent of their divorce cases involving one party having an obsessive interest in online pornography. The association's president noted, "Eight years ago, pornography played almost no role in divorces in this country. Today, there are a significant number of cases where it plays a definite part in marriages breaking up."[39]

36. Paul, "How Porn Became the Norm," in Stoner and Hughes, *Social Costs of Pornography.*
37. Struthers, *Wired for Intimacy*, 85.
38. Al Cooper, David L. Delmonico, and Ron Burg, "Cybersex Users, Abusers, and Compulsiveness: New Findings and Implications," *Sexual Addiction and Compulsivity* 7, nos. 1 and 2 (2000): 5–29.
39. Paul, "How Porn Became the Norm," in Stoner and Hughes, *Social Costs of Pornography.*

The real tragedy for marriages is that pornography not only hurts a relationship but also changes the individual's sexual character, that is, his or her fundamental capacity to enter into and sustain genuine intimacy and love. The most powerful deception of cyberporn is its promise to fulfill desire while ultimately killing it. The most ironic fallout of the pursuit of sexual gratification online is that it can render the chronic user incapable of the very sexual satisfaction he or she is seeking.

Doidge relates that many of the men he treated had become so dependent on extreme explicit imagery to arouse them that they were no longer attracted enough to their wives to be intimate with them.[40] At other times, as these men tried to focus on their wives, their minds would be flooded with scenes from their computer screens, like unwanted guests. Sex and pornography had become wired together in their brains. This echoes the musician John Mayer's observation that real life can no longer compete with fantasy. Pamela Paul also recounts that "countless men" she interviewed, including those who remained avid fans of pornography, described how their habit had destroyed their ability to relate to or be close to women. The habit became impossible to control, even when they could see its destructive effects on their interpersonal relationships.[41] Naomi Wolf puts it succinctly:

> The evidence is in: Greater supply of the stimulant equals diminished capacity. After all, pornography works in the most basic of ways on the brain: It is Pavlovian. An orgasm is one of the biggest reinforcers imaginable. If you associate orgasm with your wife, a kiss, a scent, a body, that is what, over time, will turn you on; if you open your focus to an endless stream of ever-more-transgressive images of cybersex slaves, that is what it will take to turn you on. The ubiquity of sexual images does not free *erōs* but dilutes it.[42]

This dynamic is difficult to reverse. As one philosopher puts it, when people begin to lose confidence in their ability to enjoy sex in any other way than through fantasy, then the fear of desire arises, and from that fear, the fear of love. This is the deeper, more essential risk posed by pornography. Those who become addicted to "risk free" sex face the ultimate risk: the loss of love.

40. Doidge, "Acquiring Tastes and Loves," 104.
41. Paul, "How Porn Became the Norm," in Stoner and Hughes, *Social Costs of Pornography*.
42. Wolf, "Porn Myth."

C. S. Lewis describes the ironic narrowing effect of sexual fantasy on a man's personal identity and capacity to love. Something that promises limitless frontiers of sexual discovery and satisfaction leads instead into a dead-end canyon. As Lewis describes,

> For me the real evil of masturbation would be that it takes an appetite which, in lawful [i.e., proper] use, leads the individual out of himself to complete (and correct) his own personality in that of another (and finally in children and grandchildren) and turns it back: sends the man back into the prison of himself, there to keep a harem of imaginary brides. And this harem, once admitted, works against his *ever* getting out and really uniting with a real woman. For the harem is always accessible, always subservient, calls for no sacrifices or adjustments, and can be endowed with erotic and psychological attractions which no real woman can rival. Among those shadowy brides he is always adored, always the perfect lover: no demand is made on his unselfishness, no mortification ever imposed on his vanity. In the end, they become merely the medium through which he increasingly adores himself.
> . . . After all, almost the *main* work of life is to *come out* of our selves, out of the little, dark prison we are all born in.[43]

This is one of the core contradictions of today's hypersexualized culture. In the quest for personal freedom, we have created small, dark prisons of our own choosing.

Changing the Rules of Engagement for Dating and Relationships

Another significant aspect of pornography is that it actually shifts our sexual preferences and practices. It shapes what men *expect* and what women are willing to *accept* as the rules of engagement for dating and relationships. Online pornography is changing the moral climate and expectations regarding sexuality, both within the church and the culture at large. Overwhelming evidence from a wide array of research studies confirms that consuming pornography re-forms male expectations of what is normal, meaning the perception of "what everybody else is doing."

43. Letter from C. S. Lewis to Keith Masson, June 3, 1956. Marion E. Wade Center, Wheaton College, Wheaton, IL.

A research study among first-year college students found that regular consumers of pornography developed the impression that people were generally far more promiscuous than they actually are. This led these same users to believe that sexual exclusivity is unrealistic and that sexual inactivity is bad for one's health. Not surprisingly, they developed cynical attitudes about love, affection, and marriage and family.[44]

All this would be of less concern if pornography were not becoming so broadly accepted. In one of the most rigorous and reliable studies in this area, researchers interviewed 813 emerging adults aged 18 to 26 from six colleges and universities. Two-thirds of the men agreed that pornography was "generally acceptable," while half of the women agreed. But the genders split more significantly on usage. Of the young men, 86 percent reported that they "interacted" with pornography at least once per month, and about half watched it weekly. Of the women, 69 percent said they never watched porn, while only 3 percent said they watched it weekly.[45] These findings are of particular concern because our *attitudes* toward sex and relationships eventually and inevitably shape our *actions*.

Disproportionate Impact on Young People

Although we are aware of the negative effects of pornography across the board, it is particularly harmful during the sexual formation of children and pre- or early adolescents. An important reality is that kids absorb explicit imagery differently than adults. Not only are their brains more susceptible to establishing new patterns of thought, but their minds are quite literal. Not just young children but even young teenagers are generally too unsophisticated to adequately differentiate between fantasy and reality. Sadly, they can absorb direct, unfiltered sexual lessons from pornography. They learn what women are meant to look like, how they should act, and what they are supposed to enjoy. They absorb these lessons keenly, emulating people they perceive as role models. Not surprisingly, the younger the age of exposure and the more hard-core the material, the

44. Dolf Zillmann, "Influence of Unrestricted Access to Erotica on Adolescents' and Young Adults' Dispositions toward Sexuality," *Journal of Adolescent Health* 27, no. 2 (2000): 41–44.

45. Jason S. Carroll et al., "Generation XXX: Pornography Acceptance and Use among Emerging Adults," *Journal of Adolescent Research* 23 (2008): 6–30.

more intense the effect on a person's sexual formation. Boys who look at pornography excessively become men who connect arousal purely with generic physical appearance, losing the ability to become attracted by the particular features of a given partner. As a teenage boy casually explained in an interview with the *New York Times*, "Who needs the hassle of dating when I've got online porn?"[46]

This sexual *mis*formation is a serious problem because of pornography's increasingly pervasive intrusion into children's lives. No longer like stumbling across an uncle's stash of *Playboy* magazines in the garden shed, the game has changed. Smartphones and other mobile devices make hardcore pornography available in classrooms and playgrounds, as well as in children's bedrooms and at friends' houses. The statistics are frightening. Family therapists witness to the popularity of pornography among pre-adolescents, who are increasingly being treated for compulsive habits in this area.[47] A 2004 study by Columbia University found that 11.5 million American teenagers (45 percent) have friends who regularly view internet pornography. The prevalence of teens with friends who consume pornography increases with age and is likelier among boys. In one study, 65 percent of boys aged 16 and 17 reported that they had friends who regularly viewed and downloaded internet pornography.

A government watchdog in Britain recently reported an alarming survey of fourteen-year-olds in one local authority (essentially a large suburb). The survey found that every boy and half of the girls had viewed pornography.[48] This research supports the fear of parents, teachers, and pastors that pornography has infected the innocence of modern childhood. As Mark Regnerus says, "School-based sex education is being replaced as authoritative by uncensored and unchallenged sexual content on the internet. Parents, educators, and politicians are truly fiddling while Rome burns."[49]

46. Benoit Denizet-Lewis, "Friends, Friends with Benefits and the Benefits of the Local Mall," *New York Times Magazine*, May 30, 2004, http://www.nytimes.com/2004/05/30/magazine/friends-friends-with-benefits-and-the-benefits-of-the-local-mall.html.
47. Paul, "How Porn Became the Norm," in Stoner and Hughes, *Social Costs of Pornography*.
48. Christopher Hope, "Entire School Year Groups Have Seen Porn, Children's Watchdog Says," *Telegraph*, April 3, 2013, http://www.telegraph.co.uk/news/politics/9970190/Entire-school-year-groups-have-seen-porn-childrens-watchdog-says.html.
49. Regnerus, *Forbidden Fruit*, 81.

Concluding Thoughts: Ask No Questions, Hear No Lies

We have been slow to realize the extent to which internet pornography, as well as the broader "pornification" of culture, is changing the game in terms of sexual formation. Now more than ever, there is an urgent need to talk about sex in our churches and ministry contexts in a way that engages the spirit of the age. The distorted sexual formation and expectations offered by the internet *en masse* are difficult to exaggerate. They pose an enormous risk to our young people, this generation of "digital natives."[50]

In many ways, internet pornography's power lies in its invisibility. Rather than presenting itself as an obvious problem, it is more like a hidden cancer that spreads silently through each organ until we discover that the body is riddled with it. The church has tended to adopt something like a "don't ask, don't tell" approach in this sensitive area. But our lack of attentiveness does not stop the cancer from spreading. Instead, it allows more of those under our care to fall into pornography's cycle of shame, addiction, and despair.

The Christian vision of personhood sees each of us as a whole self—mind, body, and spirit. Sexual intimacy involves the complex and all-encompassing interweaving of two selves through artful, passionate, delicate, and exclusive communication. In biblical terms, pornography's vision of sexuality is a corruption of this image into an idol. It offers us bread that can never satisfy, increasing our hunger as it malnourishes us.[51] Naomi Wolf puts it like this:

> Does all this sexual imagery in the air mean that sex has been liberated—or is it the case that the relationship between the multibillion-dollar porn industry, compulsiveness, and sexual appetite has become like the relationship between agribusiness, processed foods, supersize portions, and obesity? If your appetite is stimulated and fed by poor-quality material, it takes more junk to fill you up.[52]

The meteoric rise of online pornography is symptomatic of our culture's broader hypersexuality, which has made sex central to personal identity

50. Ibid., 60.
51. Isa. 55:2.
52. Wolf, "Porn Myth."

while ironically emptying it of its deeper meaning. Such contradictory pressures pose a significant threat to modern spiritual, emotional, and psychological identity, undermining the resilience of relationships. These mixed messages have also made it more difficult for Christians to bind themselves to the practice of chastity, that is, living faithfully in both singleness and marriage.

In the moral ecology of the modern world, Christians are pulled in several directions at once. Even as we hear the biblical call to sexual fidelity, our sex-saturated culture asks two conflicting and searching questions: Why would we deny ourselves one of life's essential experiences? And why would we go to such heroic lengths to restrain ourselves when sex is no big deal? Besides this, our culture's hypersexuality has made it more difficult to relate to each other as brothers and sisters within the household of God. When every male-female friendship is freighted with sexual overtones, it is harder to enter into the broad network of mutually nurturing relationships that we need to support our personal identity.

6

Churches without Steeples

The Loss of Transcendence and the Atomistic Worldview

Within the relational dysfunction of our romantic culture, the church's ability to live well together may be our most important witness to the gospel. Yet our God-given desire to share in a sexual relationship with an "other" has been distorted and intensified. The modern self no longer sees and expresses these human desires within the bigger arc of God's story of human redemption and reconciliation; instead of pointing to a world beyond this one, sex has become a god in its own right. This loss of cosmic vision—of transcendence—has had an enormous impact on modern sexuality, both secular and Christian.

The Atomistic Worldview and the End of Time

One of the pervasive contemporary realities, unique in human history, is the popular view that the world is a closed system of "cause and effect," with no connection to any transcendent reality. The world and everything

116

in it is seen as independent, self-sufficient, and radically cut off from God. It has become "disenchanted," as Max Weber described it. When humans tried to strip God out of creation, they succeeded in stripping created things of any higher purpose.

The influential philosopher Immanuel Kant represented an important transition toward this modern perspective. He argued that even though there may be a transcendent sphere of life—what he called the "noumenal" dimension—we cannot speak about it with any clarity, because we can only reliably experience and describe physical realities. These readily observable realities represent the "phenomenal" dimension of existence. Although the noumenal sphere is opaque for Kant, he believed that our moral sense of right and wrong still reflects divine reality, and so it gives us a small window into a higher realm—things as they *really* are.[1] Kant's philosophy of knowledge leaves one last delicate thread connecting us to our Creator, but it is vulnerable and exposed.

Friedrich Nietzsche, standing right on the cusp of the twentieth century, cut through this final thread by denying the existence of any noumenal realm. We cannot base our lives on any higher truth, he declared, but must simply embrace the void and travel in the stark reality of the world *as it is*. This resonated with the naturalistic, Darwinian worldview that was taking root at this time and formed the basis for the "modern social imaginary" as we experience it today.

In the Darwinian vision, a tree is just a tree and, more important, a human body is just a collection of limbs, impulses, and movements. This naturalistic, "scientific" view of the world eventually came to be the dominant way of seeing reality, so that every aspect of our culture is now based on the assumption that our world is purely natural and self-enclosed. This thinking has fundamentally changed the way we live and interact with each other. Whereas the world used to be seen as a "cosmos," with each part of creation connected to and reflecting its Creator to varying degrees, the world and everything in it has come to be seen as natural, neutral, and autonomous.

The modern self, then, learns to travel in a world that is rooted in a distorted and anemic vision of reality. Popular atheist Richard Dawkins

1. Immanuel Kant, *Religion within the Limits of Reason Alone* (New York: Harper Torchbook, 1960).

describes this flat, atomistic perspective—with each person or thing suspended in its own detached orbit—with brutal clarity:

> In a universe of blind physical forces and genetic replication, some people are going to get hurt, other people are going to get lucky, and you won't find any rhyme or reason in it, nor any justice. The universe we observe has precisely the properties we should expect if there is, at bottom, no design, no purpose, no evil and no good, nothing but blind pitiless indifference.[2]

This idea of a cold and meaningless world has important consequences for attitudes toward sexuality and relationships. It is summed up in the bleak vision described by the college student to Naomi Wolf: "Mystery? I don't know what you're talking about. Sex has no mystery."[3]

Myopic Vision and Moral Relativism

The atomistic worldview that Dawkins bluntly describes has resulted in the loss of any coherent vision for life. The only forces to be reckoned with in this brave new world of evolutionary biology are our instinctive impulses and the chance encounters that make up our lives. Within this "disenchanted" world, we can only choose arbitrary rules for living because there is no bigger perspective that can make sense of any particular lifestyle. This fluid moral ecology means that even the limitations or design of our bodies can be manipulated to fit with our personalized desires or preferences without any sense of contradiction.

This moral nihilism says that we are all free to have personal moral convictions about what is right and wrong, but that is all they can ever be—*personal*. Convictions have no basis in a higher truth, nor can we expect other people to live by them. Any attempt to claim authority for the Christian story is to project our personal views onto a value-neutral universe. This emphasis on living in the world *as it is*, stripped of any sacred canopy, has inevitably left us with the narrow utilitarian instincts of pursuing pleasure and avoiding pain as our primary motivations. In the end, it is hard to justify any other moral imperative.

2. Richard Dawkins, *A River Out of Eden: A Darwinian View of Life* (London: Phoenix, 1996), 155.
3. Wolf, "Porn Myth."

This backdrop of moral nihilism, with each person creating his or her own version of truth and meaning, has deeply influenced the present generation, even within the church. It makes us suspicious of any moral code that claims to be authoritative. It also helps to explain why so many Christians feel compelled to create their own unique blend of faith and practice on the basis of what suits their individual preferences and sensibilities, especially when it comes to their sexual lives.

The problem with this temptation is that it is rooted in the atomistic worldview, which has cut us off from any coherent vision of higher reality. It is worth recalling the image I introduced in the opening chapter: if Christianity calls us to see with two eyes—from both a divine and a human perspective—then the modern worldview tempts us to cover one eye and to see only the human, or "phenomenal," dimension of life. In other words, it compromises our spiritual depth perception. The Christian who designs his or her own personalized blend of faith and morality is making choices from the options available rather than seeking to reflect and participate in God's character and mission in the world.

The sad truth is that when the world and its people simply become *things* apart from God, they inevitably lose their dignity and depth. They become mere objects or resources for us to use as we see fit. Consumerism exploits this atomistic worldview, so that moderns have come to see all of life—including relationships—as transactional. When we assume this posture, the key relational question becomes, "What will this person offer me and at what cost?"

When Sex Says Nothing: Metaphysics as Sexual Ethics

This low-horizon worldview, which cuts things off from any higher reality, also strips human embodiment and life of its essential meaning. Postmodernism's refusal to provide any coherent vision of reality reduces the body to a physical machine by separating it from any animating principle, such as a soul or a guiding purpose—a telos. This denial of transcendence (higher reality) and teleology (purposefulness) leaves us with no foundation on which to think about how to engage our sexuality, except for open-ended self-expression, which fuels the confusion and destructive dynamics of modern sexual practices. The loss of any coherent cosmic structure that gives sex its real purpose—namely, God's blessing of sex within marriage for intimacy and childbearing—leads to sexual chaos. Our bodies become pleasure machines that are capable of endless different forms of sexual expression, while we have no fundamental reason for keeping this self-expression within certain boundaries.

This is inevitably what happens when we conceive of a world made up of purely natural objects that have no significance beyond themselves. We have created a neutral universe because it is an unaccountable universe, one that allows us to do whatever we want. The atheist philosopher Aldous Huxley famously confessed that he did not want there to be a God, nor any meaning, because it interfered with his sexual freedom. At least he was honest!

To my dismay, several of my Christian friends have had extramarital affairs in recent years, justifying them partly because of the conviction that their spouses were not meeting their sexual needs. The legitimization of this reasoning—which is often greeted with sympathy from peers—is given strength by the atomistic worldview. It views sex not as a sacred bonding between husband and wife but as a bodily fulfillment and natural imperative that must be satisfied for a person to be happy and healthy. In this posture, sex is a fundamental right that cannot be denied to anyone. Even within Christian marriages, this perspective can eat away at a relationship like a cancer.

When Sex Becomes a God

The growing influence of the atomistic worldview over the last century or so has resulted in sex being progressively separated from the social contexts that had traditionally given it its essential meaning. Sex has been redefined as a separate, autonomous entity in its own right, an independent commodity that can be reclassified under any category.[4] Whereas sex had always served its defining institutions, it has now become a godlike master over those contexts. Monogamous heterosexual marriage becomes just one file within the growing folder of sexual options. The "disembedding" and "liberation" of sex from its original contexts

4. Sarah C. Williams, "A Sexual Reformation? Marriage and Sexuality in the Contemporary Paradigm" (lecture, Regent College, Vancouver, April 1, 2008).

occurred in five progressive stages throughout the twentieth century with such force that the results of this journey have become unquestioned "realities" today.

The journey began with *the separation of sex from procreation*, which was enabled by a host of factors, including the invention of contraception, medically assisted conception, and the modern priority given to sex as an expression of companionship rather than as primarily for having children.

This first stage was closely followed by *the separation of sex from marriage*, so that cohabitation came to be seen by many as a sensible form of premarriage testing or even as an alternative lifestyle. The loosening of sexual relationships is reflected in our use of the term "partner," which is primarily an economic term. In the name of authenticity and honesty, we declare that we will be partners in this common endeavor for as long as it suits our perceived needs and desires.

A further fragmentation was *the separation of sex from partnership*. The commodification of sex as a form of recreational pleasure seeking means that many people have come to think of sex as a lone pursuit that just happens to involve another person.

This attitude has led not only to the disenchantment of sex but also to a further fragmentation—*the separation of sex from another person*. As the reasoning goes, why include other people if sex is purely about self-gratification? The rise of online pornography is a natural result of this cultural reasoning.

The final form of fragmentation, which is the inevitable result of this journey of progressive disembedding, is *the separation of sex from our own bodies*. Our inherited gender was once seen as normative for determining what form of sex we engaged in and with whom. But it has become a core modern intuition that "gender" and "sexuality" are things we choose, or that our "orientation" is part of a deeper "sexual personality" that transcends our gender. When I recently logged on to Grooveshark, a popular online jukebox, it asked for my name and email address, then gave me the following options to check: "I *identify* as: male or female?" Cut free from the moorings of divine design, we are now splintered and isolated by an infinite array of sexualities. In 2014 the social media giant Facebook changed its gender options from two categories (male or female) to seventy-one "custom" categories in the UK![5] This stunning transformation has been accepted as self-evident within the modern moral paradigm, and yet such a perspective has been made possible only by the progressive stages of disembedding outlined above. Today, despite the unambiguous testimony of our bodies, we are faced with an open choice.[6]

Physicality has lost its intrinsic value as an orienting force. This is true not only in the area of same-sex attraction. The normalization of anal sex among many heterosexuals also points to the mainstream view that sex is master over our bodies and relationships rather than the other way around. This becomes even clearer in light of research, which suggests that nearly one-third of Americans have experienced anal sex by age 23, although only 15 percent of the young women within this group report enjoying the experience, despite agreeing to it.[7]

Churches without Steeples: The Loss of Transcendence within Christian Relationships

This discussion leads us to ask, how is the atomistic vision of life influencing Christians? Our culture's modern social imaginary—its atomistic worldview—has made it difficult for Western people to believe in God. The guiding message, which is affirmed in every conceivable way, is that we live within a closed physical world of cause and effect. Nothing above or beyond this natural system can or should influence the way we live our lives. Although this worldview is clearly in opposition to our Christian beliefs, it nevertheless affects us in important and subtle ways. Even though we may believe in God, this secular vision has become the air we breathe, affecting our way of seeing and being in the world. It leads to a

5. Rhiannon Williams, "Facebook's 71 Gender Options Come to UK Users," *The Telegraph*, June 27, 2014. Examples include "neither," "gender variant," "pangender," "gender nonconforming," and "trans*person."

6. See Andy Crouch, "Sex without Bodies: The Church's Response to the LGBT Movement Must Be That Matter Matters," *Christianity Today*, June 26, 2013, http://www.christianity today.com/ct/2013/july-august/sex-without-bodies.html.

7. Regnerus and Uecker, *Premarital Sex*, 34, 86. For instance, a study of unmarried young women aged 18–32 asked those who had been involved in different sexual activities with their current partner if they liked it "very much." The results were only 15 percent for anal sex (although no one in Regnerus's own interviews found this desirable), 38 percent for oral sex, and 83 percent for conventional sex.

sort of "practical atheism" whereby we *believe* in God but find it hard to live *as if* he exists.

Clarifying this point, James K. A. Smith suggests that Western Christianity has been distorted in two very different ways by the modern world's insistence on a closed, natural world. At one end, liberal Christianity has been tempted to operate within these limits by essentially working on the human project within "natural" parameters. At the other end, evangelicals have fallen for the same trick by letting themselves be forced into a sort of world/spirit dualism, seeing God as a stranger to his creation who must, on special occasions, supernaturally intervene.[8]

Smith suggests that a genuine Christian cosmology rejects any such dualism—either naturalism or supernaturalism—and sees the Spirit as intimately involved within creation, including every aspect of our lives. Smith calls this a sort of "enchanted naturalism," in which God is not an alien or an occasional visitor to his creation but is already present within it. In contrast with secular ideology, which views the world as autonomous and self-standing, the Spirit remains an active and intimate presence in the cosmos just as he was in the beginning, when he hovered over the deep.[9] God's presence in the world explains both the predictability of science (creation has its own integrity) and the heightened work of the Spirit through unexpected actions (creation continues to be sustained by its Creator).

Augustine describes "miracles" as extraordinary events that focus us on the miracle of the ordinary. Such miracles do not break any so-called laws of nature, because "nature" does not have such a reified character. Miracles are manifestations of the Spirit's presence that are, in fact, "out of the ordinary," but even the ordinary is a manifestation of the Spirit's presence.[10] C. S. Lewis takes a similar approach in his view that miracles are illuminated windows into the ordinary.[11]

The naturalized secular worldview I've been describing has especially affected the way Christians approach their sexuality and relationships.

8. James K. A. Smith, *Thinking in Tongues: Pentecostal Contributions to Christian Philosophy* (Grand Rapids: Eerdmans, 2010), 86–105.

9. Ibid., 103.

10. Chris Gousmett, "Creation Order and Miracle according to Augustine," *Evangelical Quarterly* 60 (1988): 217–40.

11. C. S. Lewis, *Miracles* (New York: HarperOne, 2001).

When we experience or think about God as remote, he becomes detached from the intimate concerns and details of our everyday lives. Sociologist Christian Smith found this sort of worldview at play in the lives of young people in America. He suggests that the vast majority of teenagers, emerging adults, and their parents hold to an anemic version of "faith" that he calls "Moralistic Therapeutic Deism" (MTD).[12]

Although MTD masquerades as Christianity, it is gutted of most of the church's traditional convictions, consisting instead of a collection of benign and generalized beliefs. MTD incorporates the following beliefs: that God exists, that it is important to be kind to each other, that our ultimate goal should be personal happiness, that God is seldom personally involved in individual lives, and that good people go to heaven when they die.

Smith argues that MTD has gained such credibility because young people have largely absorbed the cultural beliefs inherent in individualism, multiculturalism, and relativism—to the point that they see little difference between various denominations or even different religions. In other words, once you have extracted the basic moral code of conduct, there's no need for religious practice. Unsurprisingly, Smith observed that this sort of watered-down faith did not have any real traction in the moral lives of those he interviewed. It translated more into a sort of relational "karma" than Christian faith.

Smith found such a strong consistency in these beliefs across the generations that he suggests MTD has colonized American churches and is now the dominant religion in America. In other words, young people tend to think about religion in exactly the way that liberal mainline Protestantism has encouraged us to do for decades in terms of individualism, pluralism, tolerance, and the authority of individual experience. Yet evangelicalism has also fostered this slide toward personal autonomy, with its anti-institutional bias and its focus on individualized Scripture interpretation.

In light of this, Christian leaders need to consider the ways in which our own teaching encourages the modern social imaginary, undermining the Christian vision of what it means to live in trusting obedience to God in every part of our lives, including our sexuality and relationships.

12. Smith, *Souls in Transition*, 154–56.

Encountering the Personal God: The Formative Power of Presence

In his research, Christian Smith found that a more connected worldview has important implications for the moral and relational lives of emerging adults. For instance, he observed a strong positive correlation between "miracles" and "sex" in the lives of young people. (It is not that keeping sex within marriage is itself a miracle!) Smith found that when people had tangible experiences of God in their lives, especially in their early teenage years, these moments retained deep significance for the rest of their lives, including their sexual lives. Specific times when they had seen miracles, experienced answers to prayer, had a moving spiritual experience, or could point to a decisive moment when they committed themselves to Jesus were all influential factors. In other words, a personal encounter with God had a profound influence on their vision and practice of sexuality.

This points to an important theme in relation to our discipling of young men and women within the church today. It is beyond dispute that the morality of Western society has been periodically renewed by spiritual revivals, such as the Wesleyan revival in Britain and the Great Awakenings in America. That same power is at work within our own communities of faith. Although a one-sided focus on Christian spiritualism and revivalism has all too often led to weak moral commitments, the counterfeit should not undermine the authentic. Whereas the vague MTD that Smith describes will have little moral traction within the complex reality of young people's practical lives, a vibrant faith and encounter with God creates a context of significance whereby all of life is nourished and given meaning by a continuing relationship to God. Miracles—by which I mean the demonstrated reality of God in people's lives—play an important role in sexual formation because they materialize the kingdom of God, giving it the force of reality in people's lives. Miracles puncture the gnostic dualism that many Christians experience, which drives a wedge between their beliefs (mind/spirit) and their behavior (body).

Drawing all this together, Smith found that emerging adults are more likely to have a vibrant faith if they believe in divine miracles *and* do not believe in having sex before marriage. He suggests that these twin beliefs help young adults to form a worldview that provides a vital narrative of resistance as well as a practical alternative to modern secular assumptions. If our culture offers an ethos of unquestioned scientific truth and unrestricted sexual happiness, then what we think about sex and the cosmos provides our most important means of resisting the closed "modern social imaginary" and its vision of life. A strong case can be made, then, for offering young people not only opportunities to encounter the living God personally but also a reasoned apologetic for sanctified Christian living.

Losing a Kingdom Perspective: Rules without Vision

A consequence of our sense of detachment from God—our practical atheism—is that we come to see our lives as consisting of an array of discrete decisions and actions rather than expressing and reflecting a comprehensive vision of life. We think about Scripture's teaching on sexuality as a "list of rules" rather than as a coherent picture of the "good life." If Christian instruction about sexuality is just a moral code, then we are tempted to question why these rules are so important. But those who hold this perspective lose sight of the fact that these are not just rules. The Christian vision of sexuality is the gracious provision of a loving God who invites us into a life of flourishing via participation in his own character, the relationships within the Trinity, and the reality of the kingdom of heaven as it takes shape on earth.

A Christian acquaintance recently announced on Facebook that she was moving in with her boyfriend. In support of her decision, she linked to an article that challenges the perceived evangelical focus on sex, what the author calls the "cult of virginity."[13] Obsessed evangelicals, the article's author complains, treat sexual sins as though they are more serious than other sins. This "unfair" prioritization of sex leaves many Christians who do have sex outside of marriage with a destructive legacy of guilt and shame, and it would be better—he suggests—to drop this negative fixation on sexual rules and to teach a more realistic approach. The article received numerous "likes" on Facebook. No wonder: it articulates a view that is becoming unquestionable within our culture of authenticity, which celebrates moral nihilism, that is, the each-to-their-own approach to life.

13. David Sessions, "What It Will Really Take to Bring Down the Cult of Virginity," *Patrol*, January 31, 2013, http://www.patrolmag.com/2013/01/31/david-sessions/what-it-will -really-take-to-bring-down-the-cult-of-virginity/.

But this approach puts the cart before the horse. The significant challenge of living faithful sexual lives does not mean that we should lower the standards of Christian sexuality. If we do, we have no solid foundation upon which to make particular choices in our sexual lives. If we let go of the ideals of Scripture, including Jesus's own direct teaching, what standards would we replace them with? Our sexual lives, of all things, leave us most open to the ensnaring tentacles of self-deception.

At a more fundamental level, this alternative approach is looking at the Christian life from exactly the wrong end—like peering down the large end of a telescope. The gospel envisions the sort of life that ultimately leads to human flourishing. Sin is destructive because it undermines the good that God has for us, not because it's forbidden candy that a cruel father keeps under lock and key. This is the age-old temptation that Adam and Eve swooned under in the garden—wondering whether God really does want what is best for us. Yet this truth sits at the heart of our faith: the Christian view of sexuality is an aesthetic vision of human flourishing just as truly as it is one of sacrificial self-denial.

The Loss of Eternity and the Idolatry of Youth

When our "naturalized" world gets cut off from any wider temporal horizon, such as God's progressive restoration of his creation, we come to see our lives through a distorting lens. In classical and traditional Christian cultures, one of the highest virtues was the attainment of maturity and wisdom, which imbued the aging process with a positive vision. But if we believe that the end of our lives really is *the end*, we inevitably focus on existential exploration and fulfillment in the here and now. If we view physical reality as "all there is, and all that ever will be," we will emphasize youth because it is in youth that we experience our physical embodiment at its peak and sexual fulfillment at its most intense.

No wonder our culture puts such a high priority on the twin fulfillments of sex and youth. Unsure of what the ultimate future holds, we cling to these symbols of immortality that offer us the chance to play god without responsibility to a Creator.

Christians profess to live according to a different vision, but the naturalistic worldview and its obsession with youth have dulled our consciousness

127

about how our sexuality fits within the greater horizon of God's story. It is only within *this* wider narrative that the sacrifices and consolations of the Christian vision of sexuality ultimately make sense. Within the modern church, we seldom travel with the deep awareness that our lives are given significance and specific shape only by our future destiny. When we do emphasize our future destiny, it is unfortunately often seen as an escape from the world and our embodied existence rather than as a transformation and restoration of life in the here and now.

Although people within the church face genuine challenges in regard to prolonged singleness and a perceived inability to enter into relationships, we have—often—overemphasized the importance of youth and the fulfillment of our sexual and relational aspirations within this compressed time frame. We feel we must live full sexual lives before middle age, or at least before our prolonged adolescence becomes embarrassing. Conversations that Esther and I have had with single Christians over the years have tended to reveal a sense of panic and doom as our culture's sexual stopwatch ticks loudly in their ears. This sense of loss is exacerbated by the feeling that celibate Christians sit on the sidelines of a sexual feast going on all around them. Many even feel that the church makes too big a deal about sex, while the sacrifices of chastity are not honored and don't even appear to be blessed by God. Those who have "had their fun" often seem to end up winning the perceived prize anyway—getting married and living happily ever after.

This raises the inevitable question: "How could God 'reward' their choices and ignore me?" One of the tragedies we have seen many times is the development of a profound anger at God and, in some cases, a loss of faith entirely. Others, out of desperation, experiment with the secular path for sexual and relational fulfillment, often with sad or even disastrous results. This disappointment in the area of relationships is a significant challenge for the church today as a growing number of single Christians move into the later stages of life.

In order to resist this overemphasis on the ticking biological clock, the church needs to articulate a strong and positive vision in relation to aging. Although peer-group ministry has some important advantages, we also need to reintegrate the different generations within the church. Mature and wise exemplars within the community train us to join confidently

*legit hated sex? said sex
but still should be allowed.*

with Paul's conviction that even as the body ages, the inner self is being renewed.[14] This is an important theme to which we will return.

Atomistic Thinking in Christian Formation

The modern social imaginary, with its denial of transcendence, has made it harder for people to believe in God. It has also made it harder for Christians to live *as if* God exists. Yet Christ calls us to live differently as his followers. As part of this calling, we need to be attentive to the subtle ways in which our culture's atomistic perspective shapes our approach to discipleship. The modern worldview encourages us to think about life instrumentally and pragmatically. In essence it asks, "What works?"

Within this vision people are reduced to flesh-and-blood machines, and even Christian formation can become focused on finding the right "technology." Provided we get the "science" or "technique" right, the rest will follow . . . or so we believe. But our role as shepherds—whether parents or leaders—is to resist the distortion of human identity along purely pragmatic lines. This resistance involves taking people beyond the modern worldview into the fullness of the Christian vision of life.

The truth is that leaders are overstretched, providing courses and services for their congregations to consume like spiritual protein shakes. But people are not robots, and as helpful as they may be, books, courses, and sermons are not *solutions* to their issues or *technologies* to promote their growth. This is the language and mentality of the modern worldview, which views human formation in *functional* terms. It is a tempting approach, because it gives us clear goals and responds to people's expectations. This functional approach is also evident in modern parenting. Children are seen as mini-computers to be filled—through endless extracurricular activities—with information and skills (or "software") that will ultimately help them to get into the best colleges and excel in the competitive world. Within this model, it does not matter who provides their care as long as the job is done.

In the modern mind-set, we view time instrumentally. We ask, "What will doing this achieve, and how can I do it more efficiently?" As a young attorney I had to record every six-minute time slot in my working day, even pausing the clock when I went to the bathroom or had a social conversation.

14. 2 Cor. 4:16.

It has taken me many years to shake off that paradigm of productivity, even as it relates to relationships. But it is actually the sacrificial, time-costly aspects of relationships that build our personal foundations and also provide the basis for loving relationships. As Sherry Turkle writes, "Relationships hinge on these investments of time. We know that the time we spend caring for children, doing the most basic things for them, lays down a crucial substrate. On this ground, children become confident that they are loved no matter what. And we who care for them become confirmed in our capacity to love and care."[15]

Concluding Thoughts: Mapping the Modern Social Imaginary

As we have seen, the atomistic worldview powerfully shapes personal identity and relationships. Although belief in God still persists, we are becoming a generation of "practical atheists," living *as if* God does not exist. Instead of living in a "cosmos" where things and people are intrinsically connected to God and each other, we live in a "disenchanted" earth, a morally neutral sphere on which we walk unconnected to and unencumbered by others. As Christians, too, we have been tempted to build churches without steeples—that is, to live our lives within the low horizons of the modern world.

In this first part of the book, we have mapped the anatomy of the modern social imaginary as well as its comprehensive formation of personal identity and relationships in the likeness of its own image. If this modern worldview has installed an idol—or false substitute—in the place of God, then what would a Christian social imaginary look like, one that effectively *counter*forms disciples in the reflection of the true image of the One who calls us his own?

15. Turkle, *Alone Together*, 291.

Part 2

Charting a New Course for Christian Formation

7

Searching for Truth
That Transforms

Introducing a Christian Social Imaginary

Our personal and social identity is being shaped primarily within the complex and yet definite vision of the "modern social imaginary."[1] Most of this formative process occurs at the subconscious level, beneath our cognitive and rational thinking. Our social and cultural context is not something we look at objectively, like a painting, but is more like an atmosphere that we exist within and cannot exist without. To paraphrase C. S. Lewis, a fish does not "feel" wet; likewise, we swim in the world rather than stand outside it as detached observers. We are involved in our surroundings in a complex and holistic way, and our context shapes every aspect of our lives, including how we see our sexuality, our relationships, and ourselves.

Despite the all-encompassing nature and palpably significant influence of the modern social imaginary, much Christian discipleship in recent times

1. See Taylor, *Modern Social Imaginaries*, 23–30.

has continued to follow the narrow, cognitive model of spiritual-moral formation. This model basically says, "Knowing and believing the right things about God will determine who we become and what we do." It is therefore natural that the emphasis of Christian discipleship has been on correct biblical teaching and doctrine.

There is, of course, much that we should affirm about this approach. In a world of relativistic reasoning, the authoritative guidance of Scripture is an anchor to which we can fasten our identities and lives. The problem is that this sort of knowledge does not get to the heart of the human condition. It may point us toward the truth, but can it form the truth within us? The cognitive model of discipleship lacks the power to *counter*form people within the rhythms of the gospel in the face of the more holistic cultural formation that occurs within the modern social imaginary. We may, then, be giving people the conceit of knowledge rather than genuine practical wisdom.

The differences between these contrasting visions of knowledge formation are best explored through an analogy. Imagine for a moment an area of a city that is of historical interest. There are two very different ways of getting to know that area. The first is the sort of knowledge that a new tour guide possesses, which he passes on to other outsiders. He gathers this information from maps, books, and other external sources, which give him important functional information that enables him to navigate the area. The map, for instance, shows him how the streets connect, where important landmarks are located, and so on. He may also pick up another level of detail that goes beyond purely functional information, such as interesting history, famous former residents, and notorious events. Yet as vast as the guide's knowledge may become, there still is a yawning gap in the *amount* of information as well as the *depth* of knowledge he acquires as compared with someone who grew up in that area.

Rather than the flat, functional knowledge of the tour guide, the "local" possesses a deep and complex intuitive understanding. This knowledge, accumulated over years of discovery and practice, has largely passed from cognitive thinking into the unconscious parts of his being. It has become part of his essential identity, and he will always be "from there." Without thinking, he knows a hundred different ways to get from one part of town to another, depending on the weather or time of day. What's more, he knows journeys and histories that don't appear on a map or in a book—such as the shortcuts across the backyards of friends and neighbors. He knows the story of the family in each house, which girls he liked when he was a boy, the different fruit trees, and when the picking is at its best. The tour guide knows a lot of helpful facts about the area, and yet her knowledge and what she passes on to her fellow travelers is fundamentally different from *what* and *how* the local knows.[2]

This example shows the deeply contrasting visions of knowledge formation at play today. Some Christian leaders and pastors are tempted to become spiritual "tour guides." At one level, this is a satisfying role. Our knowledge is clean, clear-cut, and well presented. Our responsibilities are clearly defined and fit within scheduled time frames—our Sunday tours! Yet, at the more fundamental level, tour guides create tourists rather than residents—consumers of knowledge rather than participants in actual communities. We may introduce people to the basic contours and city limits of the gospel—"map knowledge"—but how do we fundamentally reorient them within the new neighborhood of the gospel? Given the significant influence of the modern social imaginary, discipleship must be embedded within a Christian social imaginary in order to be an effective journey of *counter*formation. This will require a new vision of life, a new story to live within, a new community to be part of, and new practices to live by. Indeed, to live well as "resident aliens" in this world, we must know our true home.[3]

The second part of this book is an attempt to paint a picture of a Christian social imaginary. What does it look like, and how can Christian leaders encourage people on the journey of discipleship to live deeply within the gospel story?

More specifically, how does this vision take shape in relation to our sexuality and relationships?

---

2. I am indebted to the twentieth-century philosopher Martin Heidegger for this image from his book *Being and Time*, trans. John Macquarrie and Edward Robinson (New York: Harper & Row, 1966), 41–42.

3. Stanley Hauerwas and William H. Willimon, *Resident Aliens: Life in the Christian Colony*, expanded 25th anniversary ed. (Nashville: Abingdon, 2014).

8

Seeing the Good Life and Becoming What We See

The Role of Vision within Sexual Formation

Pearls before Breakfast[1]

On an unremarkable morning in January 2007 during the morning rush hour, a young man entered L'Enfant Plaza Station in the Washington, DC, subway. There was nothing distinctive about how he looked; a youngish guy in jeans, a long-sleeved T-shirt, and a Washington Nationals baseball cap. Taking his place against a wall at the top of an escalator, he pulled a violin from a small case and threw in a few dollars and some loose change as seed money. He played for around forty-five minutes to a restless conveyor belt of people—over a thousand in the time he was there. As he played, the preoccupied herd thundered past him; only a small boy lingered for a few minutes before his mother impatiently grabbed his arm and pulled him toward the escalator. The few who did give money tended to toss it into his

---

1. Gene Weingarten, "Pearls before Breakfast: Can One of the Nation's Great Musicians Cut through the Fog of a D.C. Rush Hour? Let's Find Out," *Washington Post*, April 8, 2007, http://www.washingtonpost.com/wp-dyn/content/article/2007/04/04/AR2007040401721.html.

case on the run, more an expression of guilt than appreciation. When he finished, the young man collected his money, packed away his violin, and left the station. No one applauded; no one even noticed. For his labors he had earned a grand total of $32.17.

The supposedly cultured crowd of largely federal government workers were unaware that morning that the young fiddler in the Metro was Joshua Bell, one of the finest classical musicians of his generation. He played some of the most complex and elegant music ever written on one of the most valuable violins ever made—a Stradivarius worth $3.5 million. A few days earlier he had played to a capacity audience at Boston's Symphony Hall, with people paying upwards of one hundred dollars per ticket. But on that nondescript Friday morning, he was just another struggler competing for the attention of busy people on their way to work. Bell's impromptu performance in the Metro was arranged by the *Washington Post* as an experiment to see if, in a mundane setting at an inconvenient time, true beauty would transcend it. The *Post* posed the poignant question: *Do we perceive beauty in unexpected places?*

The red thread running throughout this book is the conviction that we are, more than we realize, *made* by our context. The cultural philosophy that surrounds us on a daily basis provides the moral wallpaper of our lives, deeply shaping our imagination of what life should look like. To a large extent, we are not even consciously aware of this formation or that alternatives exist, especially in the area of sexuality. Rather than being a dynamic part of our character to be trained and shaped, sexuality has come to be viewed as part of our personality—something that not only is freely expressed as a reflection of our uniqueness but also helps establish that uniqueness. Indeed, the modern self sees sexual expression as a virtue that lies at the heart of human identity. We can only be fulfilled, happy, and mature when our sexuality is set free.

Power Failure: The Church's Lack of Vision regarding Sexuality

A friend recently expressed a typical frustration for single Christians. He described a mutual friend in our church who had had premarital sex and was now about to marry someone else. My friend was annoyed and disappointed because he felt that he was missing out on both counts. He had struggled for years to live out his singleness faithfully, and here was another Christian who was able to have his cake and eat it too. I had huge sympathy for him; so often, living the faithful Christian life seems like squandering the prime of our youth or maybe even forfeiting it completely. Our sacrifices just don't seem to count toward any reward in the end. In fact, those who are less faithful to the ideal often seem to flourish.

At one level, this frustration is understandable. Powerful dynamics are at play within human sexuality, exerting what sometimes feels like an irresistible force, especially within our cultural milieu. Yet this perspective also reveals a lack of vision or, more accurately, the wrong vision. What we describe as "cake" reveals what we consider deep within ourselves to be worth having—the "good life."

Mark Regnerus, at the conclusion of his comprehensive study of sex and religion among American teenagers, refuses to pull any punches about the failure of many churches to present an inspiring and workable vision of Christian sexuality to their young people. As he describes it,

> The majority of religious interviewees with whom we spoke, the ones who might possibly own some sort of religious ethic concerning human sexuality, could articulate nothing more about what their faith has to say about sex than a simple no-sex-before-marriage rule. For most of them, this is the sum total of Christian teaching on sex. For the most part, congregations are doing a terrible job of fashioning distinctively Christian sexual ethics. Abstinence organizations seem primarily interested in pragmatically doing whatever it takes to stop adolescents from having sex. In fact, despite its numeric successes, the movement is hamstrung and self-limited because of American Christians' disinterest in taking a firmer position on marriage and the family. If family formation is best postponed, and any given marriage can be undone without consequence, why should young people wait to enjoy the benefits of sex within an unstable and temporary arrangement (marriage)?[2]

The complex loop connecting marriage, singleness, and sex has been demonstrated by the True Love Waits campaign with its purity rings,

2. Regnerus, *Forbidden Fruit*, 214.

exhorting publications, and initiation events. Although it began in the United States, the campaign has influenced abstinence movements in other countries and has become an important global phenomenon. All major campaigns, like political slogans, tend to be overly simplistic in order to be clear and effective. This campaign demonstrates how something that looks like vision can in reality be a misleading distortion of it. As one writer who wore a purity ring from the ages of sixteen to twenty-five describes it, this movement encouraged her to make a "deal" with Jesus rather than to follow him. The deal was, in essence, that if you love God first, he will ultimately deliver you a husband or wife. When she was sixteen, she received from a youth leader a poem written "from God" that said, "The reason you don't have anyone yet is because you're not fully satisfied in Me. You have to be satisfied with Me and then when you least expect it, I'll bring you the person I meant for you."[3]

No doubt the True Love Waits message was presented more deftly and nuanced by other leaders. Yet this was the essential message many young people absorbed, and it highlights some of the problems involved. First, as we've already seen, it falls into the trap of defining singleness only in terms of marriage. The emphasis, then, is on "waiting." This approach distorts the Christian vision of discipleship by turning it from one of devotion and followership into a pragmatic quid pro quo. This is firmly rooted in modern individualism, which sees all relationships from the point of view of personal fulfillment and reward. Most tragically, because it gets the Christian vision of life the wrong way around, this approach inevitably leads to crushing disappointment and anger within people's romantic lives—and with God himself. As the writer poignantly describes,

> It's a graveyard of hearts, this place where single church girls crash into their late 20s and early 30s. Churches see the symptoms. They scramble to reach out to the ever-growing young adult singles crowd who feels alienated by family-oriented services.
>
> But there's something bigger behind it than that. Much bigger. There are a lot of girls out there who don't know who God is anymore—the God of their youth group years just isn't working out. Back then, that God said

3. Anonymous post, "I Don't Wait Anymore," *Grace for the Road* (blog), February 3, 2012, http://gracefortheroad.com/2012/02/03/idontwait/.

to wait for sex until they are married, until He brings the right man along for a husband. They signed a card and put it on the altar and pledged to wait. And wait they did. . . . But many of them—if they're honest—will tell you that time has passed, and it's wrecking their view of God. If this is who God's supposed to be, then He's tragically late. So some decide to chuck "Lady in Waiting" out the window . . . and possibly their virginity with it. Church goes next. God might go next, too. If He doesn't answer these prayers after they've held up their end of the bargain, why would He answer any others? Whether it was the fault of the leaders, the fault of us girls, or both, a tragedy happened back then. A lot of girls were sold on a deal and not on a Savior.[4]

This approach places people in an awkward stance when it comes to romantic relationships. While it creates an enormous amount of idealistic expectation around God's preparation and provision of a future life partner, it also puts people into a passive stance regarding relationships. We are taught not to pursue relationships because we are waiting for the perfect one. There is, however, no such person. He or she is out there in the messy throng of humanity right in front of us. Jesus calls people to follow him as the source of life, not as the giver of the sort of life we think he should want for us. If we take the latter view of God, then he inevitably becomes an inconsistent parent who gives gifts to some of his children and denies them to others—a cruelly selective Santa Claus.

The writer of this blog wonders whether this view of God "has sold people a solution for life's problems rather than life itself"—Jesus as our helper rather than our goal. The disappointment with God that many people have experienced through this well-intentioned movement shows how important the delicate project of casting vision is within Christian discipleship. In a culture where sexual expression is seen as a fundamental right, we need to give powerful significance to our sexual lives but without making them the goal of our faith. To sum this up, we worship Jesus in our sexual lives because we love and trust him, not because we love what he can do for us. This truth will not eradicate frustration and disappointment from the experience of singleness within the Christian life, but it will certainly place it within its proper perspective.

4. Ibid.

Joshua Bell's unexpected performance in the Washington, DC, subway is something like the Christian vision of sexuality today. It appears dull and inconvenient as people bustle past on their way to seemingly better and more important things. And yet if we pause to really listen, we might perceive that this vision represents the very music of heaven. Despite the awkward acoustics and bleak context of the "subway," the Christian vision of sexuality represents the divine tune played out on priceless instruments. The reality is that in the everyday shape of our sexual lives we get to play the harmonies and melodies of heaven. One day we will hear and be captivated by this tune in its unrestrained richness—in the great concert chamber—but it will be a familiar tune. The gospel, too, asks us, *Will we perceive beauty in unexpected places?*

How Do We Give Vision the Power to Direct Our Lives?

Living faithful Christian lives is impossible unless we are nourished and sustained by a vision of what human flourishing looks like—what philosophers call our picture of the "good life." Unless we really come to love this vision at the unspoken levels deep within ourselves, and come to understand our whole lives as heroic adventures to walk faithfully within this vision, our perspective will be pulled out of shape and distorted by our cultural context, tantalizing us as it does with unrealistic expectations of sexual satisfaction and relational perfection. How can we explain why so many Christians know the "dos" and "don'ts" but struggle to live within them? Christian leaders have perhaps tended to give people rules to live by without articulating a coherent vision for the Christian life that makes sense of it all—a perspective that delivers a big-enough reason to hold fast to our costly decisions when the sirens call.

The very idea that our sexuality, in the narrow sense of its physical expression, lies at the core of our personal identity is largely a twentieth-century innovation. Yet within a few generations, this view of human personhood has become for many the only conceivable way of thinking about their lives. In this vision, we can achieve personal fruition only through full, free, and honest sexual expression. Self-denial is seen as a form of self-harm or an unhealthy incursion on our self-identity. As a result, even as Christians we may begin to wonder why God and the church would want to deprive us of these essential needs. This demonstrates the grip that our culture's vision of sexuality has taken on our imaginations. That we view sex apart from marriage as "cake" shows that we are deeply suspicious of the Christian way of life. It can feel like grimly clinging to the wreckage of a sinking ship until death sets us free. This perspective sums up the depth of frustration, disappointment, and anger that so many believers experience in this area. *Why would a good God lead me into this lonely pit?* It's a familiar narrative that I've heard from many Christians over the years.

Whatever we set as our loftiest goal and make our highest priority—that is, our highest love—orders everything else that we *want* and *do* in our lives. This idea brings together two essential drivers of human identity: our nature as *desiring* beings and our nature as *moral* beings. Unlike animals, which act purely and reflexively from instinct, we have desires about our desires. This means that we are able to reflect on whether we want the desires we have and to choose other ones. If one of my core desires, for instance, is to one day sustain a committed marriage, this goal will tend to regulate my appetite for one-off liaisons.

Christian leaders should avoid defining "morality" narrowly in terms of what people should *do*—a list of rules or a moral code—without any appeal to a higher truth that gives those rules meaning or resonance. Instead, we need to focus our teaching on moral vision. Moral vision requires articulating the big picture of what the Christian life is about, as well as how to connect every aspect of our lives to this spiritual vision. This involves asking the essential questions, what are we aiming for, and how does each part of our lives contribute to this goal? When we give primary importance to our ultimate desire—knowing, following, and serving Christ—it reorders all our other desires.

I now want to sketch the outline of a Christian vision for relationships and sexuality. What does it look like? Why is this costly journey worth it, not just in the kingdom to come but also in the here and now? It is only when we come to believe in our deepest beings that God is good and that his plan for our lives reflects his goodness that we can travel with purpose and bind ourselves to his vision for life.

A comprehensive Christian vision of sexuality has four essential characteristics.

1. The vision is *eschatological*: it places our sexuality within the bigger context of God's unfolding plan for creation.
2. The vision is *metaphysical*: it aligns our sexual lives with the nature of things as they *really* are, the present reality of heaven. It attunes us to the kingdom of God, seen and unseen, which we seek to reflect.
3. The vision is *formational*: it shapes who we *are* (our character) as we journey toward maturity in the image and likeness of Christ.
4. The vision is *missional*: it shapes what we *do* (our behavior), which gives a purpose to our sexuality that expresses God's character and so witnesses to his mission in the world.

The Vision Is Eschatological

The Christian vision of life must begin with the end in sight. Our ultimate destiny provides a future horizon with which to frame our present existence. Indeed, God has put eternity in our hearts, as the writer of Ecclesiastes says, and our sexuality gives us glimpses of that eternity. It also acts as a homing instinct, drawing us toward this impending hope. Our highest priority, then, is to reorder the Christian life around our future destiny: the kingdom of God fully realized.

What Does the Future Look Like? A Vision of Hope

Scripture paints an image of our ultimate future that is summed up in John's vision of the wedding feast in Revelation 19:7–10. It depicts a state of everlasting joy and celebration in which all social barriers and pain will be set aside; we will know God and others without constraint or hostility, envy or competition. It is a picture of complete social reconciliation and relational intimacy, a time when we will know Jesus face-to-face and each other closer than any marital embrace. As the angel tells the apostle to write, "Blessed are those who are invited to the wedding supper of the Lamb!"[5] This wedding party, a joyous celebration of all who are in Christ,

5. Rev. 19:9.

is the fruition that we look for in the age to come, and it shines a very real spotlight on the ultimate horizon for our lives. This is a breathtaking vision that—if we can grasp it—can bear the weight of our present frustrations, disappointments, betrayals, and losses.

What's more, God has given all of us hints and glimpses of this vision in some of the everyday realities of our lives. C. S. Lewis's friend and fellow "Inkling" Charles Williams describes how romantic love, especially the early stages of falling in love, gives us a momentarily restored vision of one other human being—a sort of insight into his or her eternal identity. For a brief time our romantic attraction transfigures this person, allowing us to see the very best in him or her, to ignore or forgive the person's flaws, and to be endlessly fascinated by him or her. One day, we will see every resurrected person in this way, as God sees each of us now.

Some years ago friends bought us a meal at Claridge's restaurant in London, the Soho flagship of the combustible master-chef Gordon Ramsey (I'm sure we heard him screaming from the kitchen at one point!). This never-ending culinary experience was a feast for the senses, with each of the many courses expertly matched with a particular wine. What made this experience all the more enjoyable was that we had greatly anticipated it. We savored the thought of it for weeks in advance and carefully planned what we ate earlier that day so that we arrived for the meal with our appetites fully engaged. So it is with the wedding feast in Revelation 19. God has given us glimpses of this future, whetting our appetites through our present experiences and relationships. We are meant to hunger for our ultimate goal, for only then will we taste life in all its fullness.

Our present sexuality is therefore a penultimate reminder of our real destiny rather than an end in itself. Revelation 19 reminds us of the radical theological anthropology of the gospel, which views human identity and sexuality on a far grander horizon than our present lives. God's mission in the world is to invite all who will accept his welcome to this eschatological banquet, and the urgent task of the church is to share the invitation.

Biblical Sexuality: A Promise and a Warning

Scripture's imagery is almost never one-dimensional. The Song of Songs, for instance, was seen by Israel and most people throughout church history as a double-sided picture of human lovers and of the intimate relationship between God and his people. Just as this relationship comes to fruition at the eschatological wedding banquet when Christ joins with his bride, the church, it also has important implications for our present sexual lives. When we understand the marriage supper in light of the wedding customs in Jesus's day, these implications become clear.

The wedding had three major parts. First, the parents of the bride and the bridegroom signed a wedding contract, which involved the bride's parents paying a dowry to the bridegroom or his parents. This began the betrothal period, which was similar to present-day engagement except that betrothal was essentially a marriage contract that could be dissolved only in the case of infidelity. This was the crisis Joseph faced when Mary became pregnant during this stage of their marriage.[6] The betrothal period ushered in the second stage in the courting process when the bridegroom went to prepare a new addition to his parents' home, which would become his marital residence. Within the salvation story, betrothal is the moment when we are won by Jesus's blood and accept his invitation into the family of God. As we wait for his return, Jesus promises his followers that he will prepare a place for us in his father's house.[7]

The final stage in the Jewish wedding usually occurred a year later, when the bridegroom went to the house of the bride at midnight with his male friends, creating a torch-lit procession through the streets with the whole village joining in. The bride would know in advance that this was going to take place; she would be ready with her maidens, and they would join the parade, which would eventually arrive at the bridegroom's home. This custom is the basis for Jesus's parable of the ten virgins in Matthew 25:1–13. Anticipating the coming of the bridegroom, five wise maidens fill their lamps with oil but also make provision for extra oil. The five foolish maidens fail to bring extra oil for their lamps. When the bridegroom is delayed, the foolish maidens are off buying oil and miss the banquet.

The New Testament's picture of our future destiny, then, comes with an aesthetic vision—joyous intimacy with God and each other—but also with a warning. We must be ready for the bridegroom, living in faithful

6. Matt. 1:18; Luke 2:5.
7. John 14:2.

anticipation of his return even though he is delayed. It is beyond question that in the New Testament this involves not just our spiritual readiness but also the moral integrity of our lives. Referring to the man who was thrown out of the wedding feast for not wearing the right clothing, John Calvin observes that arguing about whether the missing garment was faith or a holy life is useless because the two are inextricably intertwined.[8] Indeed, the New Testament writers all place sexual fidelity at the heart of discipleship. The double-sided parable in Matthew 25 energizes us in anticipation of the bridegroom's arrival even as it creates a sense of urgency regarding the quality of our lives and relationships.[9]

Just like Paul, our goal is to present our communities as spotless and blameless when the bridegroom returns.[10] We must understand and articulate both the *hope*—or vision—of the eschatological wedding feast and the *crisis*—or warning—of the gospel. Doing so gives every aspect of our lives urgency as well as a specific trajectory. According to the New Testament, we are not merely "sinners saved" but also saints on the path to a glorious future.

Divine Affirmation of Our Sexual Lives

This bigger cosmic story gives our sexuality meaning and purpose as an essential and ongoing part of who we are. The doctrines of creation, incarnation, and resurrection all affirm this reality, so that Jesus's gendered and ascended resurrection body provides a sort of prototype for our own future existence. The coming down and joining of heaven with the new earth in Revelation 21 gives real hope and significance to our embodied material lives.[11]

Our sexuality in its fullest sense—that is, its spiritual, emotional, and physical aspects—plays an essential role in the relational vision of the kingdom of God because it speaks of our "incompleteness." Significantly, our one-sidedness as either male or female creates a homing instinct that

---

8. Matt. 22:1–14. See John Calvin, "Commentary on Matthew, Mark, Luke—Volume 2," Christian Classics Ethereal Library, http://www.ccel.org/ccel/calvin/calcom32.ii.xxxii.html?bcb=right.

9. See also Rev. 2:20; 9:21; 21:8; and 22:15.

10. Eph. 5:27; Phil. 1:10; 2:15; 1 Thess. 3:13; 5:23; 2 Pet. 3:14; and Rev. 14:5.

11. Rev. 21:1–3.

calls us beyond ourselves, to seek relationship with God and others. Sexual intimacy in marriage gives us something like a momentary glimpse of our future ecstasy. It is a fleeting and shadowy foretaste of the social intimacy we will experience in the age to come, even though sex itself will pass away.

Yet our future destiny also puts sex into perspective. In announcing the arrival of the kingdom of God on earth, Jesus declared that human history is a story that will end. This announcement gave urgency to the mission of the church, and it has important implications for Christian sexuality. Within the biblical cultures, marriage was seen as the norm, a societal obligation or necessary rite of passage. In contrast to this, Jesus's announcement of the kingdom puts our present desire for sexual and relational fulfillment in its ultimate context. The urgency of God's mission to invite all who will come to the future wedding feast focuses the church on this most important goal. As Paul observes in 1 Corinthians 7:32–35, this eschatological priority frees some from the necessity of marriage, so that singleness becomes a meaningful option for serving the community.

Both Jesus and Paul had glimpsed the future, and they each understood the greater satisfaction that is to come.[12] This new emphasis in the New Testament relativizes the importance of marriage and sexual intimacy because our future destiny so completely overwhelms all of our present sexual longing. In essence, our present sexual desires look smaller when viewed from the horizon of eternity. This balanced approach allowed both Jesus and Paul to affirm marriage while also treating it pragmatically. Paul, for instance, says it is better to be married than to burn with lust—but if you can, it is good to remain single and focused on the missional task at hand.

This approach is radical, giving singleness equal status with marriage and making marriage a *vocation* within God's mission rather than a natural or societal necessity. These parallel Christian vocations—marriage and singleness—give coherence, meaning, and purpose to each stage of our sexual lives, even if singleness is a temporary stage for most people. Viewing our sexual lives as vocational has important ethical implications. As Stanley Hauerwas says, Jesus's announcement that the kingdom of God had arrived with his own life changed the status of the world by making it part of God's kingdom. This means that the ethics of the Sermon on

12. See John 16:20–22; Rom. 8:18; and 2 Cor. 4:17.

the Mount, including the teaching on sexual purity and fidelity, are not ideal teachings but represent the new form of life for the eschatological community.[13]

Paul's Use of Eschatological Vision: The Future Made Present

The apostle Paul's sense of the ultimate future played a critical role in his pastoral ministry. He consistently contextualized the purpose and form of Christian living within the greater arc of God's cosmic story of redemption. We see this in his challenge to those Galatians who had returned to placing their confidence "in the flesh," that is, in their own ability to live according to the law.[14] Paul seeks to persuade the Galatians to return to "life in the Spirit" by contrasting the flesh (*sarx*) and the Spirit (*pneuma*).[15] As Gordon Fee explains, Paul uses these terms primarily in their eschatological and theological senses rather than in an anthropological sense.[16] Instead of referring to a conflict between each person's body and spirit, Paul contrasts life in the flesh, meaning the fallen present age, with life in the Spirit, meaning God's future reign made present. In the theological sense, *sarx* (flesh) is seen as fallen human creatureliness, which is opposed to God in every way.[17]

Fee observes that this contrast is not about our "introspective conscience" but has to do with the expression and growth of the fruits of the Spirit within the church as Christians learn to live together as God's future people in the present fallen world.[18] Whereas the age of the flesh (including trying to live out of our own moral power) leads us further into sin and creates a toxic social environment, living in the Spirit brings the socially constructive fruits of the Spirit led by love.[19] Paul explains that Christians live amid the war between these ages and so are not immune to this struggle. He is clear,

13. Stanley Hauerwas, "Living the Proclaimed Reign of God: A Sermon on the Sermon on the Mount," *Interpretation* 47, no. 2 (April 1993): 152–58.

14. Gal. 3:1–5.

15. Gal. 5:17.

16. Gordon D. Fee, *God's Empowering Presence: The Holy Spirit in the Letters of Paul* (Grand Rapids: Baker Academic, 1994), 817.

17. Ibid., 819.

18. Ibid., 883.

19. Ibid., 822. Gal. 5:19–26.

however, that we must choose decisively in which age to live; failure to choose to walk by the power of the Spirit leads to the confused ethical condition that Paul describes in Galatians 5:17, wherein the sinful nature wants to do what is opposed to the Spirit.[20] If we choose to walk by the Spirit—that is, to live in the future age made present in Jesus—then Paul assures us that we will *not* gratify the desires of the flesh. Rather, as Peter confirms, through God's own power we will "participate in the divine nature."[21]

We live in the midst of a cosmic crisis—the age of the flesh still wars against the Spirit—and yet our cultural script lulls us into believing the deception that we can live peacefully and effortlessly within these times. It tells us that what seems to come naturally will be a reliable guide. The gospel, on the other hand, acknowledges the full weight of this crisis and gives us a vision of hope to rise above it. It urges us to live like those five wise virgins in Jesus's parable, faithfully anticipating the arrival of the bridegroom.

New Testament scholar Richard Hays sums up the tension we live with in this "time between the times."[22] Although we are freed from the power of sin, we must struggle to live faithfully in this penultimate age. Referring to our sexual lives, Hays says:

> Those who demand fulfillment now, as though it were a right or a guarantee, are living in a state of adolescent illusion. To be sure, the transforming power of the Spirit really is present in our midst; on the other hand, the "not yet" looms large; we live with the reality of temptation, the reality of the hard struggle to live faithfully. Consequently . . . some may find disciplined abstinence the only viable alternative to disordered sexuality. . . . The art of eschatological moral discernment lies in working out how to live lives free from bondage to sin without presuming to be translated prematurely into a condition that is free from "the sufferings of this present time."[23]

When properly focused, the biblical vision of our ultimate future is an empowering one in which our present sacrifices and struggles are put into

20. James Thompson, *Pastoral Ministry according to Paul: A Biblical Vision* (Grand Rapids: Baker Academic, 2006), 78.

21. 2 Pet. 1:4.

22. Richard B. Hays, *The Moral Vision of the New Testament: A Contemporary Introduction to New Testament Ethics* (San Francisco: HarperSanFrancisco, 1996), 25.

23. Ibid., 393–94. See Rom. 8:18, 24–25.

proper perspective. Only this stunning reality can give direction and genuine significance to the costs and consolations of our present sexual lives.

Eschatology, then, is not tangential to Christian sexuality but essential to it. Without this clarity and assurance, we are left to the uncertain winds of cultural confusion that seek to erase eternity from our hearts.

The Vision Is Metaphysical

During World War II, when Continental Europe was occupied by fascist regimes, many people were faced with a stark choice: either join the underground resistance movements or become complicit with the foreign overlords and their native puppets. A courageous minority chose to fight for freedom, despite the costly sacrifice involved. These two choices essentially represented a battle of realities. For most Europeans at the time, reality was shaped by the overwhelming and seemingly permanent power of the occupying forces, with their pervasive symbols and agents. Meanwhile, the fledgling and vulnerable underground movements were aligned with the greater invisible reality of the Allies' future victory. Although everything in their immediate context pointed the other way, these freedom fighters were in tune with the world as it really turned out to be. On the ground, almost everyone believed in the daily reality they saw all around them, and so it was both costly and countercultural to identify with the wider perspective of the future Allied victory.

Metaphysics as Sexual Ethics

Even when we help people grasp the connection between our present lives and our future hope—how the story ends—this only gets them so far. We cannot encourage people just to cling to the wreckage of life because of a future hope. On the contrary, the core of the Christian vision is that our lives *now* can enter into and reflect the realities of heaven. Indeed, this expectation forms the climax of the church's most essential prayer: "Your kingdom come, your will be done, on earth as it is in heaven."[24] An essential aspect of Christian vision involves understanding the nature of

24. Matt. 6:10.

true reality, so that our sexual formation is embedded in and grows out of our metaphysics. Once we are clear on the nature of things as God intends them, then we can boldly seek to live "with the grain of the universe."[25] This vision of reality provides the imaginative landscape within which we can see the world and ourselves within it.

Especially in his letters to the Colossians and Ephesians, Paul emphasizes our participation *now* in heavenly realities. As he says, God has "made us alive with Christ"; he "raised us up with Christ," and we are now seated "in the heavenly realms in Christ Jesus."[26] This heavenly focus does not undermine or remove our focus from our everyday lives; it should have the opposite effect, sharpening our view of this life within the perspective of heaven.

C. S. Lewis describes how our present lives can express and take part in heavenly realities through what he calls "transposition." If we imagine heaven to be like an orchestral score, played by hundreds of different musicians on many different instruments, then we know that this same composition can also be played on a single instrument such as a piano.[27] Although there is a significant gap between the piano and orchestra in terms of nuance and complexity, the piano still can express the musical themes in a very recognizable sense. Indeed, by practicing and performing a part, a pianist can prepare to take up her place within the orchestra at the appointed time.

In this way, our lives now have the potential to express and prepare us for the realities of heaven. Lewis suggests that this relationship is "sacramental" rather than merely symbolic, which means that our everyday lives can reflect heaven but can also be drawn up into the higher reality and become part of it to some extent.[28] Our sexual lives, then, can play the heavenly musical theme now in anticipation of the great wedding feast when Jesus will be fully reconciled with his bride, the church.

The foundations for understanding our true selves are expressed in Genesis 1:26–27. Being created in God's "image" means that we were

---

25. Stanley Hauerwas, *With the Grain of the Universe: The Church's Witness and Natural Theology* (Grand Rapids: Baker Academic, 2013), 6.

26. Eph. 2:5–6.

27. C. S. Lewis, "Transposition," in *The Weight of Glory: And Other Addresses* (New York: HarperCollins, 2001), 91–115.

28. Ibid.

designed to reflect him in every way—physically, emotionally, intellectually, and socially. Sin is essentially a wedge that separates us from God and our divine-likeness, which in turn leads to fragmentation within ourselves and between one another. Within this crisis, like a physician setting broken bones, Jesus's work of atonement was the thoroughgoing act of restoring human wholeness. As the first man in the new humanity, Jesus put right all that was wrong within the human condition. As members of this new humanity we can now confidently "put on the new self, created to be like God in true righteousness and holiness."[29] *So what is God like and how can we reflect him in our sexuality and relationships?* We need to think about this within the context of the two Christian vocations of marriage and singleness.

Divine Sex: Imaging Our Creator within Marriage

The Old and New Testaments, the early church, and the whole of church history agree that sex belongs within marriage. Genesis 2 and the Song of Songs are central to both the anthropology and theology of the church. Both Scriptures express the beauty of human sexual intimacy, as well as the way in which this reflects God as the intimate and faithful Creator. Hence the title of this book: rather than being a sacrilegious double entendre, *Divine Sex* reminds us that in sex within marriage, we express something essential about God's own relationships within the Trinity, as well as point to the age when we will participate in these relationships directly.

Right at the heart of Christian confession is God's character as a *social being*, that is, his living within the community of persons in the Godhead—Father, Son, and Holy Spirit. This intimate relationship came to be understood as *perichoresis*, or co-inherence, within the divine family. It is often described as the divine dance, meaning that the generous giving and receiving by each person to the others blurs the boundaries between them. The medieval Cistercian abbot Bernard of Clairvaux even conceived of this relationship through the metaphor of the kiss from the Song of Songs.[30] Perichoresis is a dynamic in which each trinitarian person relates to the

29. Eph. 4:24.
30. Bernard of Clairvaux, "Sermons on the Song of Songs," in *Selected Works*, Classics of Western Spirituality (New York: Paulist Press, 1987), 207–78.

others in complete love, openness, and trust. Whether or not we can grasp it, it is a stunning reality that the whole cosmos rests on God's love. Even more astonishing is that we too are invited into this divine dance through the Spirit so that our own relationships may come to reflect God. Jesus summed this up in a prayer for his disciples in John 17:20–23:

> My prayer is not for them alone. I pray also for those who will believe in me through their message, that all of them may be one, Father, just as you are in me and I am in you. May they also be in us so that the world may believe that you have sent me. I have given them the glory that you gave me, that they may be one as we are one—I in them and you in me—so that they may be brought to complete unity. Then the world will know that you sent me and have loved them even as you have loved me.

This picture of divine love provides the empowering vision for intimacy within Christian marriage. Our love can enter into, reflect, and witness to the kingdom of heaven.

Charles Williams describes how our sexuality enables us to participate now in the aesthetic realities of heaven.[31] Our experience of romantic love, sexual desire, and all forms of beauty, he says, is testimony to our ultimate desire for God. In these moments we experience a sort of momentarily redeemed nature, when we feel what we were created to experience—ecstatic intimacy with God and others. In essence, we taste our origins and our future destiny. Sex and spirituality are intricately interwoven because each reflects and leads us toward the other. Sexual intimacy within marriage, then, is a visible sacrament—or icon—that participates in and reveals the unseen God.

Within our cultural moment there is an urgent need to rediscover the sacred significance and mystery of romantic love and sexual intimacy and to understand how this influences our spirituality and relationships. The Bible's holistic anthropology means that we cannot extract our "selves" from our bodies or from our relationships with other people. Sex is therefore a complex language designed to communicate and connect. This mystery is expressed in the biblical vision that two persons become "one flesh,"[32]

---

31. Charles Williams, *Outlines of Romantic Theology*, ed. Alice M. Hadfield (Grand Rapids: Eerdmans, 1990), 70.

32. See Gen. 2:24; 1 Cor. 6:15–20; and Eph. 5:25–33.

meaning that sexual relations always involve us as whole persons, "as embodied souls, ensouled bodies."[33]

Sex matters because it involves one's whole self. It is a uniquely holistic act that provides the closest analogue we have for God's own intimacy within the Trinity and our spiritual union with God. Sex outside biblical boundaries does not necessarily involve greater guilt than other forms of boundary crossing, but it does involve us more intimately. Sex is unique because it reaches closer to our core than anything else. Paul makes this point to those Corinthians who were having sex with temple prostitutes. He administers a form of moral shock treatment by explaining that they, as members of Christ's body, are joining themselves to these women and are thereby becoming "one flesh" with them.[34] He then directly compares this sexual union with another person to our spiritual joining with God: "But whoever is united with the Lord is one with him in spirit."[35] In 1 Corinthians 6:18–20, Paul gives particular significance to our sexual lives because of their intricate connection to our spiritual lives:

> Flee from sexual immorality. All other sins a person commits are outside the body, but whoever sins sexually, sins against their own body. Do you not know that your bodies are temples of the Holy Spirit, who is in you, whom you have received from God? You are not your own; you were bought at a price. Therefore honor God with your bodies.

In contrast to the modern view, sex does indeed have mystery! It is ordained as an all-consuming act of union between committed lovers that points toward our bonding with God himself. It is little wonder that our enemy has sought to trivialize and empty sex of its depth and significance. The role of sex both as a bonding agent among lovers and as a sacramental window onto the kingdom of heaven makes it a key battleground for Christian formation.

The God we seek to imitate is also a *covenant maker*. God is faithful to his promises and does not change his mind.[36] In Scripture, God's covenant with his people is often expressed as a binding marriage commitment. We

33. Karl Barth, *Church Dogmatics* III/2, study ed. (London: T&T Clark, 2009).
34. 1 Cor. 6:15–16.
35. 1 Cor. 6:17.
36. Ps. 110:4; Isa. 45:23.

are called, like God, to let our "yes" be "yes" and our "I will" be "I will."[37]
The fundamental principle underlying Scripture's preservation of sex within
marriage is that there is no such thing as real sex outside of marriage. Sex
is marriage, or else it is self-annihilation. Although sex outside of marriage
often feels like a powerful bond, it simply cannot carry the weight of this
deeper commitment and is prone to a manipulative dynamic by which it
is "traded" rather than "shared."

Within Christian marriage we covenant to be like Christ to one another.
Paul's instructions to husbands and wives in Ephesians 5 are not "rights"
to be demanded by each marriage partner; in truth, they are the generous
responsibilities of love, which each of us gives to the other. Being Christ
to each other leaves no room for domineering or manipulation and leads
us toward self-giving as the way of genuine freedom.

In light of these responsibilities, Christian marriage is a serious and risky
undertaking. The idea of binding ourselves to each other for all time, in
sickness and in health, for richer or poorer, is like standing at the foot of a
great mountain. We should feel both exhilaration and also the sacred gravity of the journey we are embarking on. In making this commitment and
walking purposefully within it, we reflect the God who has bound himself
to us for all time. It is no wonder, then, that faithful Christian marriages
are some of our most important witnesses to the gospel within our culture.
In a world where sex and love have been devalued through hyperinflation,
faithful relationships may be the only hard currency left.

Finally, but most fundamentally, in Christian marriage we seek to reflect
the God who is *creative*. The first mandate given to Adam and Eve as those
created in the image of God was to "be fruitful and increase in number; fill
the earth."[38] Having children is a Godlike act, so that sex carries the intrinsic
possibility and responsibility of being "fruitful." Sex within marriage, at
both the symbolic and practical levels, is essentially an expression of our
openness to new life beyond our exclusive relationship as a couple. Even if
we use contraception or are unable to have children for other reasons, we
are symbolically open to the possibility of children and the responsibility
of providing a stable context for them. Envisioning marriage as a Christian

37. Matt. 5:37.
38. Gen. 1:27–28.

vocation is critical because otherwise, within the soul-mate paradigm of modern culture, marriage itself can become an idolatrous fixation, a life-style enclave that we jealously guard from outside interference, so that even children become a discretionary accessory.

Singleness and the Full Christian Life

During a Christian wedding my wife and I attended recently, the convening pastor expressed what appears to have become a typical way of thinking about Christian sexuality. He explained, on the basis of the picture given in Genesis 2, that the bride and groom were by themselves two incomplete halves. Now, in their marriage, they were becoming what they had been created to be, a united whole. The wedding guests were mainly single Christians in their early twenties, and the message received was loud and clear: you are not a full self until you are a married self. Indeed, Christian discussions about sexuality often begin and end with marriage. You have either reached your destination or you are still on the way. Because of this, teaching on sexuality outside of marriage is usually also focused on marriage, meaning what *not* to do outside of it.

⌐Yet singleness has a positive and legitimate standing in its own right within Christian sexuality.⌐ The New Testament writers articulate a balanced perspective on marriage and singleness. Both are given significance within the Christian community, so that even among the apostles, Peter was married while Paul remained single. Single people are welcomed as full participants in God's service and may even have a pragmatic advantage in this respect.[39] A Christian vision of singleness is founded on a dual basis: singleness reflects God's character and also constructively engages our sexuality.[40]

IMAGING GOD'S OPENNESS TO THE OTHER

Whereas marriage reflects the intimate bond within the Godhead, singleness expresses God's ever-expanding love for his creation, as expressed in Jesus's prayer that many others would be invited into the divine family.[41]

---

39. 1 Cor. 7:25–40.
40. Grenz, *Sexual Ethics*, 181–99.
41. John 17:20–23.

The broader network of friendships and relationships available to single people expresses this divine drive for relationship within the enlarging household of God.[42] It reflects God's desire to invite and adopt all who respond. As Paul highlights in his advice to his churches, marriage and family tend to create a narrow world of commitments that focuses us on our immediate context. As a father of three small children, I can witness to this all-consuming phenomenon! Marriage and family naturally act as a strong centripetal force, drawing our time and energy into the center of these commitments. In contrast, singleness enables us to form a much broader network of friendships, both within the church and outside it. Although single Christians need to be deeply rooted within the church community, they are also freer to be God's scattered seed in the world. Within this vision, single Christians have a special and distinctive mission to reflect God's nature and his will—to be his invitation to those "others" beyond the walls of the church.

Singleness Positively Engages Sexuality rather than Denying It

The Christian vocation of singleness is one of the most countercultural expressions of life we have within the church. For this reason, we need to clearly articulate what it is and regularly affirm why we believe in it. Christian singleness must be affirmed as a positive vision of life because it constructively engages our sexuality rather than ascetically rejecting it.

Adam's recognition in the garden of his solitude and his desire to move beyond himself was sexually inspired.[43] In the same way, our one-sided sexuality compels us to seek completion beyond ourselves through relationships with others. Our sexuality, then, is at the heart of our quest for meaning and personal identity. Yet this sexually inspired search is not exclusively about sex or marriage. Whereas in the Old Testament the primary community was the immediate family, which was based on a sexual bond, in the New Testament the essential community becomes not the genetic family but the spiritual one—the household of God.[44] Indeed, the church (rather than marriage) is actually the New Testament's highest

42. Grenz, *Sexual Ethics*, 195.
43. Ibid., 32–34.
44. Ibid., 35.

form of community in this age, as well as a foretaste of our future life together—the eschatological wedding feast. As Stanley Grenz suggests, this social process is still founded in our sexuality because "sexuality is the dynamic behind the drive toward bonding in all its forms."[45] We were made for community, and the telos of the church is social reconciliation and intimate relationships.

This vision of singleness embedded within corporate relationships confronts the modern worldview, which has reduced sexuality to sex and thereby marginalized the very essence of human identity. Actually, the greater part of sexuality is "affective" or "social" sexuality.[46] Affective sexuality describes our fundamental need for relational, rather than strictly sexual, intimacy across a broad range of nurturing friendships. The challenge for Christian identity and daily living is to express our sexual energy in line with this divine purpose, thereby resisting our culture's misdirection of sexual desire into desire for sex or consumer goods. We need this range of deep and diverse relationships—with parents, friends, and elders—to properly affirm our personhood and sexuality. These networks of connections are important for single and married people alike.

For the Christian vision of singleness to be lived out in practical terms, we need to facilitate genuine communities of friendship. Leaders need to ask whether they are promoting social spaces and ministry contexts in which people's fundamental need for relational intimacy is being met and where their social/sexual energy can be expressed in line with its divine purpose. In particular, opportunities to serve together in outwardly focused mission can provide a sense of belonging and camaraderie, as well as an opportunity to work together and to get to know one another's gifts, personalities, and character without the explicit pressure of dating.

Summing Up: Vocational Sexuality

The Christian vision of life is that we seek to live in tune with the rich musical score already playing in heaven. Our greatest priority is to understand what life in the kingdom of God looks like and how our lives can reflect that form of community and help to bring it about. As we seek to

45. Ibid., 195.
46. Ibid., 17, 196.

image our Creator, we give expression to the climax of the church's most essential prayer: "Your kingdom come, your will be done, on earth as it is in heaven." We seek, then, in the small decisions, actions, and sacrifices of our everyday lives to live purposefully with the grain of the universe. This is not ultimately an ascetic vision based on self-denial or strict moral rules but rather involves entering into the fullness of God's life. This is where eschatology and ontology come together, giving us both a hope for the future and significance in the present. As Christian vocations, singleness and marriage play different harmonies within the master score, thereby reflecting the reality of heaven—the way things *really* are.

The Vision Is Formational and Missional

There has been a tendency within modern Christianity to think about *discipleship* as an individual pursuit, as though personal maturity were an end in itself. To the contrary, what I want to suggest in this next section is that *moral formation within our sexual lives leads us into healthy relationships*. This dynamic represents a prophetic witness by reimagining the world in light of the kingdom of God. Because of this intimate connection between formation and mission, I have combined these third and fourth elements of vision in what follows.

Sexual Character versus Sexual Personality

As we've already seen, our culture tends to see sexuality in existential terms. Rather than a dynamic part of our *character* to be trained and shaped, sexuality has become part of our *personality* to be freely expressed as a reflection of who we are. Modern society tends to view sexual expression as a virtue in its own right, free from any other concerns or higher priorities. Within this context, Stanley Hauerwas argues for the "necessity of the church to chart an alternative to our culture's dominant assumptions."[47] In particular, he suggests that a Christian perspective regarding the place of singleness and the family is perhaps the most important task facing the church in our society.[48] Indeed, Christian sexual ethics must regain the

47. Hauerwas, *Community of Character*, 189.
48. Hauerwas, *Better Hope*, 51.

ability to transform people and to provide a distinctive witness to the world.[49] Furthermore, Christian sexual ethics should be built upon the church's social vision of restored relationships. In other words, for the church to talk sense about sex and relationships, it must have a clear view of the nature of singleness, marriage, and family and what role they play in the church and in preserving good societies.[50] In this way, the disciplining of sex within the Christian practices of singleness and marriage testifies to the community's greater enterprise—to be the "firstfruits" of the kingdom of God. This sort of community can expose the modern fallacy that sexual relations are private and not shaped by our social contexts.[51] Indeed, according to Paul and the other New Testament writers, everything that we do as Christians, including our sexual practices, affects the whole body of Christ.[52]

Resisting Romanticism: Faithfulness versus Fulfillment

The Christian vision of marriage is rooted in the commandment to love the "other" sacrificially, as Christ loves the church.[53] As Hauerwas says, we love—first and foremost—because we are Christian, not because we are married.[54] Marriage is also one of the most powerful tools for personal formation. It forces us to put aside our own singular ambitions and to establish a pattern of self-emptying and faithfulness that extends to our children, the church, and beyond. Indeed, upholding fidelity and self-sacrifice as the animating principles of Christian love provides a weapon of resistance against the distorted conceptions of the self that we have inherited from our cultural formation—particularly the intuition of the romantic, consumerist self who seeks fulfillment over faithfulness and is driven by novelty and change. Christian marriage and family are centered on an open-ended vow, which witnesses to the belief that we are not autonomous beings but are committed to others. We should, of course, actively pursue emotional and sexual intimacy within our marriages. These are essential gifts and responsibilities to be nurtured and enjoyed, and they compose the

49. Hauerwas and Verhey, "From Conduct to Character," 12.
50. Stanley Hauerwas, "Sex and Politics: Bertrand Russell and 'Human Sexuality,'" *Christian Century* 95 (April 1978): 420–21.
51. Hauerwas, *Community of Character*, 187.
52. Hays, *Moral Vision*, 392.
53. Eph. 5:25–33.
54. Hauerwas, "Sex and Politics," 420.

aesthetic dimension of our wedding vows. Yet at the same time, our main focus cannot remain on the romantic side of love, which quickly becomes secondary to the much bigger task of keeping on with love.

This is where the missional and formational aspects of Christian sexuality come together. For our lives to witness to the kingdom of God, we must first be deeply formed in the "language" of faithfulness so that we become the sort of people who are able to hold fast to the challenges and sacrifices of fidelity and chastity, both within marriage and in singleness. In deciding *how* to think about intimate relationships, then, we need to decide *what* sort of people we want to become. As Hauerwas and Verhey say, we can live our lives "as pleasure seekers or covenant makers."[55] Sexual fulfillment and covenant faithfulness are not mutually exclusive, of course, but were fused together as the literary and literal climax of God's creation described in Genesis 2. The biblical vision of relationships says that sexual and emotional intimacy can come to their fullest expression only within the trust and security of a permanent covenant between two people.[56] And we can create this sort of environment only if we become the sort of people who can make and keep promises. This is not as simple as it sounds.

Witnessing to the Kingdom of God

As a Christian *vocation*, marriage can be sustained only if there remains a clear understanding of the role it plays within the community that created it in the first place—the church. The command for a married couple to love each other must be based on something beyond the self-enhancement or emotional fulfillment of each person. Classical and traditional Christian notions of friendship were based on Aristotle's three characteristics: affection, mutual benefit, and a shared commitment to the common good.[57] Within this scheme, the third motivation was seen as the most important foundation for a relationship. It was only the pursuit of a common purpose that would sustain friendship through the uncertainties and crises of life. For Christians, this greater common purpose lies in the church's mission to "witness" to God's kingdom in the world. This witness is not about

55. Hauerwas and Verhey, "From Conduct to Character," 12.
56. Ibid., 15–16.
57. Ibid., 15.

proving the superiority of our beliefs on modern evidential terms, such as offering scientific proof for the existence of a Creator.[58] The church bears its clearest witness to God's kingdom through practices that embody its beliefs. In this way we make claims about what the world is like and what God is like if our beliefs are true.[59] Putting it another way, Eugene Peterson observes that God reveals himself in the context of the worshiping community. "Knowledge of God," he says, "comes from Scriptures proclaimed and obeyed in the community of the people of God."[60]

We must take seriously the view that marriage and the church share a mutually reinforcing relationship, so that marriage is central to the faith community and its witness in the world, while the church provides the necessary scaffolding to sustain each marriage. We will need to provide the necessary supports for marriages at each stage in their journey. Within our church communities we will not meekly accept the "inevitable" breakdown of marriages without fighting for their survival by investing time and resources in the material, emotional, and logistical needs that must be met for marriages to survive and thrive. We will be attentive to the warning signs, coming alongside those in need with loving care. This is a critical task for the community of faith.

Resisting Realism: Biblical Vision versus Modern Fatalism

Whereas contemporary culture thinks about sex mainly as an experience, Scripture and Christian tradition have always thought about it in terms of virtue or character. Christian sexuality is primarily something we are becoming rather than something we do. In light of our eschatological destiny, this seems obvious, and yet it is completely opposite to the secular notion that has seeped into and is shaping moral intuitions within the church. Because of this slippage, the theme of sexuality as a virtue must become a priority for Christian formation. Virtues are, in essence, the practiced fruits of the Spirit. When Paul sets out his various ad hoc lists of these fruits, we have a tendency to think of them purely as personal, internal, emotional states—love, joy, peace, and so on. But Paul

58. Hauerwas, *With the Grain of the Universe*, 205.
59. Ibid., 214.
60. Eugene H. Peterson, *Five Smooth Stones for Pastoral Work* (Grand Rapids: Eerdmans, 1992), 172–73.

uses them primarily to describe the very practical love expressed through relationships within the community of faith. They are the lived expression of the command to love God and neighbor. So the fruits of the Spirit are also the social dynamics within the community—love *toward*, joy *among*, peace *between*, self-control *with regard to*, and so on. As we become more practiced in these fruits, their roots sink deeper into our lives, becoming permanent states: character traits or virtues.

The gospel's central double-command to love God and neighbor necessarily assumes salvation as a background. "Salvation" in its biblical usage means both "rescue from destruction" and "restoration to health."[61] Indeed, it is only God's healing and empowering grace that makes loving God and others possible. Eugene Peterson notes that at a certain point in Israel's history, the Song of Songs was added as the climactic reading during the Passover meal, the *seder*, which celebrates God's great act of salvation, setting Israel free from Egyptian bondage. The addition, Peterson says, demonstrates pastoral genius because it connects this giant historic salvation event (the exodus) to the everyday contexts of our most intimate relationships (Song of Songs). It communicates that we can live out God's restorative power within our relationships, marriages, families, and beyond.[62]

Similarly, the Jewish festival of Pentecost celebrated and commemorated Yahweh's giving of the law to his people. It is with some resonance, then, that the empowering presence of the Spirit came upon the first followers of *the Way* at Pentecost. The good life that the law had sketched in outline form now burst into animated life in the en-Spirited form of these believers. Applying this confidence to Christian sexuality, Paul makes a startling claim about Christian marriage. He suggests that it can reflect the love between Christ and his church. In our mutual love and responsiveness to each other, we become embodied examples of the gospel.[63]

In terms of discipleship, then, we need to teach the Christian vision of sexuality not just as a future reality but also as an expression of the future made present, albeit imperfectly. Only with this strong vision in place will we resist the brittle idealism and ultimate fatalism of the modern mindset. Christian sexuality must be given its meaning and form by Christian

61. Ibid., 28.
62. Ibid., 30–31.
63. Eph. 5:21–33.

virtues, vocations, and purposes. Its *virtues* include fidelity, chastity, and courage; its core *vocations* are singleness and marriage; its *purposes* include enriching the community of faith and witnessing to the kingdom of God.

Concluding Thoughts: Vision as Our Lodestar

Vision is not a stick that makes people obey the law, nor is it the permissive "I'm okay, you're okay" of postmodern confusion. Indeed, the dry bones of moral rules lack power to move us, while the passivity of "faith without rules" does not provide the connective tissue to give our lives integrity and coherence. By contrast, vision puts flesh on these bones and brings them to life—it animates the form of good life envisaged by the gospel. Compared with legalism, the Christian vision of sexuality is less like putting out "Do Not Walk on the Grass" signs and more like marking out the boundaries of a field so that the game of life can be played well and with conviction. Staying within the boundaries is not our primary focus, but it makes the game possible.

All too often within our times, the biblical vision of sexuality has been portrayed as narrow and naive. Yet when put in proper perspective, it represents an adventure far greater than the restricted confines of our private selves. Indeed, we have been created to launch out beyond ourselves onto the great voyage that awaits us outside the "safe" harbor of the autonomous self.

9

Getting to the Heart of Things

Redeeming Desire and Becoming Our True Selves

Sex clearly holds a privileged place within our culture; if we worship in the temple of consumerism, then sex is its god. Erotic appeal is used to sell everything from razors to race cars; even the G-rated, animated Disney movies we watch with our kids star alluring princesses with adult sex appeal. High-profile politicians and other public figures sacrifice hard-won careers and reputations for the sake of sexual liaisons they seem unable to resist. Their willingness to pay such a high price for a moment of passion points to the power of desire to direct all we do, for better or worse. In an age of rich digital media, lightning-fast networks, and aggressive consumerism, nobody is immune from this daily reality. The book of Proverbs' warning to "guard your heart"[1] becomes an important guide, because our affections and desires so easily take on a gravitational force and direction of their own.

1. Prov. 4:23.

Although the term "desire" is often used to describe our sexual urges, it encompasses a much broader spectrum of human longing. We may pour our lives into high-flying careers or respected ministries out of a desire for affirmation, security, control, or a sense of self-worth. This drive for success gets hooked to our personal identity. Even sexual longing may not present itself in the form of an aesthetic romantic attraction. One self-confessed sex addict explained to his counselor that it wasn't the sex he craved but the sense of shame that came with it. This craving sprang from his upbringing within an emotionally abusive family environment. In adulthood, his sexual desire became a force that he craved and could not control, even though he didn't like it.[2]

Human longing—sexual desire in its broadest sense—is what makes us tick. In this sense, Freud's focus on sexuality as the core of personal identity expresses an essential (albeit distorted) truth. If this is true—if desire forms the foundation of human personhood—then desire is also the decisive core of Christian formation. Contemporary culture has simply confirmed this reality in a counterfeit form, seeking to redirect this desire into the narrow pursuit of sex, consumer products, career success, and so on. The hijacking of human desire and sex doesn't just tap into our *sinful* core, as some believe, but actually taps into our *essential* sexual core. In other words, our culture did not create sexuality. It has just twisted God's good creation.

Within the context of discipleship, if vision is the bedrock on which we stand and the horizon line that we fix our eyes upon, then desire is the beating heart, the energizing core, of the Christian life. Christian leaders need to redefine and redeem people's conception of desire, which has been so heavily sexualized. Although this approach presents pastoral risks, it is our only way to get to the heart of the matter, to transform people in their faith and lives. Indeed, the most common weakness in Christians' sexual lives is not failing to *know* what to do but failing to *want* to do it. Christian living, then, is more a question of our ultimate desires than our knowledge. As James K. A. Smith observes, when we try to address discipleship through ideas and beliefs alone, "it's as if the church is pouring water on our head to put out a fire in our heart."[3] Addressing issues

---

2. "Does Sex Addiction Exist?," *BBC Magazine*, April 30, 2008, http://news.bbc.co.uk/2/hi/uk_news/magazine/7371171.stm.

3. Smith, *Desiring the Kingdom*, 77.

of sexual desire cannot simply mean checking a box in our discipleship program or covering a topic in a chapter of a book, because desire is *the* essential core of the Christian life, the wellspring from which all else flows. Unless Christian leaders attend to their hearts, disciples will be left on thin ice.

Painting a Portrait of the Desiring Self

Given the challenges we face with modern sexual relationships, we can take comfort from knowing that one of the most influential leaders in the church's history had a problem with his libido. If Paul's moral confidence seems a bit out of reach, Augustine of Hippo speaks from the trenches of the sexual battlefield. Before his conversion, Augustine describes a problematic sex life in which he failed to keep his urges under control. He notes that his singular motivation in early life was "to love and be loved" but that his pursuit of love without God led to the corruption of good things and a voracious appetite for false beauty.[4] As a brilliant young scholar, he searched through the classical philosophies and religions of his day to find truth, beauty, and goodness—that is, a vision of a bigger reality that would bring him freedom.

Some way into this spiritual odyssey, and partly through the preaching, friendship, and example of a church leader, Bishop Ambrose of Milan, Augustine came to *see* the truth, beauty, and goodness of God, going through what he describes as an intellectual conversion.[5] Seeing God as the source of all being gave him a vision of true reality. But this vision of goodness only increased Augustine's frustration and led him into a spiritual crisis. Contrary to the wisdom of Socrates and Plato, knowledge and vision of God, by themselves, proved insufficient to bring about real freedom. Seeing the goodness of God did not change Augustine nor help to curb his passions, which remained disordered and uncontrollable. In truth, this spiritual

---

4. Augustine, *Confessions* 1.1.

5. This is described as Augustine's "Platonic" or "intellectual" conversion in book 7. His subsequent "moral" conversion is described in book 8. The critical moment in this journey was when he felt compelled to read Rom. 13:13–14 and, freed from self-deception, was convicted of the depth of his own sinfulness. As he recalls, "all the shadows of doubt were dispelled" at this moment (8.16).

enlightenment shone a painful light on his brokenness and the depth of his addiction. Torn between the truth about God and the truth about himself, Augustine prayed one of the church's most honest and enduring prayers: "Lord give me chastity and self-control, but not just yet!"[6]

Augustine's full conversion happened next. Having seen a vision of God, he encountered the living Christ, who took him on a journey within himself through his "memory," meaning his whole consciousness and self-identity. Leading Augustine through his past, Jesus revealed the lies that had shaped his life and spoke truth in their place, thereby healing his whole identity, including his memory. As Augustine prayed, "Look into my heart, my God, look within. See this, as I remember it, my hope; for you cleanse me of these flawed emotions."[7] This vivid encounter of God's intimate grace brought Augustine genuine and enduring freedom.[8]

This conversion experience and his subsequent theological reflection convinced Augustine that we cannot truly love God and live freely through mere knowledge or self-discipline. On the contrary, we can only respond to God's grace through a fundamental reorientation of our whole selves, which itself is the work of God's grace. We must come to *love* the truth before it can become our guide. And we can only come to love the truth by allowing God to love us first. As Augustine writes: "Nevertheless, to praise you is the desire of man, a little piece of your creation. You stir man to take pleasure in praising you, because you have made us for yourself, and our heart is restless until it rests in you."[9] For Augustine, "longing is the heart's treasury"; or as James K. A. Smith puts it, "To be human is to love, and it is what we love that defines who we are. Our (ultimate) love is constitutive of our identity."[10]

One of the myths we still carry from Enlightenment rationalism is the idea that clarity of belief by itself will bring about personal transformation. In its simplest form, this popular model of discipleship says that if we know a biblical text or principle, then it will naturally take shape in our lives. Yet our culture's renewed emphasis on feeling and emotional resonance helps

---

6. Augustine, *Confessions* 8.7. See also Bradley P. Holt, *Thirsty for God: A Brief History of Christian Spirituality* (Minneapolis: Fortress, 2005), 71.

7. Augustine, *Confessions* 4.11; 5.1; 6.6.

8. Holt, *Thirsty for God*, 72.

9. Augustine, *Confessions* 1.1.

10. Smith, *Desiring the Kingdom*, 51.

reveal what Augustine described many centuries ago. Human identity is deeper and more complex than the simplistic cognitive model of person-hood. We certainly grow through rational understanding, but in order to come to full Christian maturity, our imaginations, feelings, intuitions, and convictions all need to be aligned with our faith.

In one of his many sermons, Augustine describes how God's original *gift* to us is our orientation to "the good"—being created in his image—and God's *promise* is that in the end we will be made like him. As we respond to this gift and promise in our daily lives, Augustine says, "the image is progressive: as false loves are sloughed off, noble desires are consummated, and the true self emerges."[11] According to Augustine, all is gift and all is desire because we can only come to discern, want, and pursue good desires to the extent that God frees us from our false loves.

I think Augustine gets to the heart of the Christian life as we actually experience it. We *do* find ourselves a battleground of desires, and yet it is desire itself that will lead us to victory. This victory is always a divine gift on the path to the fulfillment of God's ultimate promise that one day we will be completely free.[12] C. S. Lewis affirms this conviction that it is not the taming of desire that will set us free but rather the unleashing and enlarging of true desire: "It would seem that Our Lord finds our desires not too strong, but too weak. We are half-hearted creatures, fooling about with drink and sex and ambition when infinite joy is offered us, like an ignorant child who wants to go on making mud pies in a slum because he cannot imagine what is meant by the offer of a holiday at the sea. We are far too easily pleased."[13]

Chasing Chastity: To Will or to Want?

Sadly, the running battle between rationalism and romanticism in the modern world has distorted the biblical vision of who we are and what really motivates us. Rationalism has tended to set the agenda in modern ethics.

11. Augustine, "Sermon on 1 John," quoted in David Burrell, "Can We Be Free without a Creator?," in *God, Truth, and Witness: Engaging Stanley Hauerwas*, ed. L. Gregory Jones, Reinhard Hütter, and C. Rosalee Velloso Ewell (Grand Rapids: Brazos, 2005), 48.

12. Ibid.

13. Lewis, *Weight of Glory*, 26.

In turn, this has affected the way we disciple people within the church. Our cognitive model focuses on what we should *do* by setting out clear moral rules, rather than thinking about how we might *become* the sort of people who can actually live by these convictions. The flaw in this cognitive approach is its assumption that everyone is morally mature and has the power to do whatever he or she chooses to do. But the heart of the human crisis and the challenge of Christian discipleship is not a lack of knowledge but a problem within the human heart. We are not, it turns out, as free as we think.

"Chastity" is a deeply misunderstood concept today. We tend to associate it solely with sexual celibacy, but chastity is a virtue that relates equally to singleness and marriage; it is not directly about sex at all. Chastity is a disposition or orientation of the self that determines everything else we do. James Houston illuminates this by describing chastity as emotional sincerity or integrity, by which we express our feelings honestly.[14] This explains why counseling and therapy provide such a powerful experience: for many it is the first time they have spoken openly about their inner lives.

This view of chastity also explains the destructive power of Christian models of discipleship based on a "morality of knowledge." This idea is rooted in certain strains of classical philosophy that sought to dominate the emotional life by reason and to suppress the passions by an act of the will. As we've seen, this war between will and impulse was placed at the center of modern identity during the Enlightenment, creating a "head/heart" split within the modern self. The cognitive model makes the fatal mistake of believing that reason, rather than redeemed affections, can lead us into the good life.

Yet as Houston says, such a "morality of knowledge" is not Christian at all, because the heart of the gospel is God's *love* working in us and through us to transform our lives.[15] When the mind dominates, it censors and distorts our emotional life, leading us into a life of simulation rather than genuine communion with God and others. As John MacMurray explains: "To tamper with the sincerity of your emotional life is to destroy your inner integrity, to become unreal to yourself and to others, to lose

14. James M. Houston, *The Heart's Desire: Satisfying the Hunger of the Soul* (Vancouver: Regent College Publishing, 2001), 202.
15. Ibid.

the capacity of knowing what you feel. There is nothing more destructive of all that is valuable in human life."[16]

Chastity, meaning true feeling, is our goal as Christians—but it is here where we need God most. It would be a cruel irony if we sought emotional sincerity by ourselves, as an act of the will! Indeed, this is the ill-fated quest for "authenticity," as we explored earlier, that promises freedom and personal integrity but leads deeper into the disordered desires and deception of the false self. By contrast, chastity is the humble acknowledgment that we cannot love anyone or anything authentically without the love of God.

The secret of all genuine human desire is that God, not humans, is the source of love. It is he who loves in and through us. Leaders should ask themselves, then, whether they exemplify and encourage chastity as emotional integrity and honesty within their church communities.

Reforming Human Desire

How do we respond to this challenge? One of the spiritual giants of the church, the medieval Cistercian reformer Bernard of Clairvaux, offers an insight. Bernard is a helpful conversation partner for Christian leaders today because he was also trying to form disciples within a highly sexualized culture. The French courts of the twelfth century exemplified the cultural ideals of chivalry and romantic love, which were akin to our culture's expressive sexuality. Rather than simply rejecting his culture's disordered romantic impulses wholesale, Bernard sought to redirect these sexual passions toward God. He saw sexual desire as a positive and essential part of human identity that reflects both our Creator and the original human condition in Eden. Tragically, the fall led to the disorienting of these good desires. Bernard describes this in terms of humans being made in the image and likeness of God: the divine "image" refers to our being created as desiring creatures (our essential nature), while our divine "likeness" (our virtuous character) is something we lost when these desires became disordered through sin.

Bernard's goal was to encourage the reordering of these powerful desires, which had already been formed in the priorities of romantic culture, directing them instead into a passionate desire for God and each other. Bernard

16. John MacMurray, *Reason and Emotion* (London: Faber & Faber, 1942), 123.

did not focus on God in the abstract but saw the incarnation, Jesus as God in the flesh, as the key to Christian spirituality. He saw Jesus's coming as God's act of divine love, the "divine kiss." Only by immersing ourselves in this intimate gesture could our hearts be changed.[17]

The Journey into Divine Desire

Bernard taught that our desires can only be reordered as we are led by the Spirit through different stages of God's love—essentially the progressive journey from self-consciousness to God-consciousness—as God's love seeps into our deepest being.[18] As we journey deeper into God's love, we become more attuned to loving like God loves, and we better understand who we really are in light of his love. Although our desires start out as self-absorbed and self-directed, by stages they are drawn outward into passionate love for God and others until we come to a place of true self-acceptance where we love ourselves as God loves us.

True self-love, then, is not the focus but a by-product of allowing God's love to pervade and change us. When we experience this divine approval at our deepest core, we become able to love God and neighbor from our hearts. As we breathe in the Spirit's love, we breathe it out into our practical relationships in the church and beyond. This is the picture of relational joy, peace, and intimacy envisioned in Revelation 19 at the eschatological wedding feast, when all self-consciousness and envy will be set aside, and God's love will be all in all.

Bernard's progressive journey of desire shows how Christian discipleship both transforms us and exposes the counterfeit modern quest for "authenticity." This quest is a sham. It seeks to make peace with our false self or, more accurately, the self that is enmeshed in false desires. This form of "self-love" is deceptive because it denies the battle going on beneath this superficial détente. Although this sort of self-acceptance may present itself as self-assurance, what often lies at the heart of the modern "authentic" self is really self-hatred or shame. Because we have to maintain a gap between who we really are and what we present to others, false self-love sabotages

17. Holt, *Thirsty for God*, 86.
18. Bernard of Clairvaux, "On Loving God," in *Selected Works*, 173–206. Bernard thought that the experience of this fourth and final degree of love was rare in this life but would be our constant experience in the New Jerusalem.

our relationships and our ability to love others. We cannot let anyone into the inner sanctuary of our lives because we fear what they will find there. Far from being authentic selves, we become chimeric selves—shape-shifters who present whatever persona we believe will make us acceptable or lovable.

In contrast to this sham authenticity, the Christian journey of desire leads us through repentance—the "putting off" of false desires—into the soaking presence of true Life. Only within the unconditional love of divine acceptance can we come to understand and embrace our true identity.

I want to stress that this is not some esoteric spiritual quest. On the contrary, the journey of genuine desire is *the* critical hinge for Christian formation. True self-acceptance based on our experience of Jesus's love is the only firm foundation from which we can love others freely and sacrificially. Without the freedom wrought by divine acceptance, we tend to curve in on ourselves, becoming slaves to self-consciousness.

Although Bernard's goals were primarily spiritual (his monks became or remained celibate), he shows us something essential about the human condition and the project of discipleship. If we are, at our core, desiring beings, then the Spirit must reach that part of us to restore us to the image and likeness of Christ. And if our sexuality is intricately connected to our spirituality, then our sexual desires must be properly directed to God *before* they can be healthily expressed in our sexual lives.

Paul: Apostle of the Heart Set Free[19]

The apostle Paul is often depicted as the author of doctrine and destroyer of heresies. Yet like Augustine and Bernard after him, Paul was a theologian of the heart. We see this clearly in his encouragement to the Ephesian church to live as "children of light":

> So I tell you this, and insist on it in the Lord, that you must no longer live as the Gentiles do, in the futility of their thinking. They are darkened in their understanding and separated from the life of God because of the ignorance that is in them *due to the hardening of their hearts*. Having lost all sensitivity, they have given themselves over to sensuality so as to indulge in every kind of impurity, and they are full of greed.

19. See F. F. Bruce, *Paul: Apostle of the Heart Set Free* (Carlisle: Paternoster, 1977).

That, however, is not the way of life you learned when you heard about Christ and were taught in him in accordance with the truth that is in Jesus. You were taught, with regard to your former way of life, to put off your old self, *which is being corrupted by its deceitful desires*; to be made new in the attitude of your minds; and to put on the new self, created to be like God in true righteousness and holiness.[20]

Paul makes it clear that the ignorance of the gentiles' understanding and ways of living springs not from their lack of knowledge—in the narrow sense of beliefs, philosophy, or doctrine—but from the hardening of their hearts. The old false self needs to be set aside because it is being corrupted by its deceitful desires. This image of the "hardening of their hearts" is reinforced by the observation that they have "lost all sensitivity," a classical expression describing callused skin that loses any sensation of pain.[21]

Similarly, in Romans 1:21 Paul says, "They became futile in their thinking, and their *senseless minds* were darkened" (NRSV). The term "futile" is often used in the New Testament to describe idolatry, the refusal to acknowledge God as the source of life and goodness. In contrast to Bernard's journey into genuine desire, idolatry progressively conditions and numbs the mind so that eventually it becomes unable to discern or intuit goodness, and so it becomes morally disoriented. These "senseless minds," which think without feeling, lead the gentiles into confusion as their consciences become "seared"—similar to the vivid language in 1 Timothy 4:2.

For Paul, then, the desiring heart is the key to putting on the new true self, which has been created to be like God. The comprehensive transformation of our desires within the true self allows us to see life in a whole new way and to live accordingly. This is no abstract doctrine for Paul. The reorientation of our hearts has radical, real-life consequences. As an example, Paul puts his finger right on a poignant irony about human sexuality, as true now as it was then. It is not the out-of-control fires of passion that have led the gentiles into an insatiable addiction to every form of unhealthy sexual expression. Quite the opposite. It is the *deadening of desire* within their numb hearts and senseless minds that gives them a continual lust for more.

20. Eph. 4:17–24 (emphasis added).
21. F. F. Bruce, *The Epistles to the Colossians, to Philemon, and to the Ephesians*, New International Commentary on the New Testament (Grand Rapids: Eerdmans, 1984), 355.

Paul's words strike a chord in light of the hypersexual nature of modern culture. He explains why sex today has become so important and yet has also been trivialized as a form of entertainment.

As sex has lost its essential meaning as the mysterious bond between husband and wife at the center of God's creation, people have not lost interest in sex but have gone on an addictive quest for more of it and in more extreme forms. It is no surprise that as sex becomes further removed from real relationships, the insatiable quest for personal gratification has intensified. The numbing and detachment of desire empowers the forces of addiction. Describing the futile cycle of drug addiction, neuroscientist Norman Doidge explains that an addict will shoot up even if he knows that the dose is insufficient to give him a high. Such is the power of "tolerance" that the addict will take the drug even when he knows it cannot satisfy his craving.

It is no wonder that the recent growth of online pornography has turned the previously rare term "sexual addiction" into a mainstream phenomenon within counseling, pop culture, and the church. This is the age-old dynamic of idolatry. At the beginning, an idol promises total satisfaction at no personal cost. It presents the illusion that we are in full control. Unable to fulfill us, the idol draws us further in and requires more from us with each encounter. In the end, having promised us everything at no cost, the idol's false promises ultimately take everything. Having offered us control, the idol becomes our master.

We see this in the sad reality of so many marriages and relationships damaged or destroyed by the intrusion and false promises of pornography or extramarital affairs. In the 1990s the feminist Andrea Dworkin justifiably warned that online pornography risked turning men into dangerous beasts. The truth is even more tragic. Pornography, with its unrealistic fantasies of open-ended desire, actually kills genuine desire by forming men who are becoming incapable of loving their wives. Extramarital affairs offer a similar debilitating illusion. A spouse may initially be drawn to a lover who offers unbridled passion without demanding control or representing the mundane responsibilities of domestic life. The lover is always sexually engaged and never has a headache! Yet such lovers eventually demand the central role, no longer happy to sit in the background. The illusion of "free love" always breaks down under the crashing waves of reality. By offering us alluring illusions, sin distorts and captures our desires, bending them in unintended directions. Yet whereas sin disciplines and enslaves desire, the gospel heals and liberates desire from sin.

Indeed, Paul sees putting on the true self with its new desires as the key to living in the light. As children of light, we are to be imitators of God without "even a hint of sexual immorality," because this does not fit the profile for God's family.[22] These are strong words, but Paul does not expect us to constrain our sexual passions through sheer self-control, as the Stoics and others taught in his day. The healing and redirection of what we ultimately long for provides the key to living as children of light. We need to be clear that the Christian journey of desire—that is, true discipleship—will not be a smooth or speedy road. It is to be walked with hope, courage, and perseverance, always tethered to the unshakable grace and love of God.

Finding the Right Balance: Reconnecting Fragmented Selves

As we seek to usher people into the Christian journey of redeemed desire, we are faced with a problem. Our schizophrenic culture has caused a split between the head and heart—between thought and emotion—and so has destroyed the wholeness of human identity.[23] "Being rational" is seen as thinking purely with your head, trying to weed out other ways of discerning, such as intuitive feel or gut instinct. Emotions are seen as confusing, unreliable, frightening, or hard to control. A budding relationship may be subjected to an impossible barrage of overanalysis and faultfinding that pronounces it dead on arrival. The perfection trap, where no relationship will ever do, can become a form of self-protection or idolatrous fantasy. As a result, we never expose ourselves to an actual relationship.

At the other extreme, we tend to be led into relationships simply by a powerful attraction to someone, or we might set sexual boundaries according to what *feels* right. This great divorce between the rational and emotive modes has had a dramatic influence on modern sexuality and relationships. Many young Christian couples seem to be in a furious hurry to rush down the wedding aisle, often cramming their courting into a few short months.

22. Eph. 5:3.
23. Houston, *Heart's Desire*, 112–13.

The priority of these relationships seems to be getting to the altar rather than preparing for the rigors and responsibilities of a common life together.

Affirming the Deep Self: The Thinking Heart

The path to maturity in faith and life involves "learning by heart." Saint Benedict described this as bringing the thoughts of the mind into the heart so that the whole person stands in the presence of God, being transformed through this communion.[24] In a similar way, Paul prays for the Ephesians that "the eyes of your heart may be enlightened in order that you may know the hope to which he has called you."[25] In classical philosophy, "vision"—or seeing—was a way of describing the mind. Paul is asking God to illuminate their thinking hearts. If our moral compass is only oriented by what resonates within us, then our susceptibility to self-deception exposes us to being led astray by these impulses. In contrast, the thinking heart is able to discern between these different emotions and to test them within the boundaries of the Christian life. Whether we are leaders or laypeople, like Paul we need to be midwives of "the heart set free."

Sadly, some influential voices within the modern church have been tempted to define Christian "love" as neutral soil into which we can plant whatever we choose. Giving his support to same-sex marriage, for instance, former pastor Rob Bell draws on Genesis 2 to explain that we need more love, more monogamy, more fidelity, and so on. When asked if he is "for same-sex marriage," he replied, "I am *for* marriage."[26] Yet Genesis 2 is a strange text to use for such an assertion, forming as it does the cornerstone of Christian sexual anthropology. It shows that intimacy within heterosexual marriage is purposeful or teleological (it can bear new life), normative (it expresses God's intended design for sexual relationships), and comprehensive (the complementary natures and bodies of men and women in marriage are a reflection of God).[27]

24. Ibid.
25. Eph. 1:18.
26. Katelyn Beaty, "Same-Sex Marriage and the Single Christian: How Marriage-Happy Churches Are Unwittingly Fueling Same-Sex Coupling—and Leaving Singles Like Me in the Dust," *Christianity Today*, July 1, 2013, http://www.christianitytoday.com/ct/2013/july-web-only/same-sex-marriage-and-single-christian.html.
27. It is important to note that creation epics in the ancient Near East were theological, anthropological, and polemical. That is, rather than being "eyewitness" accounts of the

Bell's theological innovation replants Eden with a new moral ecology. Yet Christian love, as brought to life in Scripture, is a flourishing garden with defined walls and keen discernment regarding what we cultivate and which fruit we taste. Even more so, following our retreat from Eden, there is a presumption that what we *should* cultivate is not what naturally grows within us. Indeed, our deepest desires are likely to lead us astray, and it took nothing less than God-in-the-flesh to reverse this destructive dynamic. It is strange, then, that parts of the church have been so eager in recent years to bless almost any form of sexual expression, provided it is given and received with genuine feeling and continuity. This development is a reflection of the modern authentic self rather than the genuine Christian self. It demonstrates why Christian desire must be trained within the boundaries of Christian truth. Only this bold synthesis will enable the necessary development of the "thinking heart."

Caught in a Love Triangle

James Houston describes a helpful test for the healthy functioning of desire within intimate relationships, both with God and with others. Love, Houston states, is a triangle with three necessary and mutually supporting sides: passion, intimacy, and commitment.[28] Passion *motivates* love; it is the physiological attraction that compels us toward an "other." By itself, though, it is a fickle force that can go astray or die down after the initial heat dissipates. Intimacy *deepens* love, as physical and emotional closeness come with increasing trust, honesty, and warmth. Commitment *protects* love by providing a safe context in which it can thrive. It acts like a wall that prevents the animals of doubt, defensiveness, or competing lovers from

---

process of creation, they were designed primarily to express a vision of the nature of God and his creation. This vision was expressed over against rival creation epics. In this sense, Genesis says important and enduring things about who we are and the nature of God's intended design, thereby providing the cornerstone for Christian anthropology. This explains why Jesus and the New Testament writers draw so heavily on Genesis 2 as a framing paradigm for Christian sexuality. Paul's teaching in Romans 1 clarifies in big-picture terms that when we trade the truth about God for a lie, our culture becomes morally and sexually confused. It is ironic that some interpreters have chosen to quarantine Paul's views to his particular cultural context at just the time that his teaching is most relevant to ours.

28. Houston, *Heart's Desire*, 215. These characteristics closely resemble the three aspects of romantic love identified by Helen Fisher. See Fisher, "Why We Love, Why We Cheat."

destroying the tender fruit growing in the garden. It provides a secure place where vulnerability, trust, and exclusivity can blossom.

If, however, one or more of these sides of the triangle is consistently absent from or overactive within our romantic attachments or our relationship with God, it may point to a scarring or lack of proper attachment that we carry from our childhood. Until we allow God to get to the heart of the issue and heal our foundational desires, our intimate relationships will be lopsided, consistently marked by these dysfunctional patterns.

At the age of thirty, after a string of relational crises, Ben realized that his romantic relationships always fell into one of two categories. Either he was motivated by control and felt compelled to rescue someone in need (who then became overly dependent on him), or else he found himself entering into an emotionally detached relationship. Unnerved by this consistent pattern, he began to meet with a Christian counselor.

At a certain point, the counselor asked him to describe his mother. For as long as Ben could remember, she had suffered from depression. Unable to cope with the chaotic demands of young children, she had put Ben and his older brother into full-time day care from six weeks old, even though she was not working at the time. When they were at home, the children had to stay in their bedrooms for long periods of time because she was unable to cope with their noisy presence. They learned early on that they needed to tune in to their mother's needs rather than the other way around.

Ben realized that this lack of emotional warmth and care during his early childhood had established the pattern for his adult relationships, drawing him into consistently unhealthy dynamics. He found himself either rescuing emotionally dependent women or else becoming emotionally detached, two ways of being that were wired into his early consciousness. When his counselor gave Ben some insightful tools, he was able to identify and avoid those sorts of attachments for the first time in his life.

However, Ben soon found himself faced with the opposite problem. Because he was suspicious of the emotional intuitions that had led him astray for so long, he found that he could only think himself into relationships. Trying to navigate romantic attachments based purely on whether a relationship "makes sense" is also an unreliable guide. We can only exercise genuine discernment in our sexual and relational lives when we have both feeling/intuition and thinking/reflection working together in a dynamic balance. It is only the "thinking heart" that can lead us into healthy relationships. It is not enough just to engage both of these parts to make good decisions in our relationships. As Ben's experience shows, each part needs to be healed and restored. We cannot think ourselves into a sort of redeemed intuition. This is the work of the Spirit, with a little help from our friends.

Joy Never Ceasing

Joy is a concept that is woven throughout Scripture from beginning to end. The prophet Nehemiah proclaims, "The joy of the LORD is your strength!"[29] The psalmist witnesses that "when anxiety was great within me, your consolation brought me joy."[30] Sadly, joy has become a biblical cliché that seems to have no real meaning or significance within our culture. Yet, crucially, joy is the foundation for Christian desire and relationships.

[handwritten margin note: Our culture doesn't hate on joy — again w/ his mandate against "modern culture"]

Neurobiologists have shown that while most brain development stops sometime in childhood, the brain's "joy center"—located and observable in the right orbital prefrontal cortex—is the only part of the brain that never loses its capacity to grow.[31] Although we are born as bundles of potential, our interactions in early childhood lay the path for our future relationships, shaping our capacity as desiring beings for good or ill. As a parent—particularly a mother—tunes in to her infant, the baby mirrors the parent's responses. In this way, the brain begins the complex process of being wired for the back-and-forth communication of human relationships. These positive early interactions create a "joy reservoir" or "joy strength" that acts as the command-and-control center of the entire emotional system. As Dr. James Friesen and his colleagues explain:

> When the joy center has been sufficiently developed, it regulates emotions, pain control and immunity centers; it guides us to act like ourselves; it releases neurotransmitters like dopamine and serotonin; and it is the only part of

29. Neh. 8:10.
30. Ps. 94:19.
31. James G. Friesen et al., *The Life Model: Living from the Heart Jesus Gave You; The Essentials of Christian Living* (Pasadena, CA: Shepherd's House, 1999), 16.

the brain that overrides the main drive centers—food and sexual impulses, terror and rage.[32]

They suggest that without sufficient "joy strength" we spend the rest of our lives trying to fill the deficit. Sadly, researchers estimate that around 35 percent of children fail to make secure attachments, creating damaging and sometimes devastating consequences for their future relational lives.[33] Yet the glory of God's design is that he has wired our brains for relational connection, and he has wired them for healing.

When Amelie was first married, she thought that her struggles in life had come to an end. Family life had been difficult growing up as she struggled to connect with her emotionally distant father while needing to care for her emotionally dependent mother. But now she was turning over a new page, having married a great guy from a stable, loving family. It didn't take long, though, for the past to catch up with her. In her first year of marriage, a colleague started paying her a lot of attention. He was an older man, old enough to be her father. Rather than being put off by his advances, Amelie was alarmed to find that they triggered an inner craving she found difficult to resist. The more attention he gave her, the more she wanted. She knew that this developing relationship was inappropriate, but the attention was like a drug she couldn't resist. Fearing that the unhealthy emotional attachment might lead to a sexual relationship, she decided to tell her husband. Reflecting on that experience, she says:

> Telling my husband was terrifying because I didn't know if he would understand how out of control I felt. How could I be so convicted that the relationship was wrong, and yet have such an intense craving for it? But telling him was the best thing I did. It broke through the shame I was feeling and allowed me to seek help. I thought it was going to break us apart but in the end it made our marriage stronger.

Amelie's husband was able to see that this older man was tapping into her unmet needs for a loving and attentive father. Rather than allowing

32. Ibid., 12.

33. Marinus van IJzendoorn, "Adult Attachment Representations, Parental Responsiveness, and Infant Attachment: A Meta-Analysis on the Predictive Validity of the Adult Attachment Interview," *Psychology Bulletin* 117, no. 3 (1995): 387–403.

this experience to destroy their relationship, this insight allowed them to address the issue and become closer.

Amelie's story highlights the extent to which our deepest desires, those foundational longings that we don't choose for ourselves, are shaped in our early lives. The ability to experience healthy desire and to move beyond ourselves requires the formation of a resilient self-identity. Indeed, we cannot love others, much less God, when there is no self to do the loving. Healthy relationships require interdependence. This involves two independent people becoming bonded together through the mutual giving and receiving of time, affection, resources, kindness, and trust.

We cannot move successfully toward the independence necessary for entering a healthy, intimate relationship until we have properly experienced dependence during our earliest formation. At the heart of compulsive modes of behavior—sexual addiction, masturbation, eating disorders, overspending, alcoholism, and workaholism—lies a deep desire to fill the vacuum caused by a lack of healthy dependence and attachment as a child. Until the need to be cared for while we are totally dependent is met, we will continually seek to have those needs met elsewhere. Sadly, the unattached self tends to enter into relationships that are marked by fear, control, and self-protection. This foundational need to be cared for is an urge that seeks satisfaction, for better or worse. It's a quest that pastors and leaders need to attend to if they are to lead people into the fullness of the gospel.

Building Communities of Joy

The need to be cared for creates an important formational imperative for parents and families: to invest in building a child's identity at the beginning of his or her life. Yet the joy center's capacity to keep developing throughout life also presents a strategic opportunity for the church. If "joy strength" is developed through the constructive back-and-forth of warm and supportive relationships, then building communities of joy and friendship is a critical pastoral task for Christian leaders. Peer-group ministries, for instance, are places where faith and identity can be placed on a firm foundation.

Jesus's words in John 15:9–11 affirm the importance of this pastoral priority: "As the Father has loved me, so have I loved you. Now remain in

182

my love. If you keep my commands, you will remain in my love, just as I have kept my Father's commands and remain in his love. I have told you this so that my joy may be in you and that your joy may be complete." This may sound like strangely legalistic language, but in the Gospels of Matthew and Mark, Jesus sums up the Mosaic law as love of God and love of neighbor. We will find divine joy, then, in relationship. Belonging within a community of friendship is an important foundation for the formation of Christian identity. Only when we *belong* can we experience relational joy and the healing it brings. This is also the path to maturity, as we develop a secure identity that is able to progressively focus outward toward others, away from the suffocating focus on self.

Traveling without a Map

Our essential nature as desiring beings has important implications for our approach to discipleship in the area of sexuality and relationships. Because distorted desires can lead to the most destructive human tendencies, we need to redeem these desires and restore them to their God-given purposes. Our affections, for instance, draw us into relationship with others and should play an important role in discerning which romantic relationships to pursue. Although insufficient by itself, romantic attraction plays a more sophisticated role in relational discernment than we often acknowledge.

Like conversion to faith, passionate attraction to someone else provides an important genesis for our story together. When we hit the inevitable storms and deserts of life, remembering our "first love" reorients us with a foundational memory of how we got here and why we should keep going. The Song of Songs has traditionally been read by Israel and the church to have a double meaning, expressing and celebrating both the intimacy of human lovers and God's desire for and commitment to his people. Our relationships should also have a double orientation, characterized both by *eros* (desirous longing) and by *agape* (self-giving sacrificial love for the other).

Before meeting my wife, Esther, I struggled to imagine ever meeting someone whom I would be willing to commit to for the rest of my life. In hindsight, I had some issues centered around being too independent, but at that time, every woman I knew seemed to have more "cons" than "pros." Subconsciously, I had a long list of prerequisites, and no one could check all the boxes. Yet when I met Esther, she didn't so much check my boxes as dissolve my list. Although much about her character, personality, and gifts remained hidden for years, I instantly fell for her. Perhaps my emotional intuitions perceived the deeper levels of who she was and why I was attracted to her before the rest of me could catch up.

Of course, this attraction did not make our relationship simple. Nor is there any normative formula for how a relationship should unfold. Part of the deep mystery of romantic love is that it has an infinite array of permutations—each couple's story will be different. Yet with Esther, I did experience something of the mystery of attraction as a sophisticated intuitive guide. This force was strong enough to break through the thick wall I had constructed between me and any "other." On reflection, my intuitive reasoning, or thinking heart, was doing its job, and it played an important role in breaking through the wall of self-protection I had built through rational thinking (my checklist). Romantic love has enough explosive power to blow a hole in the barriers we erect around ourselves. Attraction can sum up a whole range of intuitive assessments that we are unable to articulate or rationalize at the time. Although the first years of our marriage were rocky, to say the least, the foundational memory of falling in love provided an important basis on which we sustained our commitment to work things out in those complex early years.

The Heart's Physician: Engaging the Spirit in Christian Formation

An important task within Christian formation is affirming and pursuing the Spirit's role in reconfiguring our loves. It is only through this spiritual-moral healing that we can live as new creations.[34] Gordon Fee describes how Paul views the Spirit's work of transformation in the believer. For the apostle, the experienced presence of the Spirit is the key to personal spirituality, leading the believer into the practical ethical life as expressed in the community of faith.[35] According to Fee, Paul's basic

34. 2 Cor. 5:17.
35. Fee, *God's Empowering Presence*, 871.

ethical imperative—from which all others flowed—is to "walk in/by the Spirit," mainly evidenced in love as the first fruit of the Spirit.[36] Indeed, the other fruits or behaviors Paul describes are examples of love, or *koinonia*, within the faith community.

For Paul, the Spirit should be a dynamically experienced reality for both the individual and the community.[37] The Spirit's progressive transformation of each person is not an ideal but an actualized reality, so that Paul believes Christians will not experience the ongoing dominance of the "flesh," or human sinfulness, in their struggle.[38]

In the Greek and Hellenistic Jewish thinking of Paul's day, the key concern was to control the "passions," or lustful desires, through self-discipline.[39] The Stoics, for instance, sought to master themselves by rejecting all forms of passion or desire. This one-sided approach represents a model of formation by amputation, and it has been a persistent temptation within Christian discipleship. Such legalistic self-discipline offers a measure of control and security but ultimately is ineffective; it actually does violence to our fundamental identity and Godlikeness. Although controlling the passions is also important for Paul, he locates the solution in the Spirit's power to restore our desires rather than extinguish them. Paul believes that "walking in the Spirit" is the key to healing our desires, which then allows us to reorient our lives and choices within the framework of the gospel. Fee challenges Christian leaders to resist the temptation to reshape Paul in our own image on the basis of a lesser experience or expectation of the Spirit's presence and work in our lives and communities.

Finally, Paul sets out the various ad hoc lists of the fruits of the Spirit *not* as systematic moral rules but as examples of "Spirit-living."[40] In Paul's approach, the Spirit is both the existential and the ethical heart of the Christian life. When we relegate the Spirit to a background figure in our lives and churches, we weaken our ability to form disciples in Christ, for it is only the Spirit who can do that. Indeed, attempting to shape Christian sexual practices only through a regime of rules and disciplines tempts us

36. Ibid., 879. See Gal. 5:22.
37. Fee, *God's Empowering Presence*, 880.
38. Ibid.
39. Thompson, *Pastoral Ministry according to Paul*, 75.
40. Fee, *God's Empowering Presence*, 882.

to make the same mistake as those in Galatia, who sought to return to the self-disciplined life "according to the flesh." This is the sort of self-help religion that Paul warns against, for it leads to the very behavior it seeks to avoid.[41] For the apostle, the Spirit is the beating heart of Christ's body, the church—the only power that can restore, heal, and remake each limb for its distinctive role within the body.

Concluding Thoughts: Shooting for the Heart

The goal of Christian formation is to form disciples within the rhythms of divine desire. This is essential to both discipleship and healthy relationships because we cannot love others well until we have experienced God's love within the deepest parts of ourselves. This is what Bernard was driving at with his progressive journey of Christian desire. First, we must be taught to love by experiencing God's love. As we travel this journey into divine desire, we are freed to become genuine lovers, like Jesus, rather than just consumers of love.

Within this model there is an important caution. Augustine reminds us that the healing of our affections is progressive, requiring disciplined training within the Christian life. We need to acknowledge and resist the way that modern romanticism has deeply shaped our commitment to both personal independence and sexual gratification as our culture's highest priorities. If we fail to resist these cultural impulses, we are likely to accommodate them into our vision of life and our approach to discipleship. Although we should affirm the wonder and mystery of sexual intimacy and romantic attraction as God's good creations, we need to set these aesthetic enjoyments within the context of the Christian virtues of fidelity, self-sacrifice, and patience in suffering.

Bringing this together, our pastoral approach should be double-edged, seeking to challenge our culture's worship of sexual desire and personal fulfillment while offering a different vision of human flourishing. Christian formation involves both *resistance* and *redirection*. But it is the redirection of our desires that enables our resistance of cultural idolatries. Failure to attend to the dynamics of our desires leads to inevitable self-deception

41. Gal. 5:16–24.

186

regarding the "freedom" of our actions. Especially within our sexual lives, our hearts must be truly captivated by the goodness of the Christian vision of life, so that our whole self is drawn toward it, or our commitment to live in tune with it will be brittle.

Focusing on the human heart as the key to Christian discipleship might sound like an ambiguous or weak affair, somehow diluting the hard realities of the gospel. But this task is the core of the gospel. As Hans Urs von Balthasar says, "God's covenant is the struggle between His love and sinful man."[42] The heart is where we encounter the most resistance to Christ's lordship over our lives. It is the heart more than the mind that clings to idols and false loves. The mind can be reeducated with good teaching and consistent preaching, but the heart stubbornly and secretly chooses its own way. Only when we get to this essential part of the self, its command-and-control center, can Christian formation push down deep roots.

We need to be clear that the Christian journey of desire will not be a smooth or easily traveled road. It is one to be walked with hope, courage, and perseverance, always tethered to the unshakeable grace of God. C. S. Lewis explains that the Christian journey of desire is unmistakably one of hard sacrifice of our cherished fantasies, as well as ultimate satisfaction in the freedom of becoming our true selves. As he puts it, "We are not necessarily doubting that God will do the best for us; we are wondering how painful the best will turn out to be."[43] Sacrifice and satisfaction, then, are the two feet that carry us on the long walk to freedom.

42. Hans Urs von Balthasar, *Love Alone: The Way of Revelation* (London: Sheed & Ward, 1968), 58.

43. C. S. Lewis, *Letters of C. S. Lewis*, ed. W. H. Lewis (Fort Washington, PA: Mariner Books, 2003), 477.

10

Living the Gospel Story

Narrative Discipleship within the Narrative Community

Dino's Story

Dino was born into a loving family and grew up within the Greek Orthodox Church community. As is so often the story, he got caught up in the wrong circles in his early teens and began to abuse drugs and alcohol. His increasingly volatile behavior eventually exasperated his parents, and he left home as a sixteen-year-old. One night, while living with some gang members who had befriended him, he was given heroin and was raped by an older man. In an attempt to dull the shame and confusion that engulfed him, he threw himself headlong into a life of drugs and alcohol, overdosing twice by the time he was eighteen and attempting suicide several times. Heroin addiction opened the door to a host of destructive experiences and other addictions. He found himself enmeshed in a web of sex, alcohol, and increasingly reckless drug use, and he fell into a pattern of highly dependent romantic relationships.

In a desperate attempt to break him out of this cycle, Dino's parents sent him to live with extended family in London—but things didn't work out as planned. While his flight from New Zealand stopped to refuel in Singapore, Dino was robbed and forced to delay his onward flight. Although he eventually made it to London, he never made the intended connection with family. Lost in a big city of endless possibilities, Dino became involved with cocaine dealers, gangsters, and a group of prostitutes who became his surrogate mothers, taking him under their wing and looking after him. He was close to being killed on many occasions, and by the time he turned forty-three he was exhausted from running. Reflecting on that time now, Dino says that his addiction began with the shame and trauma of being raped. Bad decisions and destructive ways of living snowballed, and very quickly Dino merged with the chaos he had entered. This chaos became his sense of identity. Once he was lost in it, life became a matter of mere survival.

Stepping into a New Story

A chance encounter would change everything. A guy Dino had only just met bought him lunch and asked if he could pray with him. At one point during the meal, this new friend—who knew nothing about Dino's background—said to him, "I sense God is saying that you've been running from pain and shame all your life and that you can't go on, you've had enough. God wants you to know that you don't have to, that you can stop, receive his forgiveness, and everything will be okay."

The conversation proved to be a decisive fork in the road of Dino's journey. He attended a church service a little later, where he responded to an invitation to stand up and ask God to meet with him. Dino received a glimpse of God's presence and the promise of a better way, which he describes as a sudden, deep "knowing" that he was experiencing something profoundly different from anything he had ever known before—a sense of safety and love that came from outside himself but that he experienced within.

This encounter gave Dino the resolve to end the chaotic pattern of his life. He had glimpsed another way, and as he experienced God's forgiveness, waves of relief and joy washed over him for the first time. He knew he was not yet free, but the new path opening up could lead him to freedom.

In narrative terms, he stood at the beginning of a new story. Although the specific contours were unknown, he knew that the destination was good, so he took his first steps into trusting God.

Dino describes being taken apart piece by piece: every bit of character, every addiction, every destructive relationship was brought to the surface to be tested, to see whether he'd been released and healed. The initial stages of this journey were dramatic and unsettling. As he immersed himself in prayer, Scripture, and worship, everything from his old life came rushing to the foreground. It was like someone turning over and returfing a lawn. Within this frightening mess, only the glimpse of hope he'd experienced in that first encounter with God gave him courage to keep moving.

Walking in the Company of Others

After about six weeks at church, Dino came across a Scripture passage that encouraged him to "seek good counsel." He approached the senior pastors, who prayed with him and connected him with people who came alongside him for regular coffee, conversation, and prayer. This regular contact and relational support encouraged Dino to stay connected to church and keep going, despite the struggle between his old life and the new hope that was breaking in. The most important formative process happened as Ian, a trained spiritual mentor within the church, purposefully discipled Dino, meeting with him almost every day for nearly four years. Within this relationship Dino honed the rhythms, practices, and disciplines of the Christian life. Like the early converts living in the presence of the apostle Paul, Dino was able to mimic the pattern of Ian's life, character, and way of thinking. He regularly confessed his sins and received God's forgiveness. He learned how to pray, how to read Scripture, and how to form patterns and habits that progressively displaced his old way of life. When things fell apart—as they often did—Ian was there for him to cling to, and eventually Ian taught Dino how to mentor others himself.

I have never seen anyone take hold of a vocation with such passion as Dino, and it is no wonder, given the influence of his mentor in the formation of his own faith and character. During those years, Ian acted as a pilot and pathfinder, teaching Dino through his own example and wisdom how to walk consistently within the Christian journey.

Redeemed Relationships: Meeting Lucy

One of the most destructive and addictive patterns in Dino's life had been his series of romantic relationships, in which he found himself caught in a pattern of overly dependent attachments. This proved a difficult dynamic to break, even after he came to faith. Over time and through prayer, counseling, mentoring, reading Scripture, and experiencing new patterns of friendship within the church, Dino was able to step into healthy relationships. Soon after coming to faith, he became friends with a woman at the church named Lucy. After several years of being "just good friends," the nature of the relationship changed for both of them, and it blossomed into a romantic connection. They were married a few years later. This wedding, which took place among the Christian community where Dino first encountered God, was a clear demonstration of the gospel's healing power. It was like standing at a lookout point midway up a long mountain trek: having traveled up a sustained and steep incline through dense bush, the climber suddenly gets a vista of where he's come from and the significant height he's reached. Although not the top, to be sure, it is a striking perspective on the narrative progress of the Christian life all the same.

Marriage as a New Stage of Healing

It is a myth, of course, that marriage is the end of the road. For Dino it was a vivid demonstration of God's work in his life, but it was also a new stage in the journey of healing. One night while lying next to Lucy in bed, he suddenly rolled up into the fetal position as a wave of fear washed over him. For the first time in his life he heard in his mind the words of the man who had abused him as a teenager, words that had been subconsciously locked away for a lifetime. Although he had lived out most of his adult life caught in the shame of these words, until now he had protected himself from hearing them. Finally, in the safety of a loving relationship, the diabolical voice from Dino's past began to haunt him, seeking to unravel God's restoration and suck him back into the pain of this defining experience.

Not surprisingly, he crumpled. Had the journey so far been in vain? Perhaps, he wondered, it wasn't possible to escape the deep past—those events that had formatively shaped how he thought about himself. But instead of burying this trauma, he immediately sought out several trusted friends. They prayed for healing and freedom from this experience. He felt himself decisively set free from it, and it has not troubled him since.

Dino had landed in London as a troubled eighteen-year-old with bleak prospects. Most of his friends were either dead or in prison, and he seemed destined to join them. Nearly thirty years later he flew back to his birthplace in New Zealand, a place he had vowed never to return, as an Anglican priest and loving husband. He soon became a proud father.

Dino's story is a dramatic one and certainly not the norm in our experience of discipleship, and yet it shows what narrative discipleship looks like in the flesh. This stunning transformation from addict and relationship-junkie to priest, husband, and father did not come about through any single miraculous event—he was not spiritually teleported—but through a long, uneven journey toward maturity within the community of faith.

Dino's story gives us hope as shepherds and a road map for the way ahead. It is our privilege and challenge as skilled and attentive artisans to weave each of these unique stories into the bigger tapestry of the master story—the gospel of salvation and restoration that is ours in Christ Jesus.

Narrative Formation: The Battle between Secular and Sanctified Scripts

Stories have a unique power to shape us. They enliven our imaginations, open up new possibilities, and lodge deep in our memories. I have almost no recollection of particular lessons at school when I was young, and yet I vividly remember the stories that captured my imagination as a child: *Pilgrim's Progress* read at family meal times, the Chronicles of Narnia (which birthed my love of Turkish Delight), and Rudyard Kipling's *Jungle Book*. I can still picture my dad stomping around our living room acting out the different animal characters. We retain stories so well because they are the medium that resonates most closely with our fundamental nature. Our lives are themselves unfolding stories, and narratives map onto our own experiences in a complex and comprehensive way, shaping our self-understanding.

Modern Sexual Scripts

Much of the confusion people experience in their relational lives stems from the different cultural scripts that are in play today, vying for our allegiance and seeking to direct our lives. Jane Brown, a professor of journalism, observes that the media is one of the most formative "storytellers" in the area of sexuality. The media, she says, keeps sex firmly on our radar, reinforces a narrow and consistent set of sexual norms, and rarely exposes us to responsible sexual actors. It shapes our decision making by restricting our exposure to alternative scripts.[1] As Regnerus and Uecker explain, "Popular sexual scripts have combined to generate a set of structured pathways that characterize the way forward for most emerging adults."[2] So much for the "freedom" of the modern world! Indeed, it is ironic that these restrictive scripts howl against the "stifling" boundaries offered by religious traditions.

So what are these modern sexual scripts?

In their extensive research among young adults, Regnerus and Uecker discovered a body of unquestioned convictions about modern sexuality, which the researchers found were actually *not true* most of the time. These common myths include the following:[3]

- Long-term exclusivity in relationships is not possible.
- The introduction of sex is necessary to sustain a fledgling or struggling relationship.
- Men are slaves to their lower impulses and so can't be expected to control themselves.
- It doesn't matter what other people do sexually; you're free to make your own decisions.
- Pornography won't affect your relationships.
- Everyone else is having more sex than you are.

1. Jane D. Brown, "Mass Media Influences on Sexuality," *Journal of Sex Research* 39 (2002): 42–45.

2. Regnerus and Uecker, *Premarital Sex*, 241.

3. Ibid., 236–50.

- Sex is fun and doesn't need to mean anything more.
- Marriage can always wait.
- Moving in together is a definite and positive step toward marriage.

How do we respond to these powerful themes shaping modern sexuality?

Reimagining the World as It Should Be: Gospel as Counternarrative

The gospel does not offer Christians an escape from the world. It changes the status of the world itself. The gospel reimagines the world *as it should be* rather than merely describing the world as we find it with the inevitable dysfunction of human relationships. This is the critical difference between Christian and secular anthropology. Jesus entered history and fused himself to human destiny in order to fundamentally change the possibilities of human life, not just to empathize with our struggles. And so the Christian life is to be lived within the eschatological horizon of the kingdom of God, and all moral reflection on human experience takes place within this progressive destiny.[4]

One of the most powerful characteristics of narrative is that it enlarges our moral imaginations by presenting possibilities that are bigger than our own limited horizons. Although the Christian life is coherent only when it is framed by the metaphor of "journey," Stanley Hauerwas observes that much teaching on Christian formation has been trapped within the claustrophobic metaphor of "dialogue." Within this framework, the Christian is forever caught between God's accusation through the law and his gracious invitation through the gospel. In other words, we always stand before God as hopeless sinners trapped in a closed moral loop, unable to progress to maturity. We can only ever be "sinners saved" rather than disciples on *the Way*. The narrative metaphor of "journey" draws us out of ourselves into the bigger story of the gospel, a reality that is beyond our natural comprehension or power. Indeed, the New Testament writers exhort believers to move from infancy to maturity in their faith and lives, no longer tossed about by every tantalizing new teaching or hormonal impulse.[5]

---

4. Michael Cartwright, "Stanley Hauerwas's Essays in Theological Ethics: A Reader's Guide," in *Hauerwas Reader*, 623–72.
5. See 1 Cor. 2:6; 14:20; Gal. 4:19; Eph. 4:11–15; Col. 1:28; Heb. 5:11–14; and 2 Pet. 1:4.

Eugene Peterson once observed that "truth is like pure alcohol. It is deadly. The story puts the language around the truth that allows us to understand it and assimilate it."[6] Put simply, the gospel story encourages us to climb toward our goal one step at a time, whereas the law judges us by an unyielding standard we cannot live up to. The gospel energizes the journey of discipleship, but the law enervates it. This truth, if we can grasp it, frees us from the fatalistic cycle of "back and forth." One of our culture's most powerful scripts or story lines is that our sexual identity is fixed—that it has a definite biological direction that we cannot ultimately resist. Social Darwinism, for instance, says that we are programmed with certain instincts that we cannot transcend. Yet within this closed context, the eschatological story of Christianity generates radical new possibilities for change, firing and empowering the Christian moral imagination. It breaks us free from modern fatalism by giving us a goal to aim for and a path to walk on toward that destination.

Reading to the End of the Story

Narrative discipleship also illuminates one of the most common misunderstandings within the church's moral discourse. The ubiquitous expression "Jesus meets and loves people wherever they're at" has morphed into a blanket assertion that justifies almost any behavior or form of life, especially in the area of sexuality. Although this is an accurate description of God's mission in the world—Jesus *does* meet everyone where they're at—this notion has fundamentally distorted the church's approach to discipleship. It nudges believers into the trap of getting stuck at a critical point in the gospel story.

The incarnation—that is, Jesus's life as God in the flesh—is an act of identification without comparison. Jesus describes himself as the physician who has come for the humble and sick, not the self-important elites. Yet this identification has a greater purpose, which is revealed toward the end of the story—restoration through the death and resurrection of Christ. This work of atonement is what New Testament scholar Scot McKnight calls "identification for incorporation."[7] Jesus identifies with us so that

6. Eugene Peterson, "Biblical Spirituality" (Summer School Lecture Series, Oxford University, 2000).

7. Scot McKnight, *A Community Called Atonement*, Living Theology (Nashville: Abingdon, 2007), 107–16.

through his victory we can put off the old self, which is being corrupted by its fallen desires, and be made like Christ.

Mainline Protestant liberalism has traditionally focused on Jesus's exemplary life as a way of universalizing Christianity, but the real significance of the gospel story comes toward the end. Within the modern church we have conflated and confused mission and discipleship because we are failing to read to the end of God's story, and so we remain trapped in the moral fatalism of human narratives.

Articulating the Master Story

In order to give the gospel power in people's lives, Christian leaders need to be clear about what exactly this master story is—the vision of life that is framed around the life, death, and resurrection of Jesus Christ. This story can be crowded out in the congested marketplace of competing secular scripts. For Christians, the temptation to shop in this marketplace can result in a "Christ plus something" faith. The priority of Christian leaders is to help people to focus on the pure master story as it takes shape in every part of life—a journey in which we seek to progressively make Christ's story our own.[8] For the first followers, the kingdom of God could be grasped only through the lens of Jesus's example, as told in the stories about him in the Gospels. Jesus's mission could be understood only as his followers also stepped into these stories.[9] Indeed, the story of the apostles themselves shows how difficult and necessary this personal journey is. They had to follow Jesus to Jerusalem and witness the cross in order to be purged of their fantasies and false ideas about the nature of his kingdom.[10]

This narrative understanding of discipleship finds clear expression in the apostle Paul's approach. Paul experienced the gospel as a personal and progressive story in his life and sought to pass this on to those in his care. New Testament scholar John Barclay explains the pastoral function of Paul's personal narrative in relation to Galatians 1–2.[11] Paul's introduction

8. Hauerwas, *Hauerwas Reader*, 116.
9. Ibid., 118.
10. Ibid., 121.
11. John M. G. Barclay, "Paul's Story: Theology as Testimony," in *Narrative Dynamics in Paul: A Critical Assessment*, ed. Bruce W. Longenecker (Louisville: Westminster John Knox, 2002), 139.

to the letter, Barclay says, is a testimony—or "story"—of the grace of God within Paul's life. For Paul, divine grace cannot be known apart from the lives in which it is actualized; it cannot be boiled down to a freestanding set of ideas or beliefs, like a reduction sauce.[12] As Barclay says, "Paul does not tell his stories and *then* transmit their meaning: that meaning is embodied in the shape of the stories themselves."[13] The important thing for Paul is that his entire identity and life are shaped by what God has done, so that Paul's story only has significance if it conforms to the story of the crucified and resurrected Christ—"the master pattern."[14]

Paul's approach serves several important pastoral purposes. First, it communicates the radical nature of Christ's gospel of transformation, which fundamentally reorients the convert's life. Our lives are divine gifts, not to be seized or achieved by us on our own terms. This may seem obvious, and yet it has become counterintuitive for many Christians within our culture's commitment to radical personal freedom. Second, Paul confirms the importance of "narrative knowledge" within Christian formation. As theologian Ian Scott suggests, "ethical knowledge" is not about understanding a set of moral rules or duties but involves imaginatively and wholeheartedly placing our lives within the "theological narrative," the gospel story. For Paul, this story must engulf and captivate us in order to shape our lives.[15]

Resisting the False Promises of "Authentic" Sexuality

One of the most influential yet latent themes in contemporary Christianity that reflects the culture at large is the subconscious conviction that our lives are the "primary text," while Scripture plays the role of "secondary text," helping us to interpret and make sense of our personal experience. Within this interpretive paradigm, our feelings and experiences become the decisive reality, so that biblical truth must be interpreted in such a way that it harmonizes with our deepest emotions. Most often, Scripture or Jesus's ethics get reduced to the basic principle of "love," so that anything within

12. Ibid., 154.
13. Ibid.
14. Ibid., 155. See Gal. 1:15–16.
15. Ian W. Scott, *Paul's Way of Knowing: Story, Experience, and the Spirit* (Grand Rapids: Baker Academic, 2009), 155–56.

this broad universe becomes, in a sense, "scriptural." We see this most clearly in our sexual lives. Modern culture places sexual expression and orientation right at the heart of personal identity; "authentic" sexuality has become our highest virtue and an irresistible prerogative. Yet ordering our sexual lives along these lines, even when we do consult Scripture as a guide, puts us at high risk of getting lost in the reinforcement loop of self-deception.

Teaching Scripture *as a narrative* decisively upends the distorted priorities of the "authentic" self. When we become followers of Christ, we step into a much bigger story. This gives genuine significance to our personal identities and lives because God calls us friends, but it also displaces us from the center of the story. We become followers of *the Way* rather than the heroes of our own tales. The gospel, rather than our own experience, becomes our primary text. We don't read Scripture; Scripture reads us. It challenges and reinterprets our lives, puncturing our fantasies and leading us in a new direction. Especially in our sexual lives, the gospel calls us to put off the old self and live differently, while acknowledging this to be an uncompromising journey.

The Storied Community

Developing a Shared Narrative: Whatever Happens, We'll Stick Together

We may be tempted to end the discussion here, but in exploring the personal dimension of narrative formation, we have only reached base camp. The decisive ascent is made possible only by the social dimension. Rather than just inviting us into a story, the gospel ushers us into a narrative community.

The single most important thing you can do for your family and church community may be the simplest: develop a strong common story.[16] This idea was conceived when a psychologist who works with children with learning disabilities noticed that the students who knew a lot about their families tended to do better when they faced challenges. Intrigued by this, her husband—who was also a psychologist—set out to test the idea by

16. Bruce Feiler, "The Stories That Bind Us," *New York Times*, March 15, 2013, http://www.nytimes.com/2013/03/17/fashion/the-family-stories-that-bind-us-this-life.html.

asking children a "Do You Know?" test consisting of twenty questions about their family background and history. Examples included: Do you know where your grandparents grew up? Do you know where your parents met? Do you know an illness or a sad event that happened in your family? Do you know the story of your birth?

Cross-testing the results against a range of other psychological tests that the children had taken, the researchers were struck by what they found. The more that children knew about their families' histories, the stronger their self-esteem and sense of identity. The "Do You Know?" scale turned out to be the best single predictor of children's emotional health and happiness. Even more unexpected was that within two months of their findings, the Twin Towers tragically fell in Lower Manhattan on September 11, 2001, and the researchers observed how different families coped with the stress of this shared national trauma. After retesting, they found again that the children who knew more about their families proved to be more resilient and were more able to moderate the effects of stress.

Psychologists have found that every family has a unifying narrative, some of which are healthier than others. The healthiest version is called the "oscillating family narrative," which essentially says, "We've had ups and downs in our family. We've had victories and setbacks, but no matter what happened, we always stuck together and got through it."[17] Children who have the most self-confidence and resilience know that they belong to something bigger than themselves, that they walk on a road that has been traveled by their kind before them. Likewise, organizations—from corporations to charities and sports teams—commonly seek to write a story, create traditions, and articulate a set of core values that describe who they are and where they have come from, all of which provide a coherent way forward.

Performing Traditions and Embracing Seasons

My wife, Esther, worked for several years in London alongside a Jewish woman named Mandy, and they became close friends. What impressed Esther about Mandy over time was the extent to which her life and identity were given shape and immersed within the narrative world of the Jewish faith and community. Every Friday afternoon, Mandy would leave for the

17. Ibid.

beginning of Shabbat, a social event as well as a religious ritual. Whenever her community celebrated a festival, Mandy would explain what event it recalled in Jewish history. "It's your one this week!" she would say to Esther during the Feast of Purim. Esther was struck by the way the story of God's salvation and care was kept alive within the collective memory of the community through their weekly worship and regular festivals. When we attended Mandy's wedding, this same story was woven through the traditional Jewish wedding service. The breaking of the glass and the groom circling the bride seven times symbolized that the old had passed away and that this marriage was a new creation that stood within God's overarching story of creation.

The church as the family of God also needs identity-shaping stories, or traditions, to form a deep moral order that serves us when we need it most. Christian leaders have the great privilege and responsibility of being faithful and imaginative storytellers, articulating the truth that although we will go through ups and downs, we will stick together and keep moving on, trusting that God has secured our tomorrows. The story we tell is the "oscillating narrative" of the gospel: despite threats, risks, mishaps, mistakes, and disappointments, life is ultimately going somewhere. This resists both the *fatalistic* narrative that says "you can't rely on anyone" and "life just never works out," and the *triumphalistic* narrative that says "there's no room for mess or mistakes in the church" and "life or people should be perfect."

This oscillating narrative acknowledges that our lives are a journey through mixed terrain. The gospel does not offer us a utopia on this side of Jesus's coming again. In our relationships, we will experience the exhilaration of scaling mountains and walking in the lush fields of young romance, and we will also walk through long stretches of tedious wilderness and weather bitter storms. This is the normal journey of the disciple. We need to acknowledge and embrace the seasonal nature, the oscillating narrative, of our lives. Whereas the modern world promises a smooth and uninterrupted progression toward our goals—like an idealized company profit chart—the genuine Christian life picks a coherent line through different seasons.

Eugene Peterson describes the odyssey his family would make every summer, driving across America from Montana to Maryland. At a certain point in this mammoth journey, they would travel through the Badlands of

South Dakota.[18] These are dry, desolate wastes, and Peterson compares them to a time in his pastoral ministry when the life of the church appeared to go into hibernation. Although tempted to seek fresh opportunities elsewhere, he felt called to persevere in this dry place, to discern what God was doing among this group of people. It is often in these desolate places that we most need to search for signs of life and to discern how God is at work.

Perhaps one of the most important roles of Christian leaders as shepherds is to help those in their care to orient themselves and navigate through each stage of life, especially in the seemingly lifeless waste of the "badlands." Many Christians experience prolonged singleness as a form of wilderness, while those in Christian marriages are becoming less able to travel through life's inevitable barren stages than were previous generations. The badlands have no positive meaning or place within our culture's romantic narrative. In this romantic paradigm, we are tempted as modern Christians to irrigate the wilderness out of season with an endless conveyor belt of best-selling Christian books promising a "Better You" or "Your Best Life Now."

Yet the waste places in our lives play a legitimate role in our spiritual, moral, and sexual formation. It is in the badlands where our fantasies die, where our vision is clarified, and where we come to rely on God. Although the gospel journey ultimately leads us into healing and joy, irrigating the badlands out of season reflects our culture's "anesthetic prerogative," whereby we seek to avoid or alleviate legitimate forms of waiting or suffering. Narrative discipleship gives significance and meaning to every season of life. It ushers us into maturity. Esther and I were unable to conceive children for six years. In many ways this was our badlands, a time of darkness, searching, pain, tension, and confusion. Yet that journey through infertility was a time when we came to know and rely on God in a way we simply had not needed to do before, and ultimately we received his gracious healing. Narrative discipleship involves the art of spiritual accompaniment in these seeming desert places.

Orienting Travelers within Communities of Friendship

The New Testament writers use the image of God's "family" to describe the church not just as a metaphor but as a structural reality. As Christians,

18. Eugene H. Peterson, *The Pastor: A Memoir* (New York: HarperOne, 2011), 205–8.

our goal is to conform our lives to Jesus's story, but we need a narrative community to help us learn this story. As Michael Gorman puts it, although each person may encounter Christ personally just as Paul did in his conversion/calling on the road to Damascus, the "substance and grammatical expression" of Paul's pastoral vision are irreducibly corporate. This is because our faith cannot find expression in love without others as the object of our love, and we need a context in which the master story of Christ's death and resurrection can be "nurtured, performed and contemplated."[19] For Paul, the church is both the medium for individual transformation and the telos of Christian life. As he makes clear in his key metaphors for the church—the body, temple, and family—limbs, holy stones, and children cannot be separated from the contexts that define them, nourish them, and give them their essential purpose.[20]

Christian formation should be focused on acquiring moral skills, or virtues, as they are practiced and honed in real communities.[21] Sadly, modern evangelicals have tended to underplay the significance of the church community in the area of discipleship. Yet we are social beings who are inescapably shaped by our core communities, a truth that was well understood by earlier evangelicals.

John Wesley, a master of discipleship, discerned that Christian growth can only be sustained when people are deeply rooted in a network of relationships within the church. Like a Russian doll, each disciple stands at the center of different layers of community. Wesley's "class system" provides a helpful paradigm for thinking about formation within the church today.[22]

1. The "society" was the larger worshiping community of the church, which sought to grow the disciple's understanding through prayer, worship, and preaching on Sunday.

19. Michael J. Gorman, *Cruciformity: Paul's Narrative Spirituality of the Cross* (Grand Rapids: Eerdmans, 2001), 350.

20. Fee, *God's Empowering Presence*, 870.

21. Stanley Hauerwas, *Christians among the Virtues: Theological Conversations with Ancient and Modern Ethics* (Notre Dame, IN: University of Notre Dame Press, 1997), 149–50.

22. See Kevin M. Watson, *Pursuing Social Holiness: The Band Meeting in Wesley's Thought and Popular Methodist Practice* (New York: Oxford University Press, 2014); and Watson, *The Class Meeting: Reclaiming a Forgotten (and Essential) Small Group Experience* (Wilmore, KY: Seedbed, 2014).

2. The "classes" were small groups designed to bring about behavioral change; these formed the basic structure of Wesley's churches. They were composed of twelve to twenty members of both sexes who were of mixed ages, social standing, and spiritual maturity under the direction of a trained leader. "Classes" did not gather for academic learning but focused on mutual confession, accountability, and encouragement.

3. The "bands" were designed to foster a deeper change of heart and direction. Their members were of the same sex, age, and marital status. These groups were devoted to ruthless honesty in an environment of strict confidentiality and trust, and they became the training ground for future leaders within the movement.

It will be useful at this stage to give an example of what narrative formation might look like within each of these layers of community.

Testimony within the "Society" of the Church: Reimagining the World in Light of God's Grace

A few years ago, our family enjoyed the lavish hospitality of Thanksgiving in Charlotte, North Carolina, among close friends. We all attended their church on Sunday morning. At a certain point in the service, the pastor explained that the church community had been praying for forty days for God's provision in relation to whatever practical needs people had. As he sat down, music began to play quietly in the background, and slowly, one by one, people filed forward. Without saying anything, each person faced the congregation and held up a sign with a few words on it, such as "Unemployed for nine months." After a few seconds, he or she would turn the sign around to reveal another message: "Got a job last week." This went on for about twenty minutes, until the front of the church was filled with people. The messages piled up thick and fast: "Estranged from my daughter . . . She called me," "Had debt repayments I couldn't make . . . Received a large gift," "Diagnosed with cancer . . . All clear," and so it went.

This silent testimony to God's provision was poignant and highly charged. By the end, there wasn't a dry eye in the building. The pastor's sermon about money and generosity was excellent, yet I don't remember a single word. More than five years later, however, I can still read from memory many of the silent messages on those signs describing people's breakthroughs after forty days of prayer.

Story and testimony are critical to human formation because they resonate with our essential nature as desiring creatures.[23] In contrast to propositional information, narrative knowledge—that is, the sort of understanding embedded in a story—is a more complex and comprehensive way of encountering truth. By appealing to the imagination, it engages the whole person.

The emotional intensity of that worship service in North Carolina etched those messages onto my memory. In a similar way, Dino's testimony brings to life the power of God's grace in the unfolding story of our lives in a way that theological discussion or ethical teaching simply cannot. This is a truth that the gospel writers and the apostle Paul understood and sought to pass on to the early believers.

If narrative knowledge has a unique way of communicating the Christian vision of life and reshaping our way of being in the world, then it follows that public testimony of God's work in our lives should be a regular and central part of the church's common worship. An honest account of someone's personal journey, including the struggles, uncertainties, and successes, provides hope for those listening as well as a narrative map of how God works out his restoration in human lives. Furthermore, testimony acts as a form of confession, a uniquely Christian idea in which sin is brought into the open and shown to be redeemable within the gospel story. This sort of testimonial confession not only is for the sake of the speaker but also plays an important redemptive-formative role within the gathered community; it runs counter to the pervasive secular narrative that trains us to manage and edit our personal stories, hiding weaknesses and any other signs of failure from public view.

Thriving "Classes": Telling Big Stories in a Small Group

When we first moved to London, Esther and I formed a home group in our basement apartment. It was an exciting time full of fun, honesty, and expectation. The diverse group was made up of old and new friends as well as people at very different stages of life. Because we were such a complex blend of people, each time we met one person would tell their

23. Smith, *Thinking in Tongues*, 65.

whole life story, including their journey into knowing God—or at least as much as they were willing to say, which was often more than we expected. This practice had some surprisingly significant results. With a group of nearly twenty people, all this storytelling took some time, but it quickly established a deep level of trust among us.

This mutual trust formed a platform from which we were able to share in one another's lives from week to week at a deeper level than we had been accustomed to. It enabled us to tune in more attentively to each other's needs and struggles, and it galvanized a strong sense of camaraderie. We were all foreigners in a new city, and this group created a narrative community within which we could travel securely in an unfamiliar place. Like any major city, London is a place where people can easily dissolve into anonymity and succumb to the temptations that go along with that. When our group formed, some members were tentatively coming back to faith while others were brand-new Christians, but several years later the core of that group planted a church together and still serves as its core leadership team after more than a decade.

Encouraging "Bands" of Brothers and Sisters

In our church in London, there was a group of guys who had mostly come to faith at various stages during their twenties and found themselves struggling with a whole range of issues connected to sex, relationships, pornography, and drinking. Some were frustrated; they were experiencing vibrant spiritual encounters with God in church, but in their everyday lives they were falling back into many of their old habits and patterns. Observing this collective dissatisfaction, a few of the group's natural leaders began gathering together weekly. They decided to take seriously the apostle James's encouragement to "confess your sins to each other and pray so that you may be whole and healed."[24]

Having established a safe place and clear rules of engagement—honesty and confidentiality—they shared their personal struggles and journeys: the good, the bad, and the ugly. Many people consider this sort of self-exposure to be anathema, and yet the group grew quickly. Something about their mix of courage, commitment, and candor attracted other men. The group

24. James 5:16.

became a genuine community of *koinonia*, or loving fellowship, by stepping into the sort of honest, purposeful, and supportive relationships that Augustine described in his own journey of discipleship centuries earlier. As he says: "My true brothers are those who rejoice for me in their hearts when they find good in me, and grieve for me when they find sin. They are my true brothers because whether they see good in me or evil, they love me still. To such as these I shall reveal what I am."[25]

Reviving Mimetic Discipleship

EXEMPLARS OF THE KINGDOM

In light of our culture's conviction that covenantal sacrificial love is a sort of "category error," the church requires mature living examples—storytellers who themselves personify the story—who resist this fatalistic narrative through their own faithful relationships and sexual integrity. The Christian vision of human flourishing is most clearly expressed by those people's lives that are bent toward God. It is not enough for pastors to simply *teach* Christian truth; they need to *show* what the Christian story looks like. A leader's sexual life is *not* his or her private business.

New Testament scholar Abraham Malherbe illustrates this through Paul's creative use of the philosophic pastoral tradition of *mimesis*, "imitation."[26] Paul's chosen method of shaping a community was to gather converts around himself and then, by his own behavior, demonstrate what he taught.[27] His intention was not to exert control over his converts or for them to become mirror images of him in every respect—for example, by becoming tentmakers or nomadic preachers. Instead, he would show them certain practices that they could follow in their own lives.[28] This was particularly important in gentile contexts, where the gospel called for a radically different life for Paul's converts. It would have been futile to teach abstract moral rules without showing how these might look "lived out" in their everyday lives.

25. Augustine, *Confessions* 10.4.

26. Abraham J. Malherbe, *Paul and the Thessalonians: The Philosophic Tradition of Pastoral Care* (Philadelphia: Fortress, 1987), 52.

27. See 1 Cor. 4:16; 11:1; Phil 3:17; 4:9; 1 Thess. 1:6–7; and 2 Thess. 3:6–13.

28. S. E. Fowl, "Imitation of Paul/of Christ," in *Dictionary of Paul and His Letters*, ed. Gerald F. Hawthorne, Ralph P. Martin, and Daniel G. Reid (Downers Grove, IL: InterVarsity, 1993), 428.

Living a faithful and disciplined sexual life has become equally radical in our own time, and this presents a pastoral challenge similar to the one Paul faced with his gentile converts. This vision of discipleship makes important claims on Christian leaders, as Paul makes clear in his instructions to Titus regarding the standards of life and character required for leaders within the faith community.[29] Paul is not looking for good appearances on Sundays but identifying those who publicly embody the faith in the concrete shape of their lives. His approach is founded on a cornerstone pastoral principle: leaders can only shape those in their care to the extent that they are conforming their own stories to the "master pattern."[30] Leaders must seek to be storytellers who teach through the gestures and rhythms of their lives as much as with their words.

It's an unfortunate trend within the modern church that we have largely lost the ancient Christian art of mimetic discipleship. It has become a common impulse among leaders to deflect attention from their own lives toward Jesus. The reasoning goes, "Don't look at me, I'm just like you—an imperfect human being! No, look at Jesus for an example to follow." Yet this is a misapplication of the biblical truth that Jesus should be the center and focus of all we do. It is to him that we give all glory and praise, and it is only because of him that we are able to live well. The integrity of our lives cannot be the result of a stoic act of self-mastery; it must come about through the transformative work of the Spirit. Still, the right application of this idea is that we glorify Jesus most clearly in the quality of our lives—in the Spirit's fruit, to use Paul's metaphor.

PRACTICING THE ART OF MIMETIC DISCIPLESHIP

First and foremost, we need to attend to our own lives. Just as Paul saw his life as a living expression of the gospel, we need to know this reality in our own lives. Pastors, for example, cannot preach about the transformative power of the Spirit with any genuine conviction and insight unless they know this power for themselves. Dino's story illuminates this connection. He now ministers among the most disadvantaged, to broken families, and in prisons. What makes his ministry possible and his testimony hopeful

29. Titus 1:5–9.
30. Barclay, "Paul's Story," 155.

within these bleak contexts is that he personally knows the transformative power of God.

Having attended theological colleges and seminaries in both Great Britain and North America, I've observed a lack of focus on spiritual-moral formation within these contexts once students move beyond the standard rhetoric. Even in seminaries, the overwhelming emphasis tends to be on acquiring academic knowledge. The grueling time and energy required for these studies leaves precious little space for the work of personal formation. Seminary students often confess to becoming isolated from others and not reading their Bibles devotionally for months or even years during their training. For seminaries in particular, this undervalued task of genuine spiritual-moral formation surely should be the singular most important goal in preparing leaders for Christian ministry.

James K. A. Smith observes that this typical underemphasis on worship and spiritual transformation points to a distorted vision of the self—a model that sees cognitive knowledge as the decisive core of human identity and discipleship.[31] The telling truth about many Christian seminaries and graduate schools is that when you dig below the surface, you will find a wide range of deep personal issues that are not being addressed as part of preparation for pastoral ministry. The problem is not that these issues exist but that we are doing so little to address them. We offer men's groups and counseling services, but only as voluntary add-ons rather than as core institutional priorities. Success is ultimately judged by academic precision rather than progress toward Christlikeness, even when we are careful to couch success in terms of the latter.

This deficit comes to the fore when graduates move into leadership roles in ministry, which creates enormous stress between their public and private personas. Lacking the time and space for the pursuit of genuine healing, the new leader too often finds that ministry's pressures generate waves that crash against fragile foundations, quickly undermining them. A common temptation is to try to control our environment, creating barriers that allow us to engage with the church community from a safe distance. This distance from people tempts us to *simulate* discipleship rather than to genuinely *stimulate* it, even if we sublimate our fatalism into a refined theology.

31. Smith, *Desiring the Kingdom*, 17–36.

The first step for leaders in fulfilling their mimetic vocation, then, is to attend to their own lives. This may be a long and difficult journey, but it is necessary and can be trusted to the One whose promise is to remake us in his image.

Mentoring and Spiritual Direction

SPANNING THE GENERATIONS

One of the most effective ways of teaching young Christians moral skills and discernment is to connect the generations within the church. If the Christian life is a progressive story, then it is critical for us to pool the experience and wisdom of those at different stages in the journey. This is particularly important regarding sexuality and relationships, since our culture places such a high priority on youth and short-term fulfillment. Within this context, those in later stages of life can provide significant perspective and wisdom for those on the way.

Friends of ours recently celebrated their tenth wedding anniversary. They have two small children and a strong relationship. We were surprised when they told us that the beginning of their marriage had been an unabated disaster. Nine months after their wedding, they were on the edge of pulling the curtain down on the whole thing. Yet in the midst of this looming disaster, an older couple within their church offered to meet with them every week. Their wisdom, perspective, honesty, prayer, example, and encouragement saved our friends' fledgling marriage. It is a genuine tragedy that this rich interplay between generations is so often lacking in our churches. We focus instead on the consumerist categories of peer-group ministry, keeping the generations separate. Indeed, as family researchers have found, it is the "intergenerational self" that has the most resilient foundation for personal identity and is best equipped to cope with the external pressures of life, just as a well-inflated tire can deal with bumps on the road.

WORDS THAT REVEAL AND WORDS THAT HEAL

Words have remarkable power. They can harm, heal, or destroy. The Word itself can cut like a sword to our inmost being.[32] The power of words

32. Heb. 4:12.

is demonstrated in an often forgotten or avoided Christian spiritual discipline—confession. Bringing sin into the open by verbalizing it to another person makes it tangible and collapses the disconnect between the sin and our real lives. In other words, although it is usually painful and uncomfortable, confession *integrates* us. This is what happened when that group of young men within our church chose to meet together regularly in a posture of trust and self-disclosure, determined to bring sin into the light and live "open-plan" spiritual lives. Indeed, confession is particularly important in relation to our sexual lives, where we are most likely to retreat behind a shroud of secrecy and nurse our sins in private.

Regnerus and Uecker found a strangely common and troubling theme in many of their interviews with Christian emerging adults, what the researchers describe as an "anticonversational logic."[33] This essentially is the belief that if you don't talk about something, it doesn't exist. This logic is exemplified by a young couple at college who were both deeply committed to their faith and active in Christian ministry. This couple would never consider having sex outside of marriage, and yet they engaged in oral sex almost daily for three months. As nineteen-year-old Laura explained, "We knew it was wrong, we knew we shouldn't do it, but we never brought it up, because as humans we like it. And so if you don't talk about it, then we don't have to acknowledge that it's wrong."[34]

Mentoring and honest accountability can quickly puncture this illusion, but church leaders must actively encourage the development of mentoring relationships marked by trust and honesty in order to reverse this dynamic. This is crucially important, because the shame and stigma often attached to sexual sin and dysfunction tends to drive people into isolation and hiding. Indeed, a trusted mentoring relationship may be the only place where these issues can be confessed and addressed. This is the path to freedom, but, sadly, it is the road less traveled.

The absence of mentoring relationships heightens the influence of the popular myths or sexual scripts that we identified earlier. Although it is important to affirm the development of strong peer groups within our congregations, we also need to reconnect the generations so that moral

33. Regnerus and Uecker, *Premarital Sex*, 32.
34. Ibid.

skills and wisdom can be passed down from one generation to another. Sociologist Christian Smith puts this challenge in stark terms:

> American emerging adults are a people deprived, a generation that has been failed, when it comes to moral formation. They have had withheld from them something that every person deserves to have a chance to learn: how to think, speak and act well on matters of good and bad, right and wrong. . . . They do not adequately know the moral landscape of the real world that they inhabit. . . . They need some better moral maps and better-equipped guides to show them the way around.[35]

WHEN THE STORY GETS STUCK: ADDRESSING THE CHALLENGE OF PROLONGED ADOLESCENCE

Viewing the Christian life as an unfolding story helps to clarify the places where the plot is typically thwarted, thereby undermining the journey into maturity. One of the biggest obstacles to healthy sexuality and relationships within the church and the broader culture is the recent phenomenon of prolonged adolescence. Compared to earlier generations, this generation seems to be entering adolescence earlier, at least in terms of sexual awareness and experience, and exiting this stage of life later, if at all. What used to be a relatively brief transitional stage—between childhood and the responsibilities of adulthood, marriage, and family—is now becoming, for some, a permanent lifestyle choice.

Many of the formative themes within modern culture, such as the celebration of freedom, authenticity, consumerism, careerism, youth, and sexual experimentation, have encouraged people to keep their options in play while making them skeptical about entering into ties that bind. Today, independence is presented as the ultimate expression of personal maturity. Although we still crave intimacy and social connection, self-sufficiency is lauded as the cardinal modern virtue. All this has made it difficult for many men, especially, to take the ultimate risk of entering a committed relationship.

Christian Smith observes that one of the most influential and lasting forces shaping young people's faith and practice is having elders within

---

35. Christian Smith et al., *Lost in Transition: The Dark Side of Emerging Adulthood* (New York: Oxford University Press, 2011), 69.

the church who can provide a sounding board. Those who are further along in the story can offer both example and advice for the road ahead. Smith's wide-ranging research suggests that these elder exemplars and confidants have a bigger impact over the long haul than a young person's peers.[36] This sort of connection and input is particularly important in the transitional stage of emerging adulthood, when young people are entering the uncertain waters of increased freedom and initiative but lack the fully formed maturity to make wise decisions.

Our culture's idolatry of youth has created a strange reversal within our churches: leaders tend to emulate the young rather than the other way around. Yet older mentors play a critical role in Christian formation, pointing past the adolescent period to what lies beyond. They provide a target to aim for and a path into the next stage of the story. The art of spiritual accompaniment involves sharing a way of life with young people until, as adults, they are ready to spiritually accompany someone else. Churches have an opportunity to provide contexts and relationships that anchor and shape young people's formation, helping them move through the fragile transitional stage of emerging adulthood into full maturity.

The Surprising Influence of Parents

In connection with this, Smith observes that parents have far more potential influence over their adolescent and emerging-adult children than they generally realize. Sadly, parents—including Christian parents—often shirk their potentially formative role out of a misplaced belief in the cultural myth that they have no influence over their children once they hit puberty.[37] Indeed, one of the most surprising findings of Regnerus and Uecker is the indifference of modern parents to their children's sexual lives. Most assume a "don't ask, don't tell" policy focused on "safety," ensuring a minimal protection against disease or pregnancy. The emotional, moral, and spiritual consequences of their children's sexual and relational lives are almost completely ignored. "In fact," the researchers say, "American parents' oversight of their teenage and young-adult children tends to be wide but shallow, resulting in children who long for—but seldom experience—real

---

36. Smith, *Souls in Transition*, 285.
37. Ibid., 284.

intimacy with their parents. Instead of pursuing a deeper relationship, many parents settle for just knowing that their kids are safe."[38]

This modern myth of parents' lack of influence is out of step with reality. Smith and others have found that when it comes to faith and practice, the example and advice of parents are more likely to influence emerging adults than the beliefs, perceptions, and habits of friends and peers. Tragically, Smith reports a deep yearning among adolescents to have a closer relationship with their parents at the same time that their parents are choosing to give them "space." During his team's interviews with thirteen- to seventeen-year-olds, they asked, "If there was one thing that you would change about your family, what would it be?" The most common response they received was that young people wished they were closer to their parents.

> They wanted to know their parents better, to hear more stories about their parents' pasts, to spend more time together and to get along better. When then asked why they were not as close to their parents as they wished they were, they said they did not know, they didn't know how to do that, that their parents were too busy, and they simply did not know how to make that happen.[39]

This makes for sobering reading. The modern parenting script is letting this generation down, and that is a tragedy. Christian parents can and should play a significant and constructive role in their children's lives, not just in the early formative years but also in these critical transitional phases. Here parents can offer unconditional friendship, assurance, wisdom, and rites of passage that enable their children to move into the next stage of life on a secure platform and with a well-formed self-identity.

Concluding Thoughts: Telling Stories That Are Going Somewhere

When conceived as a progressive story, the Christian life provides a compelling counternarrative to the fatalism of our culture's sexual scripts. The gospel gives us a clear hope for tomorrow while assuring us that Jesus walks

38. Regnerus and Uecker, *Premarital Sex*, 3.
39. Smith, *Souls in Transition*, 344.

with us in the present. It gives our lives—with all their struggles, sacrifices, slips, and disappointments—both significance and security. As one writer puts it, "The oriental shepherd always walked ahead of his sheep. He was always out in front. Any attack on the sheep had to take him into account first. Now God is out in front. He is in our tomorrows, and it is tomorrow that fills people with fear. Yet God is already there. All the tomorrows of our life have to pass through Him before they can get to us."[40]

Modern culture, out of fear of the ultimate tomorrow, tends to forsake any sense of the future for the sake of today. The Christian story redresses this imbalance, infusing today with peace by securing hope for tomorrow. Indeed, we can trust the plot of our lives to the Great Storyteller who has already written our names in the Book of Life.

In considering the contours of narrative discipleship, it is worth ending where we began, with Dino's story. God's powerful grace, worked out progressively in this man's life, should give us hope as pastors that, despite its seasonal variance, the Christian life is ultimately going somewhere.

---

40. F. B. Meyer, *Streams in the Desert*, ed. L. B. Cowan and James Reimann (Grand Rapids: Zondervan, 1997), 32.

11

Becoming What We Do

The Formative Power of Practices

Our culture's commitment to open-ended self-expression has led to increasing confusion in our sexual and relational lives. More than ever, we need to clearly preach and teach Scripture as an authoritative vision of life that takes shape in the practices of our everyday lives. This challenge is all the more important as our cultural moment presents social dynamics that are opposed to this formation. The growing trends of prolonged adolescence, the delaying of marriage and family, and the decision to live alone all point toward the popular desire to participate in relationships on our own terms without putting ourselves at risk.

The consumerist mind-set has also been wheeled like a Trojan horse into the sanctuary of our personal relationships. Social media, online dating, and cyberpornography encourage us to be hyperconnected, but these interactions are almost invariably one-sided—we enter into them only so long as they satisfy our "needs." They offer connection without intimacy,

215

commitment without risk, and companionship without mess. The online world all too often offers ties that preoccupy us rather than ones that bind us to each other.

Discipleship Takes Practice

The foundation of spiritual-moral formation in the New Testament is the idea that a tree produces fruit that is consistent with the tree's essential character. This is the "inside out" principle: a bad tree will produce bad fruit and a good tree, good fruit.[1] Paul affirms this theme in his letter to the Galatians. He points out that living according to the law by our own moral power ironically leads to the very behavior we're trying to avoid.[2] It is only the Spirit's work within us that enables us to live well. The tree must be made good before its fruit can flourish.

The Reformer Martin Luther placed this idea at the heart of Protestant spirituality. For Luther, only the spiritual regeneration of the "inner person" leads naturally to good actions by the "outer person."[3] We have already affirmed this important principle: we need to seek God's reshaping and redirecting of our true desires in order to be tethered to the Christian vision of life. Yet this "inside out" approach has often become one-sided within modern evangelicalism. We hold a firm conviction, rooted in our Protestant heritage, that what we *do* is merely evidence of what we *believe*. At best our actions demonstrate God's grace at work in us, and at worst they show that we are still sinners in need of ongoing grace.

Yet we need to emphasize the two-way dynamic between beliefs and practices, reinforcing the reality that our regular habits play an important *formative*—and not just reflective—role in Christian discipleship. As Richard Rohr puts it, we don't "think ourselves into new ways of living, we live ourselves into new ways of thinking."[4]

1. Matt. 7:17; 12:33; Luke 6:43.
2. Rom. 7:5–6; Gal. 5:16–21.
3. Martin Luther, *The Freedom of a Christian*, trans. Mark D. Tranvik (Minneapolis: Fortress, 2008).
4. Richard Rohr, *Everything Belongs: The Gift of Contemplative Prayer* (New York: Crossroad, 2003), 19.

The Significance of Context

The Modern Disciplined Society

Postmodern thinker Michel Foucault provides important insights on the nature and dynamics of power in the world, insights that reveal the importance of disciplines and practices in shaping our personal identity.[5] Foucault presents the individual as being constructed through relations of power and modes of discipline.[6] This means that we are inescapably shaped by our broader social context, so that even our so-called private lives are an illusion—because we are already embedded in social and cultural practices that give form to every part of our lives.

In *Discipline and Punish*, Foucault critiques power, knowledge, and discipline within modern society. He argues that knowledge shapes human identity; this knowledge is never neutral but is always *made* by those who have power, whether social, economic, political, or religious.[7] Foucault's review of the history of scientific knowledge and moral truths within Western cultures reveals their biases and roots in power relations. In his case study of the penal system, for instance, Foucault suggests that society created the prison in its own image as a "disciplined society" that conforms individuals to society's particular vision of life. He argues that power is always what shapes reality and that this reality creates our social world and, in turn, our personal identity.[8] Society's project, as seen most vividly in the prison, is to determine what is "normal" and to make people conform through numerous and diverse forms of coercion. Our context, in other words, *makes* us.

For Foucault, power is not a simple, singular force like the clumsy propaganda machine of a despotic state. Power is a complex, subtle, and ever-changing matrix of influences that nudges us toward a certain way of being. As he says, power is omnipresent in our lives, "not at all because it regroups everything under its invincible unity, but because it is produced

---

5. James K. A. Smith, *Who's Afraid of Postmodernism? Taking Derrida, Lyotard, and Foucault to Church* (Grand Rapids: Baker Academic, 2006), 102–3.

6. Taylor, *Sources of the Self*, 488.

7. Michel Foucault, *Discipline and Punish: The Birth of the Prison*, trans. Alan Sheridan (New York: Vintage, 1995).

8. Ibid., 194.

at every instant, or more-over, in every relation between one point and another. Power is everywhere: not that it engulfs everything, but that it comes from everywhere."[9]

The Gospel as a Narrative of Resistance

Foucault's picture of how we're shaped by our cultural context is like a social imaginary: it is subtle and comprehensive and has an overall consistency despite its many contradictions. Our culture's corruption of sexuality along consumerist lines provides an example. What promises to set us free actually manipulates and shapes our choices. This modern vision has become a figurative prison, with walls so high that we cannot see beyond them, even as Christians. Indeed, the sexual scripts envisioned and enforced within our culture have become the unquestioned horizon for our lives. Within this cultural matrix, the Christian vision of life is a subversive narrative of resistance. Christian counterpractices act as creative forces that shape us within alternative ways of imagining and living our lives.

Putting Paul in Context

Like Foucault, the apostle Paul understood the power of context for shaping personal identity. Paul used the raw material of existing social structures to fundamentally transform both those social structures and his converts in light of the gospel of Christ. For instance, like Jesus before him, Paul described and established each church community as a *family*—a household of God—thereby basing his communal vision for the church on a universal social relationship.[10] This was an important and risky move because the church family was called to be radically different from its cultural archetype.

The ancient Mediterranean culture of Paul's day was built upon the patriarchal household presided over by the *paterfamilias*. These families were hierarchical; every aspect of a family member's life was controlled, and each household pursued honor and glory in direct competition with

9. Michel Foucault, *The History of Sexuality*, vol. 1, *An Introduction* (New York: Pantheon, 1978), 121–22.
10. Roger W. Gehring, *House Church and Mission: The Importance of Household Structures in Early Christianity* (Peabody, MA: Hendrickson, 2004), 239. See 1 Tim. 5:1–2.

other families.[11] The rules of the game were set by accepted honor-shame codes. This zero-sum game, with each family pitted against the others, looks a lot like Thomas Hobbes's "war of all against all."

Yet in this compromised environment Paul describes the *ekklesia* as a mutually honoring family! Rather than fearing this risky template, Paul understands that context is critical for the formation of our personal identity and healthy relationships and also that the church context must be radically different from the distorted version offered by mainstream society.[12] Rather than being hierarchical and controlling, then, we are free to live as brothers and sisters in equal, loving, and open friendships, with God as our loving Father and head of the household.

As moderns with individualism in our bones, we need to be jarred by what Paul is doing here. He does not just use the *idea* of family as a romantic metaphor to add rhetorical force to his teaching, but he concretely builds the *practical* life of his churches around the dynamics of a real and different type of family. The community of faith regularly eats together, meets in homes, provides for each other's practical needs, pools complementary gifts that build each other up, and celebrates and grieves together. It is only within this sort of community that we can learn to enter into and sustain committed and loving relationships—to grow up into maturity.

The practical and sacrificial relationships Jesus describes in his Sermon on the Mount presuppose this sort of close, loyal, and transformed church family. Without this context we can treat Jesus's teaching on discipleship and community transformation only as a set of idealized platitudes. In his significant study of the Pauline house churches, Roger Gehring observes that the household *setting* provided the necessary context for understanding the church as the "household of God," while the household *structure* played an important role in ethical guidance and community formation in the Pauline churches.[13] Returning to Dino's story, an essential part of his journey to maturity was having "older brothers" in the church who came alongside him and mentored him in the gospel way of life.

If we are to foster healthy relationships—sexual and otherwise—within the church, then we need to take seriously the task of making disciples.

11. Gorman, *Cruciformity*, 362–63.
12. Ibid.
13. Gehring, *House Church and Mission*, 239.

And if we want to make disciples, then we need to organize our churches as nurturing families, not only figuratively but also in practical terms. This was a radical project in Paul's day, and it remains so in ours.

The Unquestioned Disciplines of Modern Sexuality: An Example

Foucault's description of the disciplines and practices of Western society is clearly borne out within many marriages and families today. Our culture's vision of the good life and its associated disciplines often leave little time or energy for nurturing our relationships. The universal right to have a "career," as well as the dizzying list of extracurricular activities that our children allegedly need in order to develop fully, has turned many parents into exhausted and resentful competitors rather than committed companions.

I was struck by an article whose author describes the drying up of intimacy within her and many of her friends' marriages amid the insatiable demands of modern life. Seeing that her experience reflects a broader social phenomenon, the author assesses her decision to end her marriage after twenty years. She had the most popular type of marriage today, the "companionate marriage," in which both partners have a career, co-parent, and co-housekeep according to negotiated gender-free rules. As she describes it:

> In women's magazine parlance, I did not have the strength to "work on" falling in love again in my marriage. And . . . as everyone knows, good relationships take work. Which is not to say I'm against work. Indeed, what also came out that afternoon [during a conversation with friends] were the many tasks I—like so many other working/co-parenting/married mothers—have been doing for so many years and tearfully declared I would continue doing. I can pick up our girls from school every day; I can feed them dinner and kiss their noses and tell them stories; I can take them to their doctor and dentist appointments; I can earn my half—sometimes more—of the money; I can pay the bills; I can refinance the house at the best possible interest rate; I can drive my husband to the airport; in his absence, I can sort his mail; I can be home to let the plumber in on Thursday between nine and three, and I can wait for the cable guy; I can make dinner conversation with any family member; I can ask friendly questions about anybody's day; I can administer hugs as needed to children, adults, dogs, cats; I can empty the litter box; I can stir

wet food into dry. Which is to say I can work at a career and childcare and joint homeownership and even platonic male-female friendship. However, in this cluttered forest of my 40s, what I cannot authentically reconjure is the ancient dream of brides, even with the Oprah fluffery of weekly "date nights," when gauzy candlelight obscures the messy house, child talk is nixed and silky lingerie donned, so the two of you can look into each other's eyes and feel that "spark" again. Do you see? Given my staggering working mother's to-do list, I cannot take on yet another arduous home- and self-improvement project, that of rekindling our romance. . . . I've since begun a journey of reading, thinking, and listening to what's going on in other 21st-century American families. And along the way, I've begun to wonder, what with all the abject and swallowed misery: Why do we still insist on marriage?[14]

Any parent can deeply empathize with the bone-weariness of raising a family, especially the all-consuming needs and endless chaos of little people. This inevitably takes its toll on the level of romance within a marriage, at least for a time. Yet the author is expressing more than that here. In one sense, this is a pure and popular expression of the "romantic/realist" view of intimate relationships described earlier. Being "true to oneself" means that ongoing sexual or emotional intimacy within marriage cannot be manufactured or conjured. If the love has gone, or we are simply too tired, then we must embrace this reality.

More important, the author's fatalistic approach shows how a whole range of disciplines and practices are simply assumed as essential and immovable objects. These daily rituals are so essential to the modern vision of life that they go unquestioned, even as they deprive our closest relationships of the resources they need to survive, let alone thrive. Sadly, we are prepared to let the core of our lives unravel for the sake of modern life's peripheral concerns. Indeed, the daily disciplines the author describes echo the walls and disciplines of Foucault's prison. Her description is grim and ascetic, and these arduous responsibilities take on the tone of forced labor. For many people, the demands of survival do necessitate an ascetic existence, even within the prosperous West. Yet many of the rituals the author describes are the alleged "essentials" of the good life for the modern, high-functioning, consumerist self. As if living in Foucault's prison, we

14. Sandra Tsing Loh, "Let's Call the Whole Thing Off," *The Atlantic*, July 1, 2009, http://www.theatlantic.com/magazine/archive/2009/07/lets-call-the-whole-thing-off/307488/.

have tacitly bought into the modern vision of life. But these practices and disciplines have affected our relational lives within our families and beyond.

During my time in the corporate world, I observed firsthand how people would submit to the voracious demands of their careers, at enormous cost to their marriages, families, and relationships. As the cornerstone of their personal identities, career was sacrosanct. Unfortunately, this approach is being wired into our children as we ferry them to numerous after-school activities and classes. From the outset, they are groomed for the practical demands of adult life without ever experiencing the simple joy of unstructured childhood pursuits and the unhurried affection of their parents. In many cases, we even outsource their "care," as if this was merely a practical function. Given the importance of early childhood for shaping our children's imaginations, desires, patterns of attachment, and vision of life, it makes you wonder what relational model we are forming within them.

Responding to Modern Culture

Foucault's response to the disciplines of the modern world is to reject and push back every type of outside control, especially in our sexual lives. Although this is an overreaction, his insights show us the inescapable connection between cultural practices and personal formation. Given the powerful influence of our social contexts in shaping our identity, we should seek to live in the right context. Christians, then, can cultivate a constructive view of freedom, whereby we are becoming conformed to the image of Christ within a committed community through disciplined habits, practices, and rituals. James K. A. Smith notes that we can differentiate between good and bad forms of discipline by their ultimate goals.[15] Thus we can separate a disciplinary *structure*, which is necessary and inevitable, from its *direction*, which can be good or bad.

This insight addresses two mistakes commonly made by Christian leaders. If we resonate with Foucault's suspicion of power, we're tempted to avoid prescriptive teaching that makes ethical or transformative demands on people. In this mind-set, any sort of moral boundary marking is seen as a form of violence against personal freedom and spirituality. By contrast, traditional Protestant discipleship has tended to focus Christian life around

15. Smith, *Who's Afraid of Postmodernism?*, 102–3.

knowing or *believing* certain things, with the emphasis on sermons and Bible study as the key to formation. Challenging both these approaches, Smith suggests that our greater purpose as Christians is to *become* certain people who *do* certain things. This new form of life requires a regime of practices that challenge and displace our old behaviors, aligning our lives to our faith. How does that change occur?

The Practicing Community

The community of faith must be at the center of the process of shaping Christian practices, and the character necessary to help us navigate intimate relationships must be molded within that context. Returning to the picture of the church as a family, we can learn the necessary moral skills for living in the truth only when we are initiated into them by older "brothers" and "sisters" in the faith.[16] The church community should provide an authoritative context—that is, a consensus about the best form of life—as well as a place where the moral skills needed to live that way can be learned.[17]

The critical question in relation to discipleship is this: If the church is where people grow into maturity and learn to engage in healthy relationships, what should our churches look like? New Testament scholar Mark Strom offers a challenging proposal. Paul modeled his churches on different social organizations, depending on their specific cultural context—synagogues, voluntary associations, philosophic schools, or ancient mystery cults. Paul improvised, using whatever cultural raw material he found in that context. In each case, Strom says, Paul focused his pastoral ministry around the goal and structure that maximized the process of individual and communal transformation. This involved two key strategies.

Whereas classical philosophy prioritized abstract ideals over the particulars of everyday life, Paul organized his *ekklēsiai* around, and focused their worship on, the everyday reality of living in light of Christ's dying and rising.[18] Strom suggests, for instance, that Paul's gentile churches took their particular form from Greco-Roman voluntary associations instead of the Jewish synagogue. In light of this, Strom says that the gatherings

16. Hauerwas, *Hauerwas Reader*, 141.
17. Ibid.
18. Mark Strom, *Reframing Paul: Conversations in Grace and Community* (Downers Grove, IL: IVP Academic, 2000), 13–14.

of the *ekklēsiai* were focused on equipping members through fellowship and "grace-full conversation" for life in the world outside the community.[19] Strom critiques modern evangelicalism, which he says has succumbed to the temptation to "gag the most important conversations" through its controlled, hierarchical services. These contexts, according to Strom, only offer a form of "pseudo-interaction."[20] He proposes gatherings of rich, engaged, interpersonal relationships that seek to connect the story of Christ with the everyday realities of each person within the community.

It is clear that deep, interpersonal relationships and practical spirituality were at the heart of Paul's communities and their worship. This suggests that we need to focus on tackling the practical priorities of people's lives. The annual "sex talk" or preaching series will not be enough to address the relational struggles and questions that seethe under the surface of our congregations. These issues should form part of our weekly teaching and reflections as we seek to bring the gospel to life in relation to the most important aspects of our lives. There are many contexts within the church, of course, in which these sorts of relationships and conversations can take place. Our responsibility as church leaders is to be "midwives" who nurture and encourage these critical exchanges and the contexts that foster them.

Habits That Harm, Practices That Heal: Living in a Swirl of Phantoms

Our imaginations are critical in shaping the sort of lives we live. Indeed, the key to living the new life in Christ is bringing our whole imagination under his care and direction. The imagination is an important battleground for discipleship because it is the meeting place between humans and God. Christian identity is founded on our connection to the unseen God. This relationship is nourished and sustained through prayer and meditation on Scripture, God's revealed Word. It is important, then, to understand how the imagination is shaped by modern practices.

To a large extent, the imagination feeds off images and other stimuli that are mediated through our bodily senses.[21] This explains why visual images

19. Ibid., 16.
20. Ibid., 18.
21. Smith, *Desiring the Kingdom*, 57.

have the power to shape our lives; they affect, tease, and provoke us into certain ways of living. C. S. Lewis argued that the imagination is corrupted by the excessive visual imagery that we absorb within modern culture. A diet of Hollywood products shapes and distorts real experience, he says, especially regarding ideas of love and sexuality.[22] Popular media immerses us in a "swirl of phantoms" that obscures our imaginations from the true realm that lies beyond—the truth about God and ourselves.[23]

Smartphones, for instance, have become ever-present companions. Technology allows us to access anything at any time, tempting us to fill every last moment of our day with activity. One evening recently, I stood at the back of a church. The darkness was punctuated by a sea of illuminated boxes as people caught up on emails, texts, or news. Sherry Turkle tells of being at a funeral and seeing a woman standing in the wings, texting throughout the service. Afterward the woman confessed that she found it impossible to sit through events without checking texts and emails—even a funeral![24]

These frenetic modern practices are removing the "gaps" in our lives, those times that enable us to be present to ourselves and to God. We have cluttered our imaginations with so much noise that the still small voice of God becomes a peripheral presence. Yet in a world without space for prayer and self-reflection, Christian spirituality becomes an impossible project. The endless flow of information and imagery on which we incessantly feed embalms the true imagination and cuts us off from God. It takes patience, practice, and solitude to disentangle ourselves from these illusions.

The intimate, two-way connection between our bodies and imaginations that directs our hearts and minds means that the habits we develop play an important role in shaping the vision of life that we love and pursue. Because people are being formed by the holistic practices of the modern social imaginary, Christian discipleship must focus on re-forming people's imaginations, hearts, and minds through its own comprehensive formative practices.[25]

22. Terry Lindvall, "Embalmed Images: C. S. Lewis and the Art of Film," Christian Broadcasting Network, https://www.cbn.com/special/Narnia/articles/Lindvall_LewisFilm.aspx.
23. Ibid.
24. Turkle, *Alone Together*, 295.
25. Smith calls these practices "liturgies," while Daniel Bell refers to them as "technologies of desire." See Smith, *Desiring the Kingdom*, 24–26; and Bell, *Liberation Theology*, 87.

Unleashing the Unconscious: Being Intentional about the Unintentional

James K. A. Smith highlights the importance of this project by pointing to recent psychological research into "the new unconscious."[26] This research shows that we automate a huge array of preferences, intuitions, and skills through simple repetition. As these skills or actions become automatic, our conscious choice drops out of the picture and we operate largely out of passive memory—like learning to drive or play a musical instrument. Conscious (and awkward) training eventually gives way to intuitive feel. Formational routines matter because only around 5 percent of our daily activity occurs through actions we consciously "choose."[27]

"Unconscious" formative practices can be either proactively chosen—for example, learning a musical instrument—or more passively received—for example, listening to music during our daily commutes or watching television. These practices can also be "thin" or "thick." Thin practices are trivial or incidental—for example, brushing our teeth—while thick practices shape our core identity—for example, practicing spiritual disciplines or choosing a career. It is critical, then, to understand what sort of person we become through different practices and the vision of life they carry. Even thin practices tend to get hooked to thick ones and become part of our identity formation. In this way, as Smith describes, "recognizing that there are no neutral practices . . . should push us to realize that perhaps some of the habits and practices that we are regularly immersed in are actually thick formative practices that over time embed in us desires for a particular vision of the good life."[28] Given the comprehensive challenges posed by discipleship, where do we begin?

Remaking Reality: Envisioning Creative Rituals

Redeeming Practices 1: Embracing Embodied Worship

One of the most influential trends in the modern world is the intrusion of a form of gnostic dualism, whereby mind/spirit/personality are seen as

26. Smith, *Desiring the Kingdom*, 80.
27. Ibid., 81.
28. Ibid., 83.

separate from material reality and physical embodiment. This intrusion has two important consequences for our sexual lives. First, combined with the power of the "virtual world" online, gnosticism is creating a disembodied sexual experience that tempts us to exist within an imaginary world detached from real relationships. Indeed, simulation requires immersion, and eventually we come to prefer fantasy over reality. Further, for many Christians, a gulf develops between faith (what we believe in mind/spirit) and practice (what we do with our bodies), so that these realms are not seen as inextricably connected. As the popular reasoning goes, what counts is my faith—since Jesus is interested in my heart—not what I do with my body.

In light of this challenging terrain, Christian worship must stand at the center of Christian formation, providing a passionate and intuitive understanding of the world in light of the fullness of the gospel. In response to the forces of gnostic dualism, the church needs to emphasize the unitive and formative power of its embodied worship rituals, especially its sacraments. The Eucharist, for instance, is a *material* expression of God's grace that helps connect our spirituality to our physical embodiment, thereby bonding the Spirit's transforming power to our practical lives.

Christian leaders tend to introduce the Eucharist (or Communion or the Lord's Supper) as the place where we remember what Jesus has done for us and we receive renewed assurance for the forgiveness of sins. Yet they would do well to describe the bigger vision we step into when we take the bread and wine together.

If we see the world—including ourselves—as intimately connected to God, then the Eucharist is where we share most intensely in the divine life. As we regularly enter into it, this practice has important spiritual and ethical implications for our lives and relationships. Partaking in the Eucharist, we are strengthened in faith by the Spirit and drawn into the life of the Trinity. Participation in the divine community progressively reshapes our natures to become what they are called to be—in the likeness of Christ. This is a spiritual mystery to be sure, but one that stands at the center of Christian worship within Paul's spirituality. Indeed, for Paul this meal had such power and significance that to take it in the wrong disposition could cause sickness.[29]

29. 1 Cor. 11:27–30.

The Eucharist also reminds us of the relational model that forms the foundation of our faith and identity—Christ's self-emptying love, expressed through his blood on the cross—as well as the power offered by the new life in his resurrected body. This model of self-giving love weans us off the relationships of "contract and exchange" that consumerism presents as a vision of human flourishing and intimacy. The radical Christian vision of relationality finds concrete expression in the attitude of humility and the practices of forgiveness, reconciliation, and practical love within the community of faith.

We need to creatively foster practical contexts that connect worship with our everyday lives. For example, this might involve taking Communion in our homes in small groups, spending time beforehand to allow God to show us someone we need to forgive or be reconciled to, articulating that to the group, and determining an accountable course of action together. This context helps to reinforce and materialize in our lives the new reality that we are enacting in this essential worship gesture.

In this way, the church's worship—with the Lord's Supper at its center—articulates, empowers, and enacts the vision of healthy relationships within the Christian social imaginary. The church's worship directs our ultimate purpose toward friendship with God and each other, and it enables us to be reconciled to each other through the Spirit's love. In this socially constructive practice, we seek as a community to walk into and embody restored relationships within the kingdom of God. This regular practice seeks to form a different type of community in the midst of the secular world and confronts the latter's vision of life.[30]

Redeeming Practices 2: Displacing Modern Social Practices

In the first half of this book I focused on some of the key cultural practices that are shaping our sexual and relational lives. They present themselves as benign and even beneficial, but in fact they carry a potentially damaging vision of life and profoundly influence our relational lives. My wife and I observed the formative power of embodied social practices within our young congregation in London. Despite their vibrant spiritual

30. Stanley Hauerwas, *Christian Existence Today: Essays on Church, World, and Living In Between* (Durham, NC: Labyrinth, 1988), 107.

228

lives on Sundays, many of these young people's sexual and relational lives were more directly shaped by their experience of cultural social spaces—bars, parties, and nightclubs. Many of the guys I regularly met with would struggle not to fall into the same patterns of behavior each week, despite their best intentions. Indeed, when we participate in these cultural spaces, we also enter into the subtle rules and expectations they establish. As we spend more time within these contexts, eventually we come to embody them.

Although our goal is not to create a sort of parallel universe in which the church lives cloistered away from the outside world, we need to encourage social spaces within the church where a different vision of relationships can be expressed and nurtured. This provides a context for the delicate task of being the family of God—relating to each other as "brothers" and "sisters" in Christ—while at the same time being a courting community in which romantic relationships can form, be tested, and come to fruition in an environment where people are supported and known.

If the formation of the Christian vision of life takes practice, then the more contexts we can create for these sorts of social interactions, the better. These alternative social contexts allow sexual energy to be expressed within social dynamics that direct us toward the Christian vision of sexuality. This involves learning to be part of a broad network of friendships in which not every member of the opposite sex is viewed as a potential sexual partner. This trains our sexual energy and impulses in accordance with God's will. It readies us for the twin Christian vocations of singleness and marriage.

Singleness and the Christian Vocation

I'm not sure we have, in the Protestant church at least, a clear sense of vocation in relation to singleness. If we do, we have not done an effective job of communicating it. We have tended to see marriage as the only genuine Christian goal, so that other states of relational being are, by implication, sad or simply transitional. This may happen because most Christian leaders are married themselves and because Scripture gives us a clear mandate to bless marriage. Still, it causes frustration among single Christians, as well as a perception within the church that there are "haves" and "have-nots." Singles often feel pitied or as if they are living an unnatural form of life. An invitation to a dinner party may mean being set up with a "suitable" potential partner. Although odd numbers may be the rule of thumb in interior design, there appears to be no place for them at Christian social events! This sense of frustration at least partly explains the recent rise of dedicated singles ministries.

Although the majority of people in our church in London were single, very few felt any sense of calling to remain single. On the contrary, many experienced their status as a burden, a wasteful holding pattern before finding someone and getting on with "real" life. For many people single-ness had become a strong *identity*, but one without any sense of *vocation*. How do we address this imbalance within our churches?

First, we need to regularly articulate the positive and complementary roles that singleness and marriage play within the kingdom of God, as explored earlier. Only when we understand how each vocation fits into the big picture can we wholeheartedly embrace the disciplines and costs that each role involves. As the word *vocation* suggests, we must come to see our sexual lives as particular callings within God's mission. We need to acknowledge and affirm that this is a heroic struggle, particularly in our cultural context with its emphasis on youth and free sexual expression. These Christian practices will feel alienating and at times unbearable un-less they are tethered to the greater vision of the Christian life.

One weakness in common approaches to discipleship is that we treat different areas of life as separate compartments—like discrete software packages to be downloaded. We are tempted to deal with sexuality and relationships through specialist courses or seasonal sermons. Yet the Chris-tian vision of sexuality will only seep into people's imaginations if it is constantly connected to our worship and faith. Our sexuality is an essential part of our spirituality, and it should be an integral theme in our regular teaching and worship. Teachers need to keep the Christian vision of sexual-ity before people—to continually reenvision them—much as a hot element keeps a pot on a roiling boil. To give the Christian vision power in people's lives, they need to regularly describe, communicate, and affirm the nature of the Christian life and to connect this vision with every aspect of life.

Vision is not a silver bullet for discipleship, of course. By itself, it will not take away the sense of isolation that single people often experience, nor will it inoculate us against the allure of pornography and other temptations. It does, though, provide the bedrock for Christian sexuality. Vision gives coherence, hope, and encouragement. In conjunction with regular teaching and affirmation, we need to develop practical social contexts within which people can explore a possible calling to singleness, or at least to live well while single.

The Church as a Courting Community

Taking our lead from the New Testament, we also need to keep marriage and singleness in dialectic tension within our churches. Even as we openly bless both forms of life, we can enable an environment in which people can move from singleness into relationships without the others feeling left behind or without the community dividing into separate camps of the "loved" and the "lonely lost." This is a complex and delicate balance to strike in practice as we affirm singleness as a vocation while also addressing the fact that prolonged singleness has become a problem in both our culture and our churches.

There are many reasons for prolonged singleness, but one factor is the changing social dynamics that make it difficult to meet potential partners. A woman writing in *The Atlantic* explains how she found herself single in her thirties and without an obvious context for meeting men. Her life, typical of many busy modern people, revolved around a small group of colleagues and close female friends, a circle that was unlikely to yield positive results in terms of relationships.[31] Her experience has become common with the passing away of traditional social meeting places, while new ones—such as online dating—are not yet fully formed and offer an ambiguous experience.[32]

Here the church has a significant opportunity not only for its own sake but also in terms of mission. The church is one of the few remaining social contexts that can provide the safe and coherent courting opportunities that people crave. Whereas this role used to be played by an array of social clubs and other contexts, these larger meeting places have been replaced by smaller, less diverse groups—lifestyle enclaves. As we saw earlier, these smaller affinity groups tend to come together around a shared interest or passion, such as the gym, outdoor adventure, travel, or wine. Within this narrowing of social horizons in our culture, the church can offer an alternative, but we need to recognize and seize that opportunity.

31. Bolick, "All the Single Ladies."
32. This evolution in the dynamics of courting is chronicled by Beth L. Bailey, *From Front Porch to Back Seat: Courtship in Twentieth-Century America* (Baltimore: Johns Hopkins University Press, 1989).

The church should be a coherent yet diverse courting community. Its members share some fundamental convictions about the nature of life, sexuality, and relationships—it is *coherent*; but the community is made up of people from different walks of life—it is *diverse*. It is here that a designated singles ministry can play an important role. Besides giving some vision for the single Christian life, it can provide a natural social context in which friendships can develop without the pressure of dating. Of course, people will always feel a certain pressure and exposure within this sort of "fishbowl" environment, but that is an unavoidable (and survivable) reality.

Establishing a Healthy Dynamic: Battle of the Sexes

As I explained at the beginning of this book, when addressing the area of relationships within our own church, we noticed that a mutual frustration, even anger, had developed between the sexes. The single women were annoyed that the guys wouldn't initiate relationships, while the single guys argued that the women rebuffed them whenever they did take the initiative—they always seemed to be the "wrong" guy. This led to a relationship standoff, with each group pointing the finger of blame at the other.

In addressing this dynamic, we felt the need to publicly recast the expectations and spirit in which we related together as a community of faith—a sort of "Relationships Manifesto" for our church. This involved expressing the conviction that we were, first and foremost, brothers and sisters in the family of Christ. What did this biblical mandate look like in real life? First, we acknowledged that this exhortation has profound implications for how we go about exploring, forming, and in some cases ending relationships, ways that make us different from the culture at large. This involved agreeing to treat each other with an extra measure of grace and respect in this messy and complex area, because we were all in it together. The guys were encouraged, for instance, to put themselves at risk by initiating contact, while the women were encouraged to treat the guys sensitively in their responses. Additionally, we needed to pledge support for fledgling relationships that did form within the community. This involved not encouraging gossip, allowing each party to reestablish within the community if the relationship ended, and so on.

This approach did not remove the mess and complexity of relationships within the church. In some ways, it increased for a time. Yet we were surprised by the extent to which simply articulating a common manifesto for relationships established a dynamic in which relational experimentation could flourish within safe and supportive boundaries.

Encouraging the Signs of Life

Often these social contexts need a little nudge in the right direction from people and events that act as relational catalysts. Several single people within our church developed a passion for acting as "firestarters," encouraging relationships among other singles. They broke up the potential awkwardness by creating contexts that were unthreatening yet fun, such as "speed dating" events. By providing a convivial social context and a sense of camaraderie, these events removed some of the obvious pressure people felt to impress each other or to avoid the risk of rejection. If nothing else, they were entertaining occasions where people were able to extend their circle of friends within the church.

A challenge faced by smaller churches, of course, is the lack of a sufficient peer-group population to make such social contexts viable. This can be addressed in several ways. Someone in our church, for instance, organized "Date My Friend" events that brought in people from other churches, broadening the social circle while still keeping it consistent. These occasions created a safe environment and minimized the sense of being exposed because everyone arrived with a friend with whom they could debrief afterward. In addition, kindred churches across London would occasionally come together for larger social events specifically for singles. These gatherings greatly enlarged the potential courting community while keeping it consistent within certain shared values.

Community Support

In addition to encouraging relationships, the wider church community needs to be a family, supportive of our members if they explore relationships in our midst. Those in the community who are further down the track—whether married or single—can provide wisdom, lived-out examples, and accountability in the area of relationships. This greater support network within the family of Christ fulfills the extended family's traditional role. We need this broad range of deep and diverse relationships—with parents, friends, teammates, leaders, mentors, and so on—to properly affirm our personhood. These relationships provide a solid foundation on which we can launch legitimate and healthy sexual relationships.

The church is one of the few remaining social spaces where people can come together with the express intention of forming loving friendships without the constant pressure of sexual connection. As Christian ministers, we can play an influential role within this dynamic by encouraging genuine communities of friendship in practice. Part of our task is to ask whether we are promoting social spaces and ministry contexts in which people's fundamental needs for relational intimacy are being met, as well as opportunities for people to express their affective (social) sexuality in line with its divine purpose.

Marriage Preparation as Counterformation

The Christian practice of marriage will become increasingly distinct from our culture's romanticized fatalism about committed love, and therefore it stands to become one of the church's most powerful witnesses to the kingdom of God. Yet Christian marriage has also come to be understood in contractual terms: two independent agents coming together to express a wish to be together. As a result, many Christian marriages have suffered a fate similar to their secular counterparts. Marriage preparation is often treated as a minor formality on the way to wedded bliss. With the weakening of marriage and family, preparation and support are urgent tasks for the church.

We must reframe marriage as an essential part of the community and mission of the church. It is simply not enough to wave the happy couple off into the sunset; the goal of Christian marriage is not to see two lone rangers become one lone ranger—it is that they become part of the wider faith community. By investing time in those entering into marriage, we can better help them to understand the nature of their commitment and to reach the maturity required to sustain the covenant. Our ritual practices need to reinforce this vision. Weddings, for instance, should be more than small, private ceremonies with personalized vows. Instead, we should seek to place the marriage ceremony—and so the relationship itself—within the church community that is tasked with providing nurture, wisdom, and a guiding story.

We need to articulate the significance of standing publicly before our communities and speaking the same vows that countless others have spoken. In so doing, a couple declares that their marriage is not of their own creation but is a gift from God. It reminds them and others that they are stepping into a legacy that spans millennia and testifies to Christ's continuing faithfulness to his bride, the church. Christian marriages become a clear public statement: we see these covenant relationships occurring within and for the sake of the church. When rightly oriented, married Christians refuse to fall for the illusion that they are independent beings writing their own stories. This distinctive vision provides a strong challenge to the privatization of faith—and to the pervasive sexual practices within our culture.

Concluding Thoughts: Speaking with Our Lives

The Christian life can only be learned, like a language, in conversation with others. Within the committed context of the church, we need people who are capable of being faithful to a way of life and to each other, even when that chafes against the consensus morality of our culture.

In many different ways, Christians are trained in the habits of moral excellence—or virtues—within the church, including parental training, mentoring, preaching, and our common worship. Each of these contexts helps us to learn the moral language of discipleship. We learn the basics of the language from others and exercise it through regular practice, and it forms part of our identity by becoming the basic vocabulary of our character. As in all language acquisition, we come to understand the language of discipleship in stages: first we learn the building blocks, such as words, syntax, and structure, and then how it all fits together—its meaning and coherence. Finally and progressively, we learn to use it consistently and with nuance in each new situation. As Aristotle put it: "For the things we have to learn before we can do them, we learn by doing them." The challenging question for modern Christians is whether we can be faithful people without first being part of a faithful community.

Epilogue
Melodies of Heaven

My home country, New Zealand, is often called "the land of birds." As an archipelago of lush and isolated islands in the far corner of the South Pacific, New Zealand is free from most land-based predators, which has enabled birdlife to flourish. When Captain James Cook arrived on its shores in 1769, he observed that the birdsong was deafening.

Within this symphonic mix, an especially interesting native bird is the tui. Physically beautiful, its dark, iridescent feathers are offset by a dramatic white tuft nestled under its throat. But what is most striking about the tui is its song. Regardless of where you are or what you are doing, it is difficult not to stop and tune in to its exotic and mesmerizing harmonies. This rich sound arises from the fact that the tui has two voice boxes that work together to create what could be mistaken as music from another world. The tui is literally "one flesh" with two voices. Like two instruments in conversation, a tui in song is essentially playing a duet.

This, I believe, is compelling imagery for envisioning the nature and vocation of Christian relationships. Men and women are created in God's image; they are complex, relational, and complementary beings. The bold assertion of the Christian vision of life is that human flourishing—indeed, our very telos—is to live in deep and harmonious relationships. This vision is not just the reserve of marriage but extends to social relationships within the wider community of faith and beyond.

This vision for relationships connects to the incarnational mission of the church in the world. As we pursue and progressively come to embody tender, trusting, and committed relationships, we effectively play the melodies of heaven. It is this distinctive music that causes others to stop and pay attention within the jaundiced romanticism of our culture's quest for intimacy with no strings attached.

Stewarding this journey within the church is a challenging vocation for Christian leaders, who need to be more than spiritual "tour guides" on a Sunday. It involves creating, nurturing, and encouraging contexts in which people can become known within the community of faith. Moving from good intentions to practical reality in this area will constitute a significant prophetic statement within a culture that heralds privacy and personal autonomy as cardinal virtues. Indeed, in order to protect the relational life of the church, we need to name these seemingly benevolent predators. In other words, in forging relationships of honesty and trust, we first need to acknowledge that church communities are not immune to the cultural zeitgeist.

Jesus has swallowed up death, and one day—as Paul says—we will be swallowed up by life.[1] It is the privilege of Christian leaders, indeed of all disciples, to foster communities of faithfulness and joy that begin to live into that future reality now.

---

1. 2 Cor. 5:4.

Select Bibliography

American Psychological Association Task Force on the Sexualization of Girls. *Report of the APA Task Force on the Sexualization of Girls.* Washington, DC: American Psychological Association, 2010. http://www.apa.org/pi/women/programs/girls/report-full.pdf.

Augustine. *Confessions.* Translated by Henry Chadwick. Oxford World's Classics. Oxford: Oxford University Press, 2008.

Badiou, Alain. *In Praise of Love.* New York: New Press, 2012.

Bailey, Beth L. *From Front Porch to Back Seat: Courtship in Twentieth-Century America.* Baltimore: Johns Hopkins University Press, 1989.

Balthasar, Hans Urs von. *Love Alone: The Way of Revelation.* London: Sheed & Ward, 1968.

Barclay, John M. G. "Paul's Story: Theology as Testimony." In *Narrative Dynamics in Paul: A Critical Assessment,* edited by Bruce W. Longenecker, 133–56. Louisville: Westminster John Knox, 2002.

Barth, Karl. *Church Dogmatics.* Study ed. London: T&T Clark, 2009.

Bauman, Zygmunt. *Liquid Love: On the Frailty of Human Bonds.* Cambridge: Polity, 2003.

Beaty, Katelyn. "Same-Sex Marriage and the Single Christian: How Marriage-Happy Churches Are Unwittingly Fueling Same-Sex Coupling—and Leaving Singles Like Me in the Dust." *Christianity Today.* July 1, 2013. http://www.christianitytoday.com/ct/2013/july-web-only/same-sex-marriage-and-single-christian.html.

Bell, Daniel. *Liberation Theology after the End of History: The Refusal to Cease Suffering.* London: Routledge, 2001.

Bell, Rob. *Sex God: Exploring the Endless Connections between Sexuality and Spirituality*. Grand Rapids: Zondervan, 2008.

Bellah, Robert N., Richard Madsen, William M. Sullivan, Ann Swidler, and Steven M. Tipton. *Habits of the Heart: Individualism and Commitment in American Life*. Berkeley: University of California Press, 1996.

Bernard of Clairvaux. *Selected Works*. Classics of Western Spirituality. Translated by G. R. Evans. New York: Paulist Press, 1987.

Bogle, Kathleen. *Hooking Up: Sex, Dating and Relationships on Campus*. New York: New York University Press, 2008.

Bolick, Kate. "All the Single Ladies." *The Atlantic*. November 2011. http://www.theatlantic.com/magazine/archive/2011/11/all-the-single-ladies/308654/.

Boyle, Nicholas. *Who Are We Now? Christian Humanism and the Global Market from Hegel to Heaney*. Notre Dame, IN: University of Notre Dame Press, 1988.

Bramlett, M. D., and W. D. Mosher. "Cohabitation, Marriage, Divorce, and Remarriage in the United States." *Vital and Health Statistics* 23, no. 22 (July 2002): 1–93.

Brown, Jane D. "Mass Media Influences on Sexuality." *Journal of Sex Research* 39 (2002): 42–45.

Burrell, David B. "Can We Be Free without a Creator?" In *God, Truth, and Witness: Engaging Stanley Hauerwas*, edited by L. Gregory Jones, Reinhard Hütter, and C. Rosalee Velloso Ewell, 35–52. Grand Rapids: Brazos, 2005.

Carroll, Jason S., Laura M. Padilla-Walker, Larry J. Nelson, Chad D. Olson, Carolyn McNamara Barry, and Stephanie D. Madsen. "Generation XXX: Pornography Acceptance and Use among Emerging Adults." *Journal of Adolescent Research* 23 (2008): 6–30.

Cooper, Al. *Cybersex: The Dark Side of the Force*. Philadelphia: Brunner-Routledge, 2000.

Cooper, Al, S. Boies, M. Maheu, and D. Greenfield. "Sexuality and the Internet: The Next Sexual Revolution." In *The Psychological Science of Sexuality: A Research Based Approach*, edited by Frank Muscarella and Lenore T. Szuchman, 516–45. New York: Wiley, 1999.

Cooper, Al, David L. Delmonico, and Ron Burg. "Cybersex Users, Abusers, and Compulsiveness: New Findings and Implications." *Sexual Addiction and Compulsivity* 7, nos. 1 and 2 (2000): 5–29.

Crouch, Andy. "Sex without Bodies: The Church's Response to the LGBT Movement Must Be That Matter Matters." *Christianity Today*. June

26, 2013. http://www.christianitytoday.com/ct/2013/july-august/sex
-without-bodies.html.

Dawn, Marva J. *Sexual Character: Beyond Technique to Intimacy*. Grand
Rapids: Eerdmans, 1993.

Doidge, Norman. "Acquiring Tastes and Loves." In *The Brain That Changes
Itself: Stories of Personal Triumph from the Frontiers of Brain Science*,
93–131. New York: Penguin, 2007.

Dreher, Rod. "Slouching towards Googletopia." *The American Conservative*. May 13, 2013. http://www.theamericanconservative.com/dreher
/slouching-towards-googletopia/.

Eberstadt, Mary, and Mary Anne Layden, eds. *The Social Costs of Pornography: A Statement of Findings and Recommendations*. Princeton:
Witherspoon Institute, 2010.

Englehart, Kate. "True Loves: The Search Will Soon Be Mobile, Transparent and Constant." *Maclean's*. January 30, 2013. http://www.macleans
.ca/society/life/true-loves/.

Fee, Gordon D. *God's Empowering Presence: The Holy Spirit in the Letters
of Paul*. Grand Rapids: Baker Academic, 1994.

Finer, Lawrence. "Trends in Premarital Sex in the United States, 1954–2003."
Public Health Reports 122 (2007): 73–78.

Finkel, Eli J., Paul W. Eastwick, Benjamin R. Karney, Harry T. Reis, and
Susan Sprecher. "Online Dating: A Critical Analysis from the Perspective
of Psychological Science." *Psychological Science in the Public Interest*
13, no. 1 (January 2012): 3–66.

Fisher, Helen. "Broken Hearts: The Nature and Risks of Romantic Rejection." In *Romance and Sex in Adolescence and Emerging Adulthood:
Risks and Opportunities*, edited by Ann C. Crouter and Alan Booth,
3–28. Mahwah, NJ: Lawrence Erlbaum Associates, 2006.

———. "Why We Love, Why We Cheat." *TED Talks*. February 2006.
http://www.ted.com/talks/helen_fisher_tells_us_why_we_love
_cheat.html.

Foucault, Michel. *Discipline and Punish: The Birth of the Prison*. Translated
by Alan Sheridan. New York: Vintage, 1995.

———. *The History of Sexuality*. Vol. 1, *An Introduction*. New York:
Pantheon, 1978.

Fowl, S. E. "Imitation of Paul/of Christ." In *Dictionary of Paul and His
Letters*, edited by Gerald F. Hawthorne and Ralph P. Martin, 428–31.
Downers Grove, IL: InterVarsity, 1993.

Friesen, James G., E. James Wilder, Anne M. Bierling, Rick Koepcke, and Maribeth Poole. *The Life Model: Living from the Heart Jesus Gave You; The Essentials of Christian Living.* Pasadena, CA: Shepherd's House, 1999.

Fukuyama, Francis. *The Great Disruption: Human Nature and the Reconstitution of Social Order.* New York: Touchstone, 2000.

Gehring, Roger W. *House Church and Mission: The Importance of Household Structures in Early Christianity.* Peabody, MA: Hendrickson, 2004.

Glenn, Norval, and Elizabeth Marquardt. *Hooking Up, Hanging Out, and Hoping for Mr. Right: College Women on Dating and Mating Today.* New York: Institute for American Values, 2001.

Gorman, Michael J. *Cruciformity: Paul's Narrative Spirituality of the Cross.* Grand Rapids: Eerdmans, 2001.

Gousmett, Chris. "Creation Order and Miracle according to Augustine." *Evangelical Quarterly* 60 (1988): 217–40.

Grenz, Stanley J. *Sexual Ethics: An Evangelical Perspective.* Louisville: Westminster John Knox, 1990.

Hallfors, Denise D., Martha W. Waller, Daniel Bauer, Carol A. Ford, and Carolyn T. Halpern. "Which Comes First in Adolescence—Sex and Drugs or Depression?" *American Journal of Preventative Medicine* 29 (2005): 163–70.

Hauerwas, Stanley. *A Better Hope: Resources for a Church Confronting Capitalism, Democracy, and Postmodernity.* Grand Rapids: Brazos, 2000.

———. *Christian Existence Today: Essays on Church, World, and Living In Between.* Durham, NC: Labyrinth, 1988.

———. *Christians among the Virtues: Theological Conversations with Ancient and Modern Ethics.* Notre Dame, IN: University of Notre Dame Press, 1997.

———. *A Community of Character: Toward a Constructive Christian Social Ethic.* Notre Dame, IN: University of Notre Dame Press, 1981.

———. *The Hauerwas Reader.* Edited by John Berkman and Michael Cartwright. Durham, NC: Duke University Press, 2001.

———. "Living the Proclaimed Reign of God: A Sermon on the Sermon on the Mount." *Interpretation* 47, no. 2 (April 1993): 152–58.

———. "Preaching as though We Had Enemies." *First Things* 53 (May 1995): 45–49.

———. "Sex and Politics: Bertrand Russell and 'Human Sexuality.'" *Christian Century* 95 (April 1978): 417–22.

———. *With the Grain of the Universe: The Church's Witness and Natural Theology; Being the Gifford Lectures Delivered at the University of St. Andrews in 2001.* Grand Rapids: Brazos, 2001. Reprint, Grand Rapids: Baker Academic, 2013.

Hauerwas, Stanley, and Allen Verhey. "From Conduct to Character: A Guide to Sexual Adventure." *Reformed Journal* 36 (November 1986): 12–16.

Hays, Richard B. *The Moral Vision of the New Testament: A Contemporary Introduction to New Testament Ethics.* San Francisco: HarperSanFrancisco, 1996.

Heidegger, Martin. *Being and Time.* Translated by John Macquarrie and Edward Robinson. New York: Harper & Row, 1966.

Hobbes, Thomas. *Leviathan.* Edited by C. B. Macpherson. London: Penguin Classics, 1985.

Holt, Bradley P. *Thirsty for God: A Brief History of Christian Spirituality.* Minneapolis: Fortress, 2005.

Houston, James M. *The Heart's Desire: Satisfying the Hunger of the Soul.* Vancouver: Regent College Publishing, 2001.

IJzendoorn, Marinus van. "Adult Attachment Representations, Parental Responsiveness, and Infant Attachment: A Meta-Analysis on the Predictive Validity of the Adult Attachment Interview." *Psychology Bulletin* 117, no. 3 (1995): 387–403.

James, William. *The Varieties of Religious Experience: A Study in Human Nature.* Oxford: Oxford University Press, 2012.

Kant, Immanuel. *Religion within the Limits of Reason Alone.* New York: Harper Torchbook, 1960.

Kaufmann, Jean-Claude. *Love Online.* Cambridge: Polity, 2012.

Kennedy, Sheela, and Larry Bumpass. "Cohabitation and Children's Living Arrangements: New Estimates from the United States." *Demographic Research* 19 (2008): 1663–92.

Klinenberg, Eric. *Going Solo: The Extraordinary Rise and Surprising Appeal of Living Alone.* New York: Penguin, 2012.

Levy, David. *Love and Sex with Robots: The Evolution of Human-Robot Relationships.* New York: HarperCollins, 2008.

Lewis, C. S. "Christianity and Literature." In *Christian Reflections.* Edited by Walter Hooper. Grand Rapids: Eerdmans, 1967.

———. Letter from C. S. Lewis to Keith Masson. June 3, 1956. Marion E. Wade Center, Wheaton College, Wheaton, IL.

————. *Letters of C. S. Lewis.* Edited by W. H. Lewis. Fort Washington, PA: Mariner Books, 2003.

————. *Miracles.* New York: HarperOne, 2001.

————. *The Problem of Pain.* San Francisco: HarperSanFrancisco, 2001.

————. *The Weight of Glory: And Other Addresses.* New York: Harper-Collins, 2001.

Lindvall, Terry. "Embalmed Images: C. S. Lewis and the Art of Film." Christian Broadcasting Network. https://www.cbn.com/special/Narnia/articles/Lindvall_LewisFilm.aspx.

Luther, Martin. *The Freedom of a Christian.* Translated by Mark D. Tranvik. Minneapolis: Fortress, 2008. First published 1520.

MacMurray, John. *Reason and Emotion.* London: Faber & Faber, 1942.

Malherbe, Abraham J. *Paul and the Thessalonians: The Philosophic Tradition of Pastoral Care.* Philadelphia: Fortress, 1987.

McKnight, Scot. *A Community Called Atonement.* Living Theology. Nashville: Abingdon, 2007.

Papadopoulos, Linda. *Sexualisation of Young People: Review.* February 2010. https://shareweb.kent.gov.uk/Documents/health-and-wellbeing/teenpregnancy/Sexualisation_young_people.pdf.

Peterson, Eugene H. *Five Smooth Stones for Pastoral Work.* Grand Rapids: Eerdmans, 1992.

————. *The Pastor: A Memoir.* New York: HarperOne, 2011.

Regnerus, Mark D. *Forbidden Fruit: Sex and Religion in the Lives of American Teenagers.* New York: Oxford University Press, 2007.

Regnerus, Mark, and Jeremy Uecker. *Premarital Sex in America: How Young Americans Meet, Mate, and Marry in America.* New York: Oxford University Press, 2011.

Rhoades, Galena K., Scott M. Stanley, and Howard J. Markman. "Couples' Reasons for Cohabitation: Associations with Individual Well-Being and Relationship Quality." *Journal of Family Issues* 30 (2009): 233–58.

Rohr, Richard. *Everything Belongs: The Gift of Contemplative Prayer.* New York: Crossroad, 2003.

Schoen, Robert, Nancy S. Landale, and Kimberly Daniels. "Family Transitions in Young Adulthood." *Demography* 44 (2007): 807–24.

Schwartz, Barry. *The Paradox of Choice: Why More Is Less.* New York: HarperPerennial, 2004.

Scott, Ian W. *Paul's Way of Knowing: Story, Experience, and the Spirit.* Grand Rapids: Baker Academic, 2009.

Shakespeare, Steven. *Radical Orthodoxy: A Critical Introduction.* London: SPCK, 2007.

Slater, Dan. *Love in the Time of Algorithms: What Technology Does to Meeting and Mating.* New York: Current, 2013.

———. "A Million First Dates: How Online Romance Is Threatening Monogamy." *The Atlantic.* January 2, 2013. http://www.theatlantic.com/magazine/archive/2013/01/a-million-first-dates/309195/.

Smith, Christian, with Kari Christoffersen, Hilary Davidson, and Patricia Snell Herzog. *Lost in Transition: The Dark Side of Emerging Adulthood.* New York: Oxford University Press, 2011.

Smith, Christian, with Patricia Snell. *Souls in Transition: The Religious and Spiritual Lives of Emerging Adults.* New York: Oxford University Press, 2009.

Smith, James K. A. *Desiring the Kingdom: Worship, Worldview, and Cultural Formation.* Grand Rapids: Baker Academic, 2009.

———. *Introducing Radical Orthodoxy: Mapping a Post-Secular Theology.* Grand Rapids: Baker Academic, 2004.

———. *Thinking in Tongues: Pentecostal Contributions to Christian Philosophy.* Grand Rapids: Eerdmans, 2010.

———. *Who's Afraid of Postmodernism? Taking Derrida, Lyotard, and Foucault to Church.* Grand Rapids: Baker Academic, 2006.

Stoner, James R., and Donna M. Hughes, eds. *The Social Costs of Pornography: A Collection of Papers.* Princeton: Witherspoon Institute, 2010.

Strom, Mark. *Reframing Paul: Conversations in Grace and Community.* Downers Grove, IL: IVP Academic, 2000.

Struthers, William M. *Wired for Intimacy: How Pornography Hijacks the Male Brain.* Downers Grove, IL: InterVarsity, 2009.

Taylor, Charles. *The Malaise of Modernity.* Concord, ON: Anansi, 1992.

———. *Modern Social Imaginaries.* Durham, NC: Duke University Press, 2004.

———. *A Secular Age.* Cambridge, MA: Belknap Press of Harvard University Press, 2007.

———. "Sex and Christianity: How Has the Moral Landscape Changed?" *Commonweal* 134 (2007): 12–18.

———. *Sources of the Self: The Making of the Modern Identity*. Cambridge, MA: Harvard University Press, 1992.

———. *Varieties of Religion Today: William James Revisited*. Cambridge, MA: Harvard University Press, 2002.

Thompson, James W. *Pastoral Ministry according to Paul: A Biblical Vision*. Grand Rapids: Baker Academic, 2006.

Tocqueville, Alexis de. *Democracy in America*. Translated by George Lawrence. Edited by J. P. Mayer. New York: Doubleday, 1969.

Tsing Loh, Sandra. "Let's Call the Whole Thing Off." *The Atlantic*. July 1, 2009. http://www.theatlantic.com/magazine/archive/2009/07/lets-call-the-whole-thing-off/307488/.

Turkle, Sherry. *Alone Together: Why We Expect More from Technology and Less from Each Other*. New York: Basic Books, 2012.

Vitz, Paul C. *Psychology as Religion: The Cult of Self-Worship*. Grand Rapids: Eerdmans, 1994.

Ward, Graham. *The Politics of Discipleship: Becoming Postmaterial Citizens*. Grand Rapids: Baker Academic, 2009.

Williams, Charles. *Outlines of Romantic Theology*. Edited by Alice M. Hadfield. Grand Rapids: Eerdmans, 1990.

Williams, Sarah C. "A Sexual Reformation? Marriage and Sexuality in the Contemporary Paradigm." Lecture presented at Regent College, Vancouver, April 1, 2008.

Wolf, Naomi. "The Porn Myth." *New York*. May 24, 2004. http://nymag.com/nymetro/news/trends/n_9437/.

Wolfe, Tom. *Hooking Up*. New York: Farrar, Straus & Giroux, 2000.

Wright, Bradley. *Christians Are Hate-Filled Hypocrites . . . and Other Lies You've Been Told: A Sociologist Shatters Myths from the Secular and Christian Media*. Minneapolis: Bethany House, 2010.

Wuthnow, Robert. *After the Baby Boomers: How Twenty- and Thirty-Somethings Are Shaping the Future of American Religion*. Princeton: Princeton University Press, 2007.

Zillmann, Dolf. "Influence of Unrestricted Access to Erotica on Adolescents' and Young Adults' Dispositions toward Sexuality." *Journal of Adolescent Health* 27, no. 2 (2000): 41–44.

Zillmann, Dolf, and Jennings Bryant. "Pornography's Impact on Sexual Satisfaction." *Journal of Applied Social Psychology* 18, no. 5 (1988): 438–53.

Index

247